ENDORSEMENTS

I have been asked by many to explain how I knew I was prophet. I always answer, "I could tell the future and know things that were going to happen...but then the Lord met me, the Spirit filled me, and the Word became a Living Person in my life. After that, I could seek Him and interpret time."

When I read *End Times in Real Time* by Jon and Jolene Hamill, I was caught up into another dimension. This book is one I couldn't put down. The insights, the foresights, and the incredible interpretation of now-times in the future were just amazing. This is a thrilling book. Enjoy entering into an understanding of end times today—an incredible, revelatory journey of interpreting time in the future today.

—Dr. Charles D. Pierce
Founder, Glory of Zion Inc. | Kingdom Harvest Alliance | Global Spheres Center

End Times in Real Time is a powerful, timely book. If you're a believer who wants to be equipped for the end times, then read this book. It's a compelling manual and prophetic blueprint to fight the spiritual battles of today and yet to come. One of the book's greatest strengths is its focus on Israel. In clear and compelling terms, it explains why Israel remains central to God's plan and how understanding this is crucial for discerning the end times.

I've known Jon and Jolene for years and admire them as spiritual forerunners. I believe this is their Holy Spirit-inspired gift to equip the body of Jesus "to understand, shine, and overcome" in these end times.

—Chris Mitchell
CBN News, Middle East Bureau Chief

We are living in this most historic time in the history of the world and in the beginning of the greatest awakening and move of His Spirit in the history of Christianity. The Lord is issuing forth the clarion call to rise above the chaos, to *come up higher* and see and discern the times we are in from His throne room perspective. The more of His "awakening glory" in us, the more of His glory in the land!

You and I are His called and chosen ones, whose presence has been requested by the King with great purpose. There is a summoning to His church, His surrendered ones, His army of valiant warriors to awaken, arise, discern the times and advance in His Kingdom of Heaven plans in this unprecedented *kairos* season. It is time to have ears to hear what the Spirit is saying and to say yes to the summoning to be His called ones to overcome. Thank you, Jon and Jolene, for this strategic, real-time, relevant and timely message!

—**Rebecca Greenwood**
Co-founder, Christian Harvest International
Strategic Prayer Apostolic Network

In a time when our nation stands at a critical crossroads, *End Times in Real Time* by Jon and Jolene Hamill is both a battle cry and a road map for the body of Christ. This book doesn't just diagnose the darkness we face; it equips believers with essential decrees and a fresh spiritual lens to intercede for our land with renewed passion and purpose. Through powerful insights and Spirit-led strategies, Jon and Jolene call on all of us to partner with God in bringing a "born-again" renewal to America, a rebirth that aligns us with Heaven's vision for true freedom.

The Hamills direct our eyes toward our Sovereign Ruler, Jesus, and His Kingdom authority. They strategically highlight the prophetic tools needed to discern the signs of the times and counter the antichrist agenda that seeks to undermine our nation and our faith. Drawing on timeless scriptural truths, there's an active mobilization of the body of Christ to cry out for the last days outpouring of God's Spirit to witness the powers of darkness dismantled over the nation.

This book is a profound invitation to pray boldly, to discern wisely, and to decree with authority—transforming both our hearts and our nation in the process. *End Times in Real Time* is essential reading for every believer who desires to see America redeemed and restored to God's purposes.

—Myles and Leza Milham
Pastors, Kingdom Awakening Ministries
Kingston, NH

This book is the embodiment of the powerful experiences of two proven prophetic intercessors and watchmen, Jon and Jolene Hamill. We have walked with them for over 25 years and can attest that they live what they teach. I love the honesty and transparency with which they address difficult issues, such as clergy abuse in the prayer movement.

As shown in the book of Daniel, the end times are about needed character and not just an order of events. May this book enable you to not just survive, but to thrive in the end times.

—Rick Ridings
Founder, Succat Hallel (24/7 house of prayer overlooking the
Temple Mount in Jerusalem)
Author (with his wife Patricia) of
Shifting Nations through Houses of Prayer

Jon and Jolene! Thank God for His grace on you to write this excellent book. I love how you've related these three together: early American history, present American happenings as they are unfolding, and personal experiences. I was especially blessed by the study questions and prayer at the end of each chapter. It helped me process the chapters on multiple levels. I appreciate that God can do things on global and national levels but at the same time, He could use those things to minister to me personally.

—**Andy Leong**
Worship Director, Church on the Rock OKC

How can something be this ethereal—beautiful in a way that is almost otherworldly—and yet be this biblically accurate at the same time? How can something be this riveting and yet be this factual? As writers, historians, and prophetic prognosticators, Jon and Jolene keep taking their readers from one journey of investigative truth into the next unfolding of progressive revelation for our days. Welcome to their next saga of prophetic journalism: *End Times in Real Time!*

—**James W. Goll**
God Encounters Ministries
GOLL Ideation LLC

Jon and Jolene are dear friends and prophetic forerunners whose book *End Times in Real Time* has laid out a road map to equip the body of Christ for the days ahead. Unlike books of past eras, focused on the enemy and his players on the global scene, *End Times in Real Time* focuses on our Bridegroom King and His purposes to have a pure and spotless Bride in the last days—the days in which we live. This book gets deeper with every chapter and draws the reader into an ever-expanding place of intimacy, purpose, and surrender.

I was especially blessed by the chapter about the "rescued lampstand"—a powerful word for this season. I highly recommend this book for the ones looking to be voices crying out, preparing and hastening the day of the Lord.

—Jamie Fitt
Director, Philadelphia Tabernacle of David

End Times in Real Time carries a strong anointing that will awaken the God-given destiny within you and strengthen your faith to walk in supernatural victory. The Lord has given Jon and Jolene Hamill great prophetic insight concerning the end times and a practical strategic blueprint to help His Body win the war on every level as we enter the midnight hour of redemptive history.

It's been my honor and great privilege over the past eight years to partner with Jon and Jolene on many strategic Kingdom assignments, which have borne the fruit of divine turnaround even on a national level. I highly recommend this prophetic exposition; it will give you clarity concerning the Church's end-time mandate and the ability to navigate the days of the climax of God's story.

—Ed Watts
Zion Gate Ministries

Another literary masterpiece for the Kingdom! The Hamills have written a must-have resource for the body of Christ. Even if you've avoided the subject of the end times, it will prove life-changing. The message is real, simple, and profound. Jon and Jolene are very approachable as they share prophetic stories and dreams. The insights in the book are easy to understand, engaging, and thought-provoking.

The greatest value for most will be how American history is woven into God's overarching calendar and timing. The reader will also gain significant understanding of the Hebrew foundations impacting both the Christian faith and today's current situations.

Your captivating invitation to connect in God's cosmic story, unfolding right now, will cause your faith to soar. And a clear, biblical foundation to build upon is provided for you as a runway. You won't be able to put this book down!

—**Jen Mallan**
Jen Mallan Ministries
Host of *Come Home!* Christian Television Network

In *End Times in Real Time*, Jon and Jolene have skillfully woven the scriptures and prophecies of the Bible together and connected them with the events we are seeing today for both Israel and America. With clear prophetic insight and a call to action, they are sharing with us Heaven's preparation for our future. And especially for the success He will bring to see the Kingdom of God established! This is a great book to see how the plans of God unfold even when it takes centuries to come to pass.

—**Dr. John M. Benefiel**
Presiding Apostle, Heartland Apostolic Prayer Network
Founder and Senior Pastor, Church on the Rock, Oklahoma City

End Times in Real Time is right on time. With great prophetic insight and revelation, Jon and Jolene open up our path into the future moves of God and help us see and understand the times and seasons we are in. You will perceive your assignment and find great faith, even for the end times. This is a must-read for our day!

—**Garland Thomas**
Lead Apostle, New Life Worship Center
National President, The Priesthood Motorcycle Ministry

END TIMES
IN REAL TIME

DESTINY IMAGE BOOKS
BY JON AND JOLENE HAMILL

*White House Watchmen: New Era Prayer Strategies
to Shape the Future of Our Nation*

*Turnaround Decrees: Disrupt the Enemy's Plans and
Shift Your Circumstance Into Breakthrough*

*End Times in Real Time: Discern the Signs of the
Times and Annihilate the Antichrist Agenda*

END TIMES
IN REAL TIME

DISCERN THE SIGNS
OF THE TIMES AND
ANNIHILATE THE
ANTI-CHRIST
AGENDA

JON AND JOLENE HAMILL

DESTINY IMAGE® PUBLISHERS, INC.

P.O. Box 310, Shippensburg, PA 17257-0310

"Publishing cutting-edge prophetic resources to supernaturally empower the body of Christ"

This book and all other Destiny Image and Destiny Image Fiction books are available at Christian bookstores and distributors worldwide.

For more information on foreign distributors, call 717-532-3040.

Reach us on the Internet: www.destinyimage.com.

Photos and graphics by Jon Hamill.

ISBN 13 TP: 978-0-7684-8105-1

ISBN 13 eBook: 978-0-7684-8106-8

For Worldwide Distribution, Printed in the U.S.A.

1 2 3 4 5 6 7 8 / 29 28 27 26 25

CONTENTS

FOREWORD

Every generation of Christians has undoubtedly felt they were in the end times, and they were! God's clock started ticking the moment Jesus ascended to Heaven. However, I feel I can safely say that if we were minutes away from the return of the Messiah, we are now seconds. We know that, and satan knows that. According to Jon and Jolene Hamill, the "holy clock" is ticking.

We see manifestations of the clash of kingdoms on vast levels and broad landscapes. Indeed, satan (the dragon) has come down knowing that his time is short. (Revelation 12:12). The antichrist spirit rages against believers, the values and principles of the Word of God, and the core tenets of faith.

So, what do we do? We overcome! And we learn how to read the prophetic signs before us. Not with charts and timelines, although some may be called to do that, but rather with the Issachar anointing of those who know the signs of the times through the power of the Holy Spirit.

Jon and Jolene know how to do that. They are forerunners. Their lives are lived as those who are prophetic watchmen on the wall and passionate lovers of the coming Bridegroom.

This book prepares you to do what the end of "THE book" challenges us to achieve—"to those who overcome, I will give." To do that, one needs a road map. One could say we need instructions on how to do just that—overcome!

I love the stories they tell of prayer journeys taken to not only disrupt satan's plans but to build a road map for our lives and nations, particularly Israel.

In addition, they have lived through real-life pain. The enemy wants to shipwreck us to move us off of God's purpose for us in these end times. They have walked through some deep valleys and share in a transparent way how they forgave and walked out of the depths of betrayal and pain. They are an example of being ready to be that bride without spot or wrinkle. Each of us needs help, at times, to overcome the challenges satan sends our way. Sometimes by the boatload!

We have all heard the stories of abuse by Christian leaders. If we are being real, we all need to say that the leadership in our churches has often dismally handled situations where those under them have been victimized. God is requiring us in these last days to repent, rectify, and recognize behavior that is absolutely criminal. *End Times in Real Time* addresses this as they decry the egregious actions of the leader of the International House of Prayer in Kansas City.

I don't want you to think the whole book is so serious that you will not be uplifted by its contents. You will laugh at the portion where, as a young Christian, Jolene was deeply disappointed in God and, in her own words, decided that she was "breaking up with Jesus!" (It didn't last long!)

For those of you waiting for a spouse, Jon and Jolene's last story will both amaze you and give you hope. It is supernatural!

As a couple, the Hamills are called to watch over the nation and are strategically placed in Washington, DC. This has given them key insights as they intercede for the nation. Jon is a direct descendant of

Paul Revere, whose historic ride saved many lives during America's war for Independence. He is a historian who knows how to weave the past into the fabric of today to give us language on how to pray and is masterful in sharing relevant issues.

Get ready to go on an adventure as you read these pages. Absorb the relevance of the end-time points into your current situations, and you will certainly be an end-time overcomer!

—**Cindy Jacobs**

INTRODUCTION

The world is a chaotic place. Headlines scream of wars and rumors of wars, natural disasters ravage the globe, and a palpable sense of unease seems to hang in the air. For those familiar with the biblical text, these events are not merely random occurrences; they are the birth pangs of a new era, the undeniable signs of the end times unfolding before our very eyes—in real time.

But fear not. *End Times in Real Time* is not a book born of despair, but of revelatory insight, equipping us to not only understand the times but to overcome! My friends Jon and Jolene Hamill have poured their very lives into the truths presented here. I know this because I have had the honor of running with them for almost a decade, witnessing firsthand the intersection of God's end-time purposes being unveiled in real-time moments.

Jesus, the living Word, is described in the book of Revelation as "the One who was, who is, and who is to come." In the pages ahead, you will discover how the One who is—working with us in real time—reveals what was, for the purpose of giving us insight and authority for what is to come. Our seemingly ordinary days are not so ordinary after all!

Hidden in each one is an invitation to come up higher and live from the place that covenant has secured. As you will soon learn, covenant is the key to accessing the counsel of God in these days both for ourselves and the spheres entrusted to us. A return to fidelity and first-love devotion has been at the core of everything Jon and Jolene have pursued and what they have chronicled here. The book you hold in your hands is not just ink and paper but carries with it grace to impart the substance of the things spoken of.

These journeys and prophetic revelations will also act as a template to help you interpret where you are in God's timeline while giving you the tools to navigate it. You will be empowered to live out His storyline for your life and become the burning and shining lamp He is calling for in the last days.

—**Chris Mitchell Jr.**
King's Gate International
Williamsburg-Virginia Beach, VA

SECTION 1

INAUGURATION

Peace Monument by Capitol, Washington, DC.

CHAPTER 1

Chapter Topics: Forging Your Future in Real Time | The Call to Overcome | Jesus' Vigil! End-Times Prophetic Encounter

A RELENTLESS VIGIL

"IT'S THE END OF THE WORLD AS WE KNOW IT!"
Back in the day, the song by iconic band REM topped the charts with rap-filled lyrics none of us could understand and a chorus few of us could get out of our heads. "AND I FEEL FINE!"

Feeling fine in the end times? I guess. Or maybe the 1980s were simply the "age of innocence." I was a young radical then. A budding journalism student who became a counter-cultural revolutionary in the eyes of family and friends, simply by coming to Jesus Christ in college. Note that most of my family identified as Unitarians, and nominal ones at best. So my "come to Jesus" moment wasn't taken too kindly. The memories!

But now, in an era of cryptocurrency and Covid, "X" diplomacy and existential threats, weaponized government, weaponized pronouns and marginalized faith, there's a vibe in the air that feels somewhat like the end of the world. At least as we know it. Especially from the vantage point of our watchman's perch overlooking Washington, DC.

We have the honor of living and ministering in our nation's capitol. And as you will discover in the book, much of the private conversations in these corridors of power center on challenges of biblical proportions that are prophesied for the end times. Why? Because these very issues are now at hand.

How can you be sure you are living in the end times? What can you do? What should you do? How should you feel—fine?

And more importantly, how can you lean into God to gain direction, protection, and breakthrough through these days? How can you gain His heart? How should you pray?

EXPLORE AND BE EQUIPPED

If you're asking these questions, this book is for you. *End Times in Real Time* is an equipping manual for apostolic and prophetic advancement through Jesus Christ. Please note it is neither a review nor a debate of different theological paradigms on the end times, which many readers have come to expect from this genre. We're not going to suggest you jump for "rapture practice," nor are we going to reveal the secret identity of the antichrist, nor are we going to compel you to store food and ammo in your underground bunker.

Not that we have a problem with any of this. If you have a bunker, save some room for us.

But these teachings largely miss God's overarching purposes for the period known as the end times. Most equip you only to escape. We're going to equip you to understand, shine, and overcome.

Many of the most important biblical themes on God's heart for the end times remain undiscovered treasures. We hope to open the "Promise Box" a little wider for you to explore. We will broaden your horizons with historical perspectives that shed light on present and future realities. You'll gain biblical strategies to implement, removing intangibles and providing you with consistent, proven results. You'll discover the significance of covenant.

Conversely, you'll discover God's abhorrence of idolatry, and why confronting idolatry here and now is such a big part of end-times advancement. You'll grow in experiencing the Lord, hearing His voice, discerning His direction, and securing His turnarounds in your world.

But here's the key. You have to have a hunger within you for more. You must gain the courage to explore. To push beyond the tree line to the summit of the mountain.

BE A REVOLUTIONARY

In many teachings on the end times, our greatest victory is pictured as our ultimate escape from the enemy's grasp. We get raptured. And maybe we will. There's a lot of scriptural precedent for it.

But historical precedent shows that virtually every generation must come face to face with a manifestation of the antichrist spirit, with no other option than to prevail. So far no anti-gravitational exfiltration has ever been presented as an option. Instead every generation has been mandated by God to recognize the evil for what it truly is, confront it, and pay the price to overcome.

"To him who overcomes, I will give...." Jesus conveys a consistent message to all churches in the book of Revelation, chapter 2. Victory can be obtained. But friend, you cannot gain the legitimacy to turn the battle against antichrist forces on a national or global level without first overcoming the antichrist expression within your own life and your own backyard.

End Times in Real Time is your summons to become spiritual revolutionaries, capable of moving yourself and your camp beyond the undermining paralysis so many believers have succumbed to. Maybe without even knowing it.

And as you will see, it all begins with covenant. This cannot be stated enough. Securing covenant with Jesus Christ divorced from idolatry, and stewarding your authority to empower His justice and freedom in your sphere, is the foundation for His victory in our hour.

FORGING YOUR FUTURE IN REAL TIME

You know how the Lord sows a word into your life and then cultivates it to maturity? Sometimes the words manifest quickly, but sometimes the fullness only comes through years of journeying through life. We know only in part until what He speaks is fully developed.

We have structured this book according to this pattern. First we take a journey. Many themes introduced in the next few chapters are more fully developed in later chapters. There's great intentionality in leading you this way. Because it's actually how God works with you to forge your future *in real time.*

MY GREATEST END-TIME VISITATION

Throughout the book Jolene and I will draw from many personal experiences as well as revelation from the Lord that we believe are vital to your understanding. I would like to begin with the most powerful, and most personal, visitation with the Lord in all my life.

Jesus came to me back in 2002, late on a hot spring evening in Kansas City. I was working for what was then the International House of Prayer. The encounter revolutionized my understanding of the end times.

As background, my wife, Jolene, is my dream come true. We met during the final period of the most difficult season of my life. Previously I was married to a very broken young woman who had engaged in a series of affairs throughout our marriage, the last of which brought us to divorce. Early in my previous marriage, the Lord spoke for me to love as Hosea loved and that through the experience I would come to understand His love for each of us personally and for our nation.

It proved true. But as anyone who has been through this magnitude of betrayal understands, the experience nearly broke me.

Historical precedent shows that virtually every generation must come face to face with a manifestation of the antichrist spirit, with no other option than to prevail.

For a while it looked as though the vicious cycle of affairs had ceased and healing had been gained. But during a ministry trip a friend gave me a prophetic warning that my then-wife had once again become unfaithful. Back then landlines were still predominant, and when I returned home I felt strangely directed to pick up my home phone and push the redial button. A receptionist from a cheap hotel outside of town answered the call. And I knew my friend's warning was true.

When confronted, my former wife simply confessed that she had fallen in love. Again. Though I tried to keep the family together, the writing on the wall was clear. Soon she decided she did not want to be a mother anymore, or a wife. I became a single dad with full custody of my children.

The times in between this decision were the hardest. One night, half the bed remained empty well after midnight. Thoughts of what was transpiring defied my bravest attempts to attain any measure of sleep. I made my way to the living room, switched on a light, grabbed my Bible and collapsed on the couch. Face in hands, my prayers succumbed to angry tears as yet another midnight vigil progressed.

Suddenly God's tangible presence moved in the room. I could not see Him but I strongly sensed Him. A powerful warmth filled my spirit as this unseen Being took a seat beside me, right on the couch. It was unmistakably Jesus. All I can say is that when He truly comes, you know it.

Though I felt His compassion, He spoke to me no audible words or revelatory direction. Jesus the Christ was simply there. Somehow trading His eternal Throne of glory for the other half of a faded blue couch.

At once my heart knew why. And the solidarity between us grew deeper than words could ever convey. Because just as I was keeping watch through the night for my bride to come home, I knew Jesus was keeping watch for His bride to return home to Him.

Want to understand the end times in real time? Here it is, at the most basic level. Jesus is the Bridegroom, and He is longing for His bride to fully join with Him. To fully return.

Though I did not understand it, through my midnight vigil I became aware I was giving Jesus solace even as He was strengthening me. Only later did I come to realize the fuller implications of His "Bridegroom watch," when exposure of covenant-breaking, of clergy sexual abuse at the highest levels of the prayer movement I was serving, came to light.

"Watch therefore, for you do not know what hour your Lord is coming" (Matthew 24:42 NKJV). Most of us know Jesus' admonition to keep watch through the end times. But maybe we haven't yet discovered His relentless vigil over you and over me. Keep this at heart as you read. Nothing more needs to be said right now. Except to keep watch.

STUDY QUESTIONS AND PRAYER

1. What does the phrase "the end times" mean to you? Does it stir fear in you? Anticipation? Hope? Why?

2. What subjects related to the end times do you want to learn more about?

3. Do you pray regularly for a person, an institution, or a cause? Have you experienced answers to prayer?

4. What real-life experiences have opened your heart more to the Lord? How has He used them to draw you closer to Himself?

Father God, from the outset of this journey through End Times in Real Time, *please speak deeply to me. Confirm perceptions You have already given. Shake up my worldview where I need to realign. Get me in sync with You! Help me to gain Your counsel and implement Your precepts in my life. Help me to pray. Help me to see.*

Expand my capacities. And strengthen me to become a more effective catalyst for Your Kingdom in the end times. In Jesus' name, amen!

Bicentennial reproduction of the Paul Revere lantern.

CHAPTER 2

Chapter Topics: The Forgotten Forerunner Call | 2017 Prophecy—Midnight Crises Beginning in 2020 | When God Ignited our Lamp

TWO BURNING LAMPS

"The fate of the nation was riding that night."

—Paul Revere describing his midnight ride on April 18, 1775. The year 2025 marks the 250th anniversary of his freedom ride, torch outstretched, igniting the American Revolution.

Have you ever noticed that the treasure right in front of you is sometimes the hardest to perceive? Your wallet, for instance. Your car in a Costco parking lot. Or a mobile device. You hit the "Find my iPhone" button and then leap out of your skin as the alarm blares from your own pocket.

To a large extent that's what Jolene and my journey into *End Times in Real Time* has been like. For us the subject of the end times was once relegated to a forgotten pocket in our spiritual lives. When the alarm began to sound, it took us completely by surprise. Especially as He began to show us how we have neglected this aspect of our calling for decades. As you will see, He actually prophesied it into our lives from the very beginning.

Probably like you, we simply did not perceive the full scope of the revelation entrusted to us. That is, until the alarm went off.

A prophetic word related to the end times was given to me by Cindy Jacobs in the year 2000. The world had just entered into a new millennium. Both the hope and dread of "Y2K" ignited an extreme hunger to understand the end times. Prince sang about it. Kirk Franklin rapped about it. Street preachers raved about it. Toby Mac rapped about street preachers raving about it. Fiction novelists wrote about it. Don't be left behind!

Strangely, the fivefold ministry leaders you expected to hear from the most were actually the most silent. Though many prophets shared insights into the end times, very few seemed brave enough to actually touch last-days scenarios related to real time. Probably because of the danger of getting it wrong in real time. It's a genuine risk!

Fortunately, fear has rarely seemed to hold back our friends and mentors Mike and Cindy Jacobs. I had the honor of working for their ministry Generals International for a season just around Y2K. One day Cindy returned from a ministry tour and summoned me immediately into her office.

"Please sit down," she said. "I have a word from the Lord for you."

At once Cindy's prophet finger, known around the world for its power of conviction, began to rise toward me. I literally ducked. This was followed by immediate, internal repentance of everything I had ever done, as well as many things I had never done or even thought of. Just to be safe.

"Jon Hamill, the Lord says you are a spiritual Paul Revere. And just as with Paul Revere during the American Revolution, God is sending you on a midnight ride. You are going to go from city to city, holding out a burning lamp. But instead of saying, 'The British are coming! The British are coming!' You are going to say, 'The Lord is coming! The Lord is coming!'"

She later added, "And everywhere you go, revival will break forth!"

THE LORD IS COMING

Paul Revere, iconic forerunner, holding out a burning lamp and releasing a midnight cry. My jaw hit the floor. First because of the raw power of the anointing on her word. Second because without even knowing, Cindy had just repeated a prophecy, word for word, that was given to me by an unknown prophet in Kansas City two years beforehand. The sheer prescience remains amazing.

Yet strangely, I did not give the admonition about the "return of the Lord" a second thought. To me Cindy's word clearly meant that the Lord was coming in awakening to our nation. That's what I lived to hear. In 2007, Jolene and I stepped into full-time ministry to fulfill this calling, and we haven't stopped since. In 2016 we even ministered from city to city through all 50 states, declaring the Lord is coming in revival and turnaround! Our Glory Train journey was soon met with one of the most comprehensive governmental turnarounds in modern American history.

All that to say, though I thought we were fulfilling Cindy's word, I still missed a major aspect of it. Like the part where she prophesied Jesus' second coming. Jolene and I knew we were being summoned as forerunners. But until 2017, I had never given a thought that the prophecy clearly referred to being forerunners of the actual return of Jesus, Messiah to Israel and all mankind. How does that even work?

Then during Passover 2017 the alarm sounded, and my eyes were opened to the calling that's been right in front of me this whole time.

"BY 2020, SERIES OF MIDNIGHT CRISES..."

At the time I was praying from our watchman's perch overlooking Washington, DC. Across the Potomac, the White House, the Capitol, the Supreme Court were all in view. Suddenly, Holy Spirit interrupted my prayer with a dire warning that as of 2020 a midnight hour is coming upon America. His actual words:

> By the year 2020 there will be a series of midnight crises. How you confront these challenges and overcome them will even become a road map for believers in the very last days.

Through the prophetic experience, it became clear that beginning in 2020 we were being given the honor of literally preparing the way of the Lord, in a way that would influence even the final moments of the end times. That's pretty heavy, right? It boggles the mind. We introduced this word in our 2017 book *Midnight Cry,* and touched on it in both *White House Watchmen* and *Turnaround Decrees.* We'll be sharing additional insights in the chapters ahead.

But if you know anything about the year 2020, the prophetic warning about a "midnight crises" proved accurate. End times in real time—it came to pass.

First there was Covid, a manufactured virus that accidentally escaped a Chinese lab, sweeping millions of people from the earth and paralyzing our nation in an election year. This was followed by a controversial vaccine created at "warp speed," overseen by the guy who, according to documented evidence, helped develop the virus strain and then provided China with the research.

Massive riots erupted in Washington, DC and across the nation as anger over police brutality boiled over. The focus of ensuing protests shifted from racial justice to "woke" ideologies such as LGBTQ dominance, democratic governance, and leftist ideology. "Capitalism is murder," declared graffiti that was spray-painted on the White House grounds. "Until you elect a democrat as president, these riots will continue!" declared a protest speaker in southern Georgia during a rally we attended.

As part of the protests, Antifa took over entire city blocks in Portland and Seattle. Their name Antifa is a clever reference to "intifada," two murderous terror campaigns of Palestinian radicals in 1987 and 2000. Maybe not a coincidence that in 2024, Antifa and BLM leaders helped coordinate nationwide anti-semitic, anti-Israel, pro-Hamas protests.

Back to 2020. Both fake news and false prophecy saturated social media feeds, making it challenging to discern truth from error. In a totalitarian kind of way, propaganda manufactured to deliberately deceive American citizens even influenced the 2020 elections.

On one hand, the highest authorities in intelligence and media accused former President Donald J. Trump of "Russia collusion." Only later was it discovered the entire assertion was baseless, initiated by rival Hillary Clinton to boost her failed campaign.

On the other hand, just before the 2020 elections the highest levels of intelligence and media thoroughly dismissed documentation of criminal activity and sexual abuse on Hunter Biden's laptop as "Russian propaganda." Finally in 2024 the president's son was convicted of the criminal activity after the FBI confirmed the documentation was real.

Not playing politics here. Just stating facts. Disinformation and propaganda were generated to deceive "we the people." By our own government, in an election year.

Then the US presidential elections erupted in controversy over further allegations of deceit and voter fraud. Already besieged by the trauma of Covid and riots, the election drama pushed a divided America almost to the brink.

MIDNIGHT CRY—THE BRIDEGROOM IS COMING!

Hindsight, they say, is 2020. Which basically sums up the fierce admonition from Holy Spirit that we must consider, confront, and overcome the challenges of 2020 that caused us to spiral. Our nation still needs recovery. And future believers will absolutely need our road map as we continue to overcome.

But the first road map Holy Spirit highlighted through the crisis was a parable from Jesus Himself. Matthew 25 records His discourse on the 10 virgins and the Bridegroom. And I discovered that long before Paul Revere embarked on his midnight ride, Jesus Himself prophesied about a company of midnight riders who would be sent ahead of Him to prepare the way for His return. They would literally be lamplighters! The sound of their midnight cry would awaken God's people to light their lamps and follow Him through the midnight hour.

Here's the simple phrase that awakens the world: Behold the Bridegroom. He is coming. Rise up to meet Him!

Then the kingdom of heaven shall be likened to ten virgins who took their lamps and went out to meet the bridegroom.

Now five of them were wise, and five were foolish. Those who were foolish took their lamps and took no oil with them, but the wise took oil in their vessels with their lamps. But while the bridegroom was delayed, they all slumbered and slept. And at midnight a cry was heard: "Behold, the bridegroom is coming; go out to meet him!" Then all those virgins arose and trimmed their lamps. …Watch therefore, for you know neither the day nor the hour in which the Son of Man is coming (Matthew 25:1-7,13 NKJV).

Here's another insight that's pretty heavy. The book in your hands is largely written to activate this company.

BREAKING THE CYCLE OF ANTICHRIST DICTATORSHIPS

Paul Revere was a patriot of the American Revolution. He was a forerunner. He was a horseman. He was a spy. He was a pretty good silversmith as well. Most of all, he was a powerful catalyst for freedom. But without the prescient wisdom of, say, Cindy Jacobs, you might never consider him an action figure for the end times.

However, no legitimate book on the end times would be complete without at least a segment on the rise and fall of antichrist dictatorships, including monarchies that got off track. And when it comes to conquering monarchies that got off track, Paul Revere stands among the giants.

A little history. From biblical times through the 1700s, bloodline dictatorships tied to idolatry ruled most of the nation-states around the world. Whether Pharaohs in Egypt, the kings of Babylon, the Aztecs in Mexico, the Zulu chieftains of Africa, or Roman Caesars, virtually all monarchical rulers established their thrones in covenant with the highest levels of occult forces. Across the world the pattern is exactly the same.

Which means that, with the exception of Israel, virtually all governments around the globe were influenced by the very powers cast from Heaven for rebellion against the government of God.

Which, actually, explains a lot.

The American Revolution largely broke this cycle. The newly birthed government set a never-before seen precedent of constitutional governance empowering freedom for all, with a balance of power that ensured no man, woman, or party would again gain authoritarian dominion. One nation under God alone—through national covenant with Jesus Christ.

ONE SMALL CANDLE

My forefather Richard Warren was among the Pilgrims who crossed the stormy Atlantic, signed the Mayflower Compact, and helped establish the original covenantal foundations for our freedom nation.

Similar to Moses and Joshua, the Pilgrims believed they had received a holy commission from the Lord to cross these waters and establish "a new Israel," a nation wholly in covenant with God. The Pilgrims actually viewed their journey as an exodus from Babylon. They considered the monarchies of Europe to be so entwined with spiritual darkness that the only proper comparison was the biblical depiction of antichrist Babylon in the end times. And they were determined to make their exodus from Babylon permanent, founding America as a covenantal beachhead against antichrist dictatorship.

In the early 1700s, this covenant was met with holy fire. A massive Great Awakening ignited all New England. Led by Jonathan Edwards, unprecedented numbers of settlers turned to Jesus with astonishing manifestations of Holy Spirit. Many quaked in His presence. Many travailed. All bowed and wept in repentance as they came to Christ. Quite literally they saw the very words of the Pilgrim covenant come to pass—with tangible manifestations of the glory of God, and the rapid advancement of the Christian faith.

Jonathan Edwards called this revival "a divine attack upon society." Not coincidentally, in the midst of the awakening a vision to fully break with England began to take hold. From the very beginning, the governance of America was established through covenant—not with fallen powers but with the Lord Jesus Christ Himself.

The Lord always confirms His covenant with holy fire. No wonder Pilgrim governor William Bradford likened the colony to a newly lit candle, spreading the light:

> Thus out of small beginnings greater things have been produced by His hand that made all things of nothing, and gives being to all things that are; and, as one small candle may light a thousand, so the light here kindled has shone unto many, yea in some sort to our whole nation; let the glorious name of Jehovah have all the praise!

But as the Revolution began to take hold, the purity of the covenant became severely tainted through the embrace of Freemasonry and other forms of the occult. More on this later.

TWO BURNING LAMPS

Just before midnight on April 18, 1775, Paul Revere spotted two burning lamps in the upper room of the Old North Church. The lamps conveyed a covert signal that the British army was invading by sea. Revere mounted his horse and began his legendary midnight ride, awakening citizen soldiers to engage in a war for America's freedom. Against all odds they prevailed. The year of release for *End Times in Real Time* marks the 250th anniversary of Revere's ride.

The next day in Lexington, as the first battle lines were formed, a British envoy was sent to negotiate peace. The only non-negotiable aspect was for the 13 colonies to remain under the monarchy's sovereignty. A now legendary reply of the patriots said it all, "Sir, we will have no Sovereign but God, and no King but Jesus."

No King but Jesus! With those words, thousands of years of global dominance by dictators simply began to crumble. A new, forerunning expression of representational governance under God was soon birthed—with government of the people, by the people, and for the people.

Maybe it's not a coincidence that Revere's midnight ride occurred in the middle of the Jewish feast of Passover. It was as though the Lord declared once again to the earth, "Let My people go!" That said, beginning in 2025 it's time once again to hold out the burning lamp and prepare the way for God's freedom movement.

FORERUNNER FIRE

Messiah's love is described as an unquenchable fire. Throughout the Bible, fire is a symbol of God's covenant. A better way to put it is that fire is a seal of His covenant, an affirmation that His covenant blessings are either released or restored. Really, the burning lamp symbolizes God's glory.

> Set me as a seal upon your heart, as a seal upon your arm, for love is as strong as death, jealousy is fierce as the grave. Its flashes are flashes of fire, the very flame of the Lord (Song of Songs 8:6 ESV).

When the Lord came to Abraham, He cut covenant with Himself for the land and people Israel. The sign was a burning lamp. David, Solomon, and Elijah all saw fire fall from Heaven, sealing again God's covenant with Israel. Even the disciples experienced this in the upper room. Pentecost. Wind and fire. They bore witness to the literal restoration of God's glory.

THE MIDNIGHT CRY IS A SUMMONS TO A WEDDING

Jolene and I experienced our own measure of holy fire during our marriage ceremony. Seven years beforehand, Jolene consecrated herself fully to the Lord, and even purchased a wedding ring to wear as a symbol of her covenant. Not long after, she received an invitation in the mail from the Lord.

To clarify, the invitation was given in a dream. Jolene opened the mail and received a surprise invitation—to her own wedding. Featuring yours truly, of course. But all Jolene could remember from the dream was that the

Messiah's love is described as an unquenchable fire. Throughout the Bible, fire is a symbol of God's covenant. Really, the burning lamp symbolizes God's glory.

date "December 20" was highlighted. Too bad she couldn't remember any details about her future husband. Tall, dark and ruggedly handsome. Okay well maybe medium-build, tanned by midsummer, and still ruggedly handsome. Because beauty is in the eye of the beholder!

But the entire experience provoked Jolene to pray for our wedding through many years. Her most relentless request was very simple. "Lord, please come. Please visit. Please make Yourself known."

You have to understand that all of this revelation about our soon-coming wedding was conveyed to me only after I proposed to Jolene, in the fall of 2003. I figured we'd wait at least a year to get married. Both of us wanted a Saturday wedding so our friends could join us. But in 2004, December 20 fell on a Monday, not a Saturday. And from year to year, the dates just spiraled further down. The only year of convergence between a Saturday and the 20th day of December was in 2008 and 2025. A little too long to wait!

Oh. And then there was December 2003. Only two months away from our engagement. We both took a huge leap of faith.

WHEN GOD LIT OUR LAMP

To our astonishment December 20, 2003, marked the first day of Hanukkah. For those not familiar with Jewish feasts, the "festival of lights" celebrates the reconsecration of the Temple after it had been desecrated by foreign powers who performed idolatrous rituals within its sacred walls. You have to understand that the Jerusalem Temple was more than a church on a corner. It was the centerpiece of Israel's entire culture. The Greco-Syrian army, which occupied Israel at the time, desired to shame that culture to bring the land further under subjugation.

Just married! Jon & Jolene wedding, with son Jonathan
and best man Will Ford, December 20, 2003.

One of the first commands God ever gave was for the Temple menorah to be continually kept lit. The big shot army blew out the candles, confiscating the holy oil used for fuel.

But God had a plan. Spiritual revolutionaries known as the Maccabees broke through this vicious army on the Temple Mount. They fought their way through to recapture the Temple. Their first priority was to become Lamplighters. They relit the Temple menorah to reconsecrate it to the Lord after its harrowing desecration.

To Jolene and me, the fact that the Lord prophesied our wedding date seven years beforehand, only to have the very date converge with the first day of Hanukkah, sealed everything. It projected God's love and care straight into our hearts. Especially after the personal "desecrations" we both had endured.

In honor of the day, Jolene and I purchased a special "Hanukkiah" (modern Hebrew spelling) menorah to serve as our unity candle for the ceremony. And as we were worshiping the Lord, literally singing "Glory, glory, send Your glory," a holy awe suddenly settled in our midst. My best man, Will Ford, pointed toward our menorah, tears streaming down his face. Our unity candle had supernaturally lit! In front of everyone. Again on the first day of Hanukkah, as we were singing "Glory, glory, send Your glory!"

Can't make this stuff up. Needless to say, we were in awe. Seven years of tearful prayers were answered in a moment. The Lord visited us, consecrated our marriage to Himself, and commissioned us with holy fire.

BURNING AND SHINING LAMPS

Looking back, our wedding ceremony was also an inauguration—into a new era of God's unrelenting blessing, of redeeming love, of running together through life, of gaining a stability and wholeness I always knew was possible but had never experienced long term.

It also marked a new era of God moving in our midst, eventually directing us into full-time ministry. Through all 50 states, from Faneuil Hall in Boston to Rome and Jerusalem, from the wilderness of Alaska to the US Capitol and even the White House, we have seen God impact countless lives and even change the trajectory of our nation.

Best of all we have had the privilege of walking together with the One who drew us together, and who invigorates us still today. Two burning lamps for Jesus. The journey has only just begun.

That said, the Light of the World never intended for us to live without His glory defining us. But glory and covenant are joined together. He is the Bridegroom. And He reserves His most intimate blessing, personally and corporately, for those who fully embrace His covenant.

Not a coincidence that John the Baptist was known to Jesus as "the burning and shining lamp." He carried the torch of Christ's covenant and prepared the bride for His real-time appearing. To a large extent that's your calling and mine in this hour. You and I must become burning lamps for Jesus, released to prepare the way of the Lord. It's where we're going in this end-time movement.

In the midst of great darkness, the Bible clearly predicts that those with Heaven's understanding will shine like the stars (Daniel 12:3). Let's become Lamplighters. Forerunners of the new. Devoted to Jesus Christ, with an understanding of the times, a recalibration of the heart, and a clear pathway forward to secure your families and spheres of authority, and even your nation, in His covenantal blessing. No king but Jesus!

STUDY QUESTIONS AND PRAYER

1. Have you ever encountered a "midnight hour" of personal crisis? How did the Lord answer your prayers?

2. Give a synopsis of a prophetic word which has impacted your life. What are your takeaways? Do you perceive any obscured revelation or direction pertaining to your life?

3. How is the Lord working to redeem your potential and cause you to flourish?

4. What is a primary biblical symbol of God's love?

———————————

Father God, I want to experience Your fire at a greater level. Shine Your light! Give me revelation beyond my own understanding. Prepare me for what You have prepared for me, even in the end times. In Jesus' name, amen!

Marine One at the White House.

CHAPTER 3

Chapter Topics: End Times, Real Time | Revelation—Come Up and See | Jesus' Inauguration | Jesus, America, Last Days | End Times—When? | Trump & Harris | 2025: Inaugurating New Era

INAUGURATION

*"Mine eyes have seen the glory of
the coming of the Lord!…"*

—"Battle Hymn of the Republic," Julia Ward Howe

You have been born into an unprecedented crossroads in history, where the "end times" is intersecting with "real time." Events prophesied in Scriptures thousands of years beforehand are now coming to pass. The most defining example is the rebirth of Israel in 1948. But there are many more examples. Some of them are occurring right before your eyes.

For this reason, billions of people around the globe are coming to embrace an extraordinary conclusion. We are now living in an era described in the Bible as the *"time of the end"* (Daniel 12:4 NKJV) or the end times.

In Matthew 24, Jesus shared that the culmination of the end times would bring the emergence of birth pangs, gradual at first but increasing in frequency as the great crescendo draws close. From Israel's war to President Trump's near-assassination, the urgency of the hour is clear. Our role to advance His Kingdom in the midst of these birth pangs is a primary focus of this book.

That said, the following are just a few challenges we face today:

- Hypersonic bombs bursting in air. Key Bridge collapsing—cyber warfare? Fabricated virus, tainted vaccinations. Compromised borders, mass migration. Terrorists and gangs cross us virtually unchecked. Illegals are covered while our veterans are wrecked.

- Compromised sovereigns, stolen elections. Weaponized government, global deception. China, Russia, Iran all take aim. United Nations rule that the Jews are to blame. Deep fakes, deep state, Nazi propaganda brings a holocaust fate.

- Chip in your brain makes a virtual feast—humanity's gain or the mark of the beast? AI tracks you with its all-seeing eye. Tower of Babel, are you now on the rise? Flash from Amazon, across from the Pentagon.

- Trafficking. Trauma. Fentanyl. Obama. Hollywood occultists as cinematic priests, luring our children to their ancient beasts. Girl or boy, you must decide by first grade. Cancel mom and dad, they alone block the way!

- Tabernacle down, call 911. Trusted pillars tumble, smashing all the humble. Compromised church, compromised state, compromised leaders, great falling away.

- Who will repair the breach?

End times in real time—my best lyrical summation. But that's just a little of what's actually before us. Jolene and I are spiritual watchmen. Our counterparts in the intelligence world have been facing down Armageddon-like scenarios at an increasingly frequent basis, trying to avert a magnitude of destruction that sometimes now seems inevitable. We owe them our prayers!

Biblically, where are we on the last-days timetable? How can we know for sure? What is the role of prophetic ministry through the end times? What is the role of strategic prayer? And the big questions—how much of the antichrist agenda, so clear in our present hour, can we actually defeat?

Then there's you. Why is it that the God who frames history somehow decided to *inaugurate you* into His timeline for this era? Right here, right now?

What role do you have to play?

MINE EYES HAVE SEEN THE GLORY

Jesus the Son of God was once cradled as a baby while His earthly parents fled the wrath of kings. He is returning to fully liberate humanity from their grasp. The war is first spiritual. Revelation 19:11 (NASB) conveys the procession of a freedom movement as Jesus Himself bridges dimensions between Heaven and earth.

> *And I saw heaven opened, and behold, a white horse, and He*
> *who sat on it is called Faithful and True, and in righteousness*
> *He judges and makes war.*

We are all praying for our eyes to fully see the glory of His coming. Yet before His Throne and in the battlefields of our spheres, already His freedom movement is at hand. Already the God who identifies as Love is rendering His righteous sentences, and making war to uphold them.

> Jesus the Son of God was once cradled as a baby while His earthly parents fled the wrath of kings. He is returning to fully liberate humanity from their grasp.

Already it is glorious.

It's hard to imagine the White House as a portal for end-times revelation. But the truth is that prophets, presidents, students, and scientists are all wrestling through global challenges that have been accurately prophesied only within the scrolls of Holy Scripture.

All who seek shall find. Including you. The Bible remains the best source of intelligence that can be gained. Followed directly by authentic, real-time prophetic revelation gained by the Spirit of God.

Across from the White House on a bone-chilling November morning in 1861, the Willard Hotel glowed gray by dawn's early light. A sleep-deprived abolitionist reached for a stubby pencil and raced to capture prophetic truths that were suddenly flooding her heart. The result was a defining vision of Jesus entering into America's freedom struggle. He took the lead. Even through the end times.

Just before Abraham Lincoln was sworn into office, the Willard Hotel played host to America's final, failed summit to avert the Civil War. Division succumbed to open insurrection. America was poised to be X-ed out. But the Lord of hosts chose to re-enter this same portal to unseal a verdict of His divine intentions, which power and politics had failed to gain.

> Mine eyes have seen the glory of the coming of the Lord! He is trampling out the vintage where the grapes of wrath are stored. He has loosed the fateful

lightning of His terrible, swift sword. His truth is marching on!

Abolitionist writer Julia Ward Howe received what we today would call a prophetic song. "As I lay waiting for the dawn, the long lines of the desired poem began to twine themselves in my mind," Howe recalled. "I said to myself, I must get up and write these verses down, lest I fall asleep again and forget them!"

With this, the "Battle Hymn of the Republic" was birthed. Even though it wasn't ready by Abraham Lincoln's inauguration, in many respects it became his inauguration song. The stanzas formed an astonishing picture of Jesus—at war, for freedom, securing His original intentions for America. Even through the end times.

Instantly the imagery became iconic. The freedom mandate within the Civil War began to be seen more clearly—for both sides. And for more than 160 years, the "Battle Hymn" has mentored hundreds of millions of Americans through generations—on the end times, on Jesus' return, and even His engagement to redeem our freedom nation.

What a priceless gift. Can you imagine what would have happened—or worse, what would *not* have happened—if Julia Ward Howe had decided just to sleep in? No "Battle Hymn"! Take her wisdom to heart. Write down your revelation from the Lord the moment you receive it. Take seriously your impressions, your dreams, your visions. Record them. Create a system so that you can access your words, pray into them over time, and celebrate when they come to pass.

And further—never underestimate the power of a prophetic song! This one changed the trajectory of the entire conflict, and still shapes our nation today.

> I have seen Him in the watchfires of
> a hundred circling camps;
> They have builded Him an altar in the
> evening dews and damps;
> I can read His righteous sentence by
> the dim and flaring lamps;
> His day is marching on....

The scrolls you are opening are in many ways an overflow of this hymn. Through both waning light and fiery circumstance over the previous few years, the Lord has endeavored to unveil His righteous verdict. We have endeavored to perceive it, write it, and pass it on to you.

THE END TIMES—WHEN?

The "Battle Hymn of the Republic" was released in an era when most Americans were Christians. Culturally at least. Biblical scholarship was fundamental to any education. When the bright embers of the Second Great Awakening succumbed to the mass bloodshed of the Civil War, many Christians concluded that the final days were at hand.

"If America is lost, the world is lost!" thundered a prominent Boston minister in 1863, in a Thanksgiving message titled "The War and the Millennium." Like many of his peers, his understanding of the times may have been a bit off. Yet his core message is even more accurate today.

Let their example instruct you. It's wise not to presume too quickly regarding the times we are in. Yet God wants us to be like the sons of

Issachar, by His Spirit understanding the times (1 Chronicles 12:32). Further, we are clearly commanded by Jesus Himself to yearn for His coming, and even keep watch as though His return is immediately at hand (Matthew 25:13).

It is hard to live with real-time expectations of a future reality. Engage anyway. There is tremendous intentionality behind Jesus' directive, forging within you an unyielding hope that will in time be overwhelmingly fulfilled.

"Jesus is coming—look busy!" This sage advice from a 1990s bumper sticker is second only to the "Battle Hymn" when it comes to end-times Americana. It actually begs a few questions. How would you live differently if you absolutely knew you were living in the end times? How would your priorities shift? Would you try to make every moment count? What would you pursue?

What would you stop?

I ask this because Scriptures clearly confirm that you are actually living in the end times. Very likely more toward the finish line. According to the Bible, the dispensation between Jesus' birth and His return is defined as the end times. How do we know? After Jesus was resurrected, Holy Spirit blew through Jerusalem during Pentecost. The apostle Peter framed the experience as a fulfillment of a promise for *"the last days"* by quoting the book of Joel:

> *"And it shall be in **the last days**," God says, "That I will pour out My Spirit on all mankind; and your sons and your daughters will prophesy…"* (Acts 2:17-18 NASB).

Paul the apostle adds understanding in his epistle to the Hebrews. He sees the inauguration of Jesus to redeem mankind as the demarcation of the last days:

*God, after He spoke long ago to the fathers in the prophets in many portions and in many ways, in **these last days** has spoken to us **in His Son**, whom He appointed heir of all things...* (Hebrews 1:1-2 NASB).

Wait a minute. The last days began with Jesus? Not with Nero, Hitler, September 11, or the rise of the Deep State?

Honestly, it was a shock for us too. But from these passages and many others we can see that the dispensation the Bible refers to as the last days actually began with the birth, death, resurrection, and inauguration of Jesus Christ as King, followed by the release of Holy Spirit to mankind. It culminates with Christ's second coming.

NEEDED: REAL-TIME REVELATION

Prophetic Scriptures provide clear signposts of the end times and instruction. But they don't necessarily fill in the details. Instead they provide a plumbline of truth for direction to be gained from the Lord through real-time revelation.

To better understand this, let's look at Jesus' triumphal entry into Jerusalem. It was a procession leading to an unimaginable inauguration:

Rejoice greatly, daughter of Zion! Shout in triumph, daughter of Jerusalem! Behold, your king is coming to you; He is righteous and endowed with salvation, humble, and mounted on a donkey, even on a colt, the foal of a donkey (Zechariah 9:9 NASB).

To prepare for His final days, Jesus withdrew to Bethany beyond the Jordan, on the other side of the Jordan River. Earlier in Israel's history Joshua led the people across the river from this same location to possess their covenant land. Elijah ascended to Heaven there, and passed his mantle to Elisha. In the spirit and power of Elijah, John the Baptist immersed multitudes there, including Jesus Himself. Holy Spirit descended as a dove.

Likely from there, Jesus began to perceive that it was time for the fulfillment of Zechariah 9:9 *as His inaugural procession.* He would make His ascent from the wilderness to Jerusalem, City of the Great King, where details of the passage would convey to all Israel His true identity.

As King, He would then be crucified for their sins.

The messianic Scripture highlights many details. He would enter Jerusalem on a humble donkey instead of a horse-drawn chariot or even a camel. People would be fervent to welcome Him. But other details are strangely missing. When should this procession occur? Should it mark a feast day? Which one? And how should the donkey be obtained?

For Jesus to accomplish His mission He needed clear direction from Scriptures, but He also needed real-time revelation. Likewise we are living in an era when many end-times Scriptures are in process of being fulfilled. You likely have a role to play. But if Jesus Himself needed immediate direction from Holy Spirit to fulfill His destiny, how much more do you need accurate, real-time revelation to fulfill yours!

Within the gates of Jerusalem, Jesus was brutally tortured by Roman soldiers and died while being mocked as King of the Jews. He took the full punishment that was meant for you and me because of our sins (Isaiah 53). Holy Spirit then resurrected Jesus from the dead. He is risen indeed!

But the procession does not end there. Jesus then ascended to the Father, to present before Heaven's Court His own body and blood for the redemption of mankind. Let's pick up right where our previous book *Turnaround Decrees,* published in 2022, left off.

OPENING THE SCROLLS—
INAUGURATING THE END TIMES

John the Beloved was exiled on a remote Greek island in the Aegean Sea when he suddenly found himself before the Throne. Here's how it happened. He was in the Spirit on the Lord's day. The piercing cry of a shofar suddenly broke a prolonged silence. Within the sound a command formed:

> **Come up here**, *and I will show you what must take place…*
> (Revelation 4:1 NASB).

And boom there he was. With God the Almighty before him, senses overwhelmed, immersed in a realm of majesty far surpassing human description. Before the Throne, the exiled apostle was shown the inauguration of Jesus to rule over humanity, unleashing the last days.

Or more biblically, unsealing them.

As recorded in the book of Revelation, *"I saw in the right hand of Him who sat on the throne a scroll, written inside and on the back, sealed with seven seals"* (Revelation 5:1).

Note the most guarded storyline in Heaven was still communicated first on paper. With written symbols forming words. In the beginning was the Word, the genesis or origin of all things. Before the content could be experienced, it first had to be written and read. In the midst of unimaginable Throne Room glory, all creation remained captivated by simple words on a scroll.

And if you only knew the prophetic treasures embedded within the book you call your source, you would be just as captivated.

In Heaven, John perceived how the destiny of mankind depended on the unsealing of these scrolls. He wept in travail for their release. Many high-level intercessors today are following John's example, travailing for Heaven's scrolls to be perceived and birthed in a way that frames the very last days. You can join them, and gain the same for your family and sphere!

The apostle's tears were soon met with an answer. Jesus Christ approached the Father to receive the scrolls of mankind's redemption. Heaven's Court had fully scrutinized the offering of Christ's body and blood. All requirements of His Father's covenant were authentically fulfilled, so that Jesus could literally *become* God's covenant for all humankind.

Here's a revelation for us all. Gaining earned authority was mandated by the Father for Jesus, and it is mandated for you as well. No entitlement, no shortcut. He was tested. He paid the price in full to gain Heaven's justification to justify you. And there is a price for you to pay as well. First and foremost by living out basic covenantal morality, from a heart of love.

Before the Throne, the evaluation of Jesus' life brought a unanimous verdict, summed up by one word: "Worthy!"

> *...behold, the Lion that is from the tribe of Judah, the Root of David, has overcome so as to be able to open the scroll and its seven seals. And I saw...a Lamb standing, as if slaughtered.... And they sang a new song, saying, "Worthy are You to take the scroll and to break its seals..."* (Revelation 5:5-6,9 NASB).

Jesus arose and received the scroll out of the right hand of Him who sat on the Throne. Heaven roared in celebration. The sacred exchange marked the inauguration of Jesus as Redeemer and Ruler. It also marked the inauguration of a new era in which the Father's scroll for mankind's redemption was released. A freedom movement encompassing every tongue, tribe, and nation.

Given the emphasis on redeeming every ethnicity, the focus on Yeshua's Jewish identity may be surprising. Especially in John's era when the covenant people were persecuted and enslaved by the Roman Empire, the globalist federation of his day. Through Jesus, God's covenant with the Jewish people was not negated, it was instead fulfilled. And the Jewish Passover Lamb, slain yet standing, became the conquering Lion of Judah, ruling the world.

The inauguration of Jesus as King also inaugurated a new era on earth known as the end times. Accompanied by the greatest prophetic anthem ever sung!

> And they sang a new song, saying, "Worthy are You to take the scroll and to break its seals; for You were slaughtered, and You purchased people for God with Your blood from every tribe, language, people, and nation. You have made them into a kingdom and priests to our God, and they will reign upon the earth" (Revelation 5:9-10).

INAUGURATING AMERICA'S NEW ERA

Prophetically, we sense that the inauguration of America's president in 2025 also marks the inauguration of a new, defining era for America and the world. A scroll has been unfurled. Times have sovereignly been set. And a greater acceleration into a final segment of the biblically defined end of days is at hand.

As a prophet representing God's covenant for America, writing this book amidst the extreme presidential challenges of 2024 has been daunting. As you'll see, we've given many prophetic words that have played out before our eyes during this time, both warnings and wonders. For instance, by the Spirit's prompting we warned consistently throughout our book *White House Watchmen* about potential assassination attempts against former President Trump, and equipped readers to effectively pray. July 13, 2024, will be forever memorialized by the defiant fist of a bloodied president who narrowly escaped death. It was truly a miracle turnaround.

That said, we *must* continue a vigilant watch for Trump against assassination attempts.

Open the Scrolls

On July 4, 2021, the Lord awakened me with a prophetic vision. The experience is highlighted in our book *Turnaround Decrees*. I saw a blank scroll hovering over our bed. It looked similar to the parchment on which the Declaration of Independence was written. But it was completely blank. I knew immediately the Lord was requiring us to perceive, receive, and write Heaven's scrolls to decree America's future—and that if we failed to do so the enemy's globalist policies would fill in the blanks and prevail by default.

One way or another the "turnaround decrees" formed on these blank scrolls would carry a similar weight to our founding documents to turn the nation in this hour.

In another experience chronicled in *Turnaround Decrees*, I saw the Lion of Judah roaring His redemptive decrees over the United States.

He came virtually unseen, in a midnight hour, to do so. Note again that the only place Jesus is revealed as the Lion of Judah is when He receives and opens the scrolls. But we're in this midnight hour right now.

A Severe Redemption

Clearly Jesus wants to redeem us, to heal our land. But the Spirit of God is saying that what He is granting America in the era ahead is actually a severe redemption.

As with John the beloved, the Lord is calling us all to come up higher. Leaders especially. Our nation will be tested. A turnaround that realigns with basic covenantal standards of biblical morality is mandated. Movements within the body of Christ are already being tested and purified, including the prophetic movement. It goes without saying that our role in the end times is far too vital not to be rescued from our current state.

In the midst of this severe redemption, Jesus is going to be revealed as the Bridegroom to Israel and the United States of America. Even Hosea nations will be summoned to fully return to Him. Why? Because in this season Hosea intercessors are destined to prevail. Through your prayers and mine and countless others, His bride will return.

Inauguration of End-Time Awakeners

Just before July 4, 2024, Holy Spirit spoke to me an unusual phrase. "I am inaugurating My end-time awakeners. I am inaugurating My end-time awakening!" This is great news. Kind of like Paul Revere, end-time awakeners will soon be released to stir a slumbering army, holding out their burning lamps to ignite us all with revolutionary fire. An anointing of holy conviction will again sweep the nation. The false "woke" awakening that has promoted antichrist ideologies of witchcraft, cultural marxism, antisemitism, and the sexualization of our children will be deflated and repudiated. We will come to our senses. We will return.

God's move will be strengthened by the grace of Holy Spirit exemplified biblically through the ministry of Elijah. A forerunner anointing to turn the hearts of the fathers to the children, the children to their fathers, and to turn many of the sons of the covenant back to the Lord their God (Malachi 4:6, Luke 1:52).

Not only is a new era being inaugurated but a defining new season of worship is also being inaugurated. Awakening songs. Throne room anthems. Corporate encounters in the spirit of Isaiah 6 where our worship draws down the holy awe of God. The gates will shake!

A New Way Forward—Jesus' Way!

It was astonishing that presidential candidate Kamala Harris chose as her campaign theme, "A New Way Forward." My heart leapt. Because back in 2018 the Lord gave me this very phrase as a prophetic word for the White House. We were hosting our Revolution gathering at the Trump Hotel at the time. And I knew the word was for the governmental seat.

When Kamala Harris cast vision for the "New Way Forward," many of the themes of my prophetic message were front and center. Most of all the need to unify the nation around ideas we all agree on.

The word came from a vision of "the Glory Train" leaving the station. Remaining on the platform were two "cancel culture" groups the train was leaving behind. To the left were Antifa members, dressed in black. To the right were KKK members, dressed in white sheets. I knew we had to move beyond these two hateful embodiments of cancel culture to see our nation recover.

I'm not sure Vice President Harris ever shared that aspect. In fact she's long been a proponent of "cancel culture." But we all need to give opportunities for people to change, and honor their progress when they do.

TRUMP AND LINCOLN—END-TIMES INAUGURATIONS

As presidents, Abraham Lincoln and Donald Trump both presided over America during extremely perilous, divisive times. Let's draw a few lessons from their watch that will prove invaluable.

"So help me, God." By all accounts Abraham Lincoln did not own these words when he first took his inaugural vow on March 4, 1861, one month before the Civil War broke out. But he fully owned them by its culmination. He was known for clinging to God in prayer over pivotal battles. On April 14, 1865, Lincoln was targeted for assassination with a bullet fired toward his head. This one stole Lincoln's life before he could oversee the reunion and turnaround he longed to secure.

During the war, Lincoln had grown not only in his personal relationship with the Lord, but also in revelation that could only have come from the very Throne of God. Including an understanding of His end-times judgments, which surpasses most theologians then and now. A portal to glory had seemingly opened at the White House. Please join me in praying this portal opens once again. And that President Trump grows like Lincoln in his relationship with the Lord.

With President Lincoln's inauguration, all America was inaugurated into a new era of history. The "Battle Hymn of the Republic" soon came to define it.

"So help me, God." Now Donald Trump has returned to the throne. Age has made it slightly more difficult for Trump to ascend the Capitol stairs for his second swearing-in ceremony. But it has also brought more wisdom and maturity to govern. This is truth, not speculation.

Just four days before the 2020 elections, *Rolling Stone* magazine dubbed Donald Trump "the End Times President." It was actually an accurate assessment. Love him or hate him, many Americans intuitively perceive that his presidency became a true sign of the last days.

And it proved especially true after Trump decided to run again. This time the primary opposition did not come from within the government but from the outside. Even from rogue nations. And it nearly proved lethal.

On July 13, 2024, Trump was leading a campaign rally in Butler, Pennsylvania (Butler PA), when an undetected sniper took aim and fired. At the last moment Trump turned his head. The sound of a supersonic burst screamed past, while the bullet grazed his right ear. By all odds this bullet should have marked Trump's last day on earth. But it failed.

Bloodied but clear, Trump arose. His protective detail tried to quickly exfiltrate him from the stage, but Trump demanded they stop. He engaged the crowd. With fist raised in godly defiance, he shouted, "Fight!"

Facing death, Trump's immediate resolve was to inspire us all to fight for the nation he so clearly loves. His resolve immediately re-energized the American spirit. Politics became secondary. It earned him the right to genuinely become a father of our nation. Even without a return to Washington, DC as president.

In the early fall of 2024, the FBI took the unprecedented step of briefing Donald Trump on Iranian attempts to assassinate him as well as other former members of his administration. It was also disclosed that the Butler PA shooter possessed on his phone encrypted communications with other nations. Iran was not specified. But their ultimatum was very clear. Iran had hired people in America to take down the former president.

And if that were not enough, the FBI disclosure was followed up by messaging from President Biden, both publicly and through back channels. Any assassination attempt sourced by Iran against Donald Trump would be considered an act of war against the United States, and we would respond accordingly

For Trump's former rival to so clearly invoke the power of the entire US military, intelligence, and diplomatic communities toward this end, in an election year, shows the seriousness of the issue.

Trump ran and nearly died to make America great again. And despite the fiercest efforts of czars, dictators, and ayatollahs to kill him while a candidate and disrupt our election process, our peaceful transfer of power once again attained the highest aspirations of our enduring greatness.

No disrespect here, but I'm not referring to the capabilities of our best governmental leaders to rule, Trump included. Instead, I'm making reference to the foundations of our freedom—government under God—which alone preserve our greatness. By these sacred foundations our liberties are perpetuated largely unhindered to ensuing generations, while protecting our citizens from the ceaseless threat of subjugation by government itself.

The light still shines. Brightly. No King but Jesus.

THE RESURRECTION OF DONALD JOHN TRUMP

In our book *White House Watchmen,* we felt checked to prophesy that Trump would win the 2020 election. But we felt strangely led to share many prophetic words casting vision for Trump's second term, as well as policy shifts that would be solidified. Only now does this make sense.

One word was on "the resurrection of Donald John Trump." In a dream I saw the president sinking in the Potomac, chained to a cement block. "They tried to leverage him but it did not work," the Lord spoke to me. "So they decided to throw him overboard!" Our job was to pray until chains were broken so Trump could resurface. Then I heard the Lord proclaim, "The resurrection of Donald John Trump." Given his extraordinary return to office, I believe this word is now being fulfilled.

A second dream is worth noting. A bridge from our home to the White House appeared, and the doors of the White House opened. President Trump was at the top of the stairs, kneeling as if in prayer. He invited me to join him. To my surprise, Trump was praying over a sculpture of the Capitol. In the White House!

Was this some kind of hostile takeover? A violation of the separation of powers? The opposite, in fact. In the dream the Lord spoke to me, "What I desire to do next in this nation requires peace between the offices!" Zechariah 6:13 provides a scriptural reference for the phrase.

That was certainly not the case at the time of my dream. Nancy Pelosi presided. You might remember she tore up President Trump's State of the Union Address in front of a global audience. Let's just say there was no peace between the offices!

But in a surprising turnaround, Mike Johnson arose to the House speakership in 2023. As you will soon read, by the grace of God we even had a small part to play in this breakthrough. Speaker Johnson has long been working to synergize efforts between the House, the Senate, and the White House for a dramatic turnaround over the 100 days. The way is prepared.

Here's a final prophetic word for you regarding President Trump, originally shared in our book *White House Watchmen*. Early in Trump's first administration, friends from Israel warned that he could be a Hitler for our time. I went to the Lord in prayer and received a surprising answer: "Donald Trump is not a Hitler, he is instead a Churchill. Then you must ask, why does America need a Churchill for this time?"

Winston Churchill presided over the United Kingdom through World War II, in what might be called a season of severe redemption. Known as "the Roaring Lion," against all odds Churchill prevailed against the Nazis.

As noted, President Trump continues to preside over one of the most divisive eras since the Civil War. Perils from within and without have exponentially increased. The mandate remains the same as the first, to make America great again. But how?

And on a global scale, what's next?

NEW BIRTH OF FREEDOM

Midway through the Civil War, on a cold November day in 1863, President Lincoln traveled to the Gettysburg Battlefield, seeking a new way forward for his generation. As with the prophet Ezekiel, the president walked through a literal field of dry bones, with many soldiers from both north and south still remaining unburied.

Lincoln gained the conviction that only a "born-again experience" on a national level could actually redeem our land. It is the same in our day. From the Gettysburg Address:

> That this Nation, under God, shall have a new birth of freedom; and that government, of the people, by the people, for the people, shall not perish from the earth.

Always remember this. God often confronts the greatest magnitude of evil with the travail of a new birth. It happened with the birth of Jesus. It happened with America in Lincoln's day. And it can happen again today.

On 7-22-2024 (July 22), the Lord showed us that Lincoln's decree of a "New Birth of Freedom" is in fact being reconstituted as a turnaround verdict for this hour. Those familiar with our books know we have often referenced it as a foundational prayer. What's different is my compelling sense that Heaven's Court is authorized to nationally grant these words.

What changed? I submit to you this verdict has now been unsealed in response to

God often confronts the greatest magnitude of evil with the travail of a new birth.

the US Supreme Court's annulment of the covenant with death and hell through nationally legalized abortion. Maybe not coincidentally, the "scroll" of this verdict was released on a date Catholics honor the birth of John the Baptist.

FOLLOW-UP VISION

Early in the process of writing *End Times in Real Time,* the Lord gave me a follow-up vision to the verdict. I had hit a roadblock. And I felt drawn to ask Him to heal any wounds within my spirit hindering the birthing of what this book represents. Instantly, I saw a vision of a stillborn baby coming awake, smiling, and coming to birth with ease. The child was immediately followed by another beautiful baby. Both babies were born healthy!

In the midst of great calamity, America is being released into a double-portion season. It is an Elijah movement, Jesus' original intent in granting a new way forward for America. Forerunners are being sent before His face to prepare the way of the Lord. And even the two covenant lands of Israel and America are being ushered into this move.

Some scholars say the US doesn't actually have a destiny in the end times. We say different. By verdict from Heaven's Court, America remains a covenant nation under God. Therefore as the "Battle Hymn" conveys, Jesus' freedom movement remains twined with ours. It is no less vulnerable now than in Lincoln's day. Probably it is more.

But Jesus is taking His place at the head and is leading the charge. The battle for the Exodus of humankind continues to unfold before our eyes. And the embers of ancient watchfires are still burning hot, reaching for you today.

See Him. Catch the fire. The Lord of hosts is in your midst. He is re-entering spheres where power and politics have failed. Redemption is in His hand. May you have eyes to perceive the sentence of His unfurled scroll, and may you be inaugurated into His fiery camp.

A note on history. Prior to the 20th century, March 4 was the inauguration date for presidents as specified in the Constitution. The date happens to be Jon's birthday. On March 4, 2024, the Supreme Court ruled that former President Trump must remain on the ballot as a candidate for president. And entirely coincidentally, March 4, 2025, is also the date selected by Destiny Image Publishers for the release of this book. The Lord marches forth as a warrior... (Isaiah 42).

STUDY QUESTIONS AND PRAYER

1. When did you first encounter "The Battle Hymn of the Republic"? Growing up? In school or church? How do the words impact you now? Do you see them as prophetic for our time?

2. Are we living in the end times? How do you know for sure?

3. What does "end times in real time" mean to you? How is the Lord leading you today? Do you feel you are currently receiving real-time revelation personally?

4. Was it a surprise to discover how, after the cross, Jesus was inaugurated into His position?

5. God is inaugurating a new era for the United States of America in this hour. What are the characteristics prophesied?

6. How do you feel about the 2024 elections? The 2025 inauguration? How are you praying for our president?

7. What did Lincoln mean by a "new birth of freedom"? How can we see this today?

Father God, I ask for Your personal inauguration for my life. Grant me a new birth of freedom. Let me see Your glory! Help me to realign my worldview with Your worldview of the end times. Help me to understand times and seasons. Grant me real-time revelation. And help me to see and understand Your real-time work in my life, in my spheres, and even in my nation. Sharpen me as an effective prayer warrior for the new season we have entered into. Help me to pray for our leaders, including the president. In Jesus' name, amen!

SECTION 2

END TIMES
IN REAL TIME

Vision of Armageddon clock over Tel Megiddo. Illustrative graphic.

CHAPTER 4

Chapter Topics: Armageddon Vision | Warning of Israel War | Gideon & Elijah | X Eclipse, Earthquake, Passover | God's Time Clock | Antichrist Timing | Throne Room Timing | Redeem Your Time

THE ARMAGEDDON CLOCK

"We are living in a time of unprecedented danger, and the Doomsday Clock time reflects that reality."

—Dr. Rachel Bronson, President, *Bulletin of the Atomic Scientists,* January 2023

"TICK TOCK TO THE HOLY CLOCK. Do you know what time it is?" Words from a spontaneous prophetic song raced through Jolene's heart as we gazed across the Jezreel Valley from Tel Megiddo, a large hill by the Carmel mountain range in northern Israel. We had come to the covenant land to fulfill a prophetic assignment by the Jordan River the following day.

Tel Megiddo is better known as Har Megiddo or Armageddon. The summit is a watchman's perch that overlooks the best-known battlefield in the world. Scripture instructs us that the kings of the earth, their demons and their armies will one day gather in this cross-roads of continents for *"the war of the great day of God, the Almighty"* (Revelation 16:14-16 NASB).

Our visit in December 2022 was not so action-packed. In fact it was saturated with peace. A rising sun glistened over vast fields of produce in the land known as Israel's breadbasket. A weighty, fragrant haze partially lifted. To the east, Mount Gilboa and Mount Tabor revealed their rounded summits.

Jesus' hometown of Nazareth and other northern points finally came into view. It is shocking to realize that Nazareth's most famous resident grew up overlooking Armageddon. Likely it is where He learned to pray.

We began to seek the Lord. Jolene received a vision. A huge grand-father clock lay over the Jezreel Valley, its hands demarcating the time. According to God's timetable, it was ten minutes to midnight.

Ten months later almost to the day, on October 7, 2022, Iran proxy Hamas crossed into Israel and brutally killed some 1,200 people in an unforeseen invasion from Gaza. At least 32 Americans were among the dead. It was the largest wholesale slaughter of the Jewish people since the Holocaust. And it occurred on the final, most celebratory day of the Feast of Tabernacles. Some 250 hostages were abducted, many of them violated sexually on camera while being forced into captivity. Israel immediately declared war.

Astonishingly, the most brutal strike in Israel's history soon sparked the most widespread surge of antisemitism in global history. Even in the United States, violent protests on college campuses erupted across the entire nation with chants of genocide "from the river to the sea." For weeks on end US intelligence agencies publicly warned of a dramatic spike in terror threats.

No clarification was needed as to why. "We are Hamas," exclaimed one protester at Columbia University. "We are all Hamas!"

PASSOVER—A MIDNIGHT DELIVERANCE

On April 13, 2023, just a week before Passover, the midnight skies burst with what looked like fireworks above the Temple Mount. Iran was bombing the covenant land of Israel. From Eilat to the Golan Heights, flaming streaks of armaments rained down across Israel's darkened horizons. Fighter jets roared through the skies, firing rockets to intersect and decimate incoming munitions.

If this were a movie, it could legitimately have been called "Armageddon." Note this was just before Passover 2024.

More than 300 drones and cruise missiles were intercepted, largely preserving Israel from harm. "It was like Top Gun meets Star Wars!" exclaimed one Israeli pilot in an interview with the *Times of Israel*.

Reporters, military strategists, rabbis, and scientists all referenced it as a "Passover miracle." An Exodus moment when *death literally passed over.*

ISRAEL—GOD'S TIME CLOCK

Israel is God's time clock for the US and for the nations. The Bible is unapologetically Israel-centric. When prophets received words from the Lord, they interpreted them from the vantage point of the Covenant Land to the horizons of the earth. Even while they were in exile this remained true. Prayers were always directed to Jerusalem, and from Jerusalem to the world.

Of course, the entirety of prophetic projections within both the Old Testament and New Testament culminate with Israel. Both in Jerusalem and in the fertile harvest fields below a large mound called Tel Megiddo.

The Jezreel valley is referenced continually by biblical prophets as a parabolic symbol of Israel as a nation. The name *Jezreel* is actually a variant of *Yisrael* or *Israel*. Note that the word *Jezreel* in Hebrew means, "God sows." And as Israel's most fertile farmland, it is now living up to its name!

Because of its legendary hill, Jezreel is also known as the Valley of Armageddon. They are one in the same. It's no surprise that the harvest fields hosting the "great war of God" have already hosted countless wars through thousands of years, including many of the conflicts recorded in scripture between the forces of God and satan, Christ and antichrist.

Gideon's 300 warriors converged there—after the valiant warrior tore down his father's altar to Baal. They blew their trumpets, unsheathed their lamps, and invading forces were supernaturally routed. Conversely, the witch of Endor practiced her sorcery in the valley, invoking for kings the spirits of the dead.

Abraham, Isaac, and Jacob all sojourned through the fields. Deborah led and won there. Saul led, lost, and was killed there. Solomon romanced the Shulamite girl there. Hosea romanced his wife Gomer there. He lost her there, wept over her there, and found her once again as a prophetic witness to God's unfathomable restoration.

> *"I will remove the names of the Baals from her mouth,"* [Hosea prophesied,] *"...I will betroth you to Me in righteousness and in justice, in favor and in compassion, and I will betroth you to Me in faithfulness. Then you will know the Lord"* (Hosea 2:17,19-20 NASB).

The Lord then focuses on the harvest restoration over drought-ridden seeds of grain in the fields, seeds of grapes in the vineyards, and seeds of olives in the orchards. "They will respond to 'God sows' or the God who sows. They will all respond to Jezreel!" (See Hosea chapter 2.)

"Throughout history Megiddo and the Jezreel Valley have been Ground Zero for battles that determined the very course of civilization," writes George Washington University professor of anthropology Eric Cline. "It is no wonder that the author of Revelation believed Armageddon, the penultimate battle between good and evil, would also take place in this region."[1]

Perhaps most importantly, the region was also home turf for the historic clashes between Elijah and the prophets of Baal—Ahab and Jezebel included. Fire was called down from Heaven overlooking these fields, turning Elijah's nation back to the Lord.

Here's a takeaway for you. As it was in the days of the prophet so it is today. Armageddon is a backdrop for the spirit of Elijah.

HEBREW TIME IS CYCLICAL

As anthropologist Eric Cline infers, great battles of God the Almighty have already been fought on the Megiddo soil, both in the spirit and the natural. What once was, again will be. And the end times is like that. Hebraic understanding of time is not so much linear as cyclical, much like the dial of a clock. It is patterned after God's orchestration of times and seasons through the sun,

> As it was in the days of the prophet so it is today. Armageddon is a backdrop for the spirit of Elijah.

moon, and stars. Within the broad arc of time are many revolutions, where similar challenges to the past come back around in somewhat different forms.

Sometimes the cycle seems like ascending through a tornado! The good news is that as you move through time with Jesus, you're not just going around in circles, you're coming up higher. By gaining revelation of God's victories in the past, you can better comprehend the scope of challenges, how to approach them, and how to secure the victories He desires to unleash for your present and future.

Likewise, to understand future challenges, you need to look both to the past and to the present. This dimension of remembrance is a primary reason we recommend every Christian celebrate the biblical feasts. Purim, Passover, Pentecost, Rosh Hashanah and Yom Teruah, Yom Kippur, Tabernacles, Hanukkah. Each feast brings a celebration of God's intervention that unveils a dimension of His nature and character. You are invited to relate to Him in a new way through this revelation. By rehearsing the miracles granted to our ancestors and putting a demand on Heaven for His intervention, you and I can access the anointing to see the same breakthroughs in our day.

Tick tock to the holy clock!

ANTICHRIST TIMING

God's timing is always perfect. There's a natural flow to His supernatural rhythm. Conversely, the antichrist spirit has a counterfeit timing he seeks to impose on individuals, on governments, and on the masses.

We are seeing this imposition today. And in every case, timing is used as a function of the enemy's dark mission to steal, kill, and destroy.

For instance, in satan's dark timing sex education should begin in kindergarten, include every form of deviant sexuality, and be taught to the schoolchildren by drag queens. That's actually going on today.

In global affairs, dark forces have sought again and again to spark an Armageddon-like war way ahead of God's permitted timetable. The mission remains to take out as many human beings as possible, causing mass heartbreak and trauma, depleting nations of generations and resources, while robbing God of His precious harvest.

Daniel shows how the antichrist spirit seeks to change times, seasons, and laws: *"And he will speak against the Most High and wear down the saints of the Highest One, and he will intend to make alterations in times and in law; and they will be handed over to him for a time, times, and half a time"* (Daniel 7:25 NASB).

Haven't you seen this today? Not just from the Oval Office but from your local school board, your city council, your local news station.

But the good news is that *"The court will convene for judgment, and his dominion will be taken away, annihilated and destroyed forever"* (Daniel 7:26 NASB). This is a facet of the Daniel 7:22 verdict He has already granted. It's your job to appropriate it to your life and world.

The Lord calls us to *"walk circumspectly...redeeming the time, for the days are evil"* (Ephesians 5:15-16 NKJV). In other words, the evil of our time mandates we appropriate His verdict to redeem time! Through Jesus we can repair the past to redeem the present and secure His dream for our future.

We are part of a team working on this now. Long before our time, an ancient ruler named Constantine co-opted Christianity and shifted the entirety of Christendom from God's rhythm of time to idolatrous Roman time. In a "cancel culture" move George Soros would be proud of, Constantine literally canceled the biblical feasts from his yearly time clock. The pagan holidays of Rome and Greece then gained new "christian" identities. Which is why, when you scratch the surface, many of the "christian" holidays we celebrate actually have pagan roots.

RECOVERING THE TRUE MEANING OF CHRISTMAS

The December celebration of Christmas, for instance, is rooted in the worship of Zeus. And if you ever wondered why the resurrection of Jesus is called "Easter," look no further than the ancient idolatrous worship of "Ishtar." This subject is touchy, and we are not looking to disrupt your holiday celebrations. Our holiday traditions have actually been greatly enriched by gaining a more accurate biblical understanding.

For instance, according to Messianic Jewish scholars such as Asher Intrater, Dan Juster, and others, Jesus was likely born during the fall feasts, not on December 25. And if you count nine months backward, it's a joy to discover that Jesus was likely conceived over Hanukkah. A Jewish holiday which often converges with the Christmas season, the "Festival of Lights" commemorates a miraculous breakthrough where God's people relit their lamp, or menorah, to reconsecrate their Temple back to the Lord.

When we discover the Light of the Word likely came into the world over the Festival of Lights, the true meaning of Christmas becomes even more cherished. Because through Jesus' greatest gift to you, His redemption, your temple has been forever consecrated to Him, and His sacred fire has been imparted to your life. It's what He came to do!

You may find it interesting that, since the days of Constantine, we've been celebrating the birth of Christ at His actual conception.

Just in case you're wondering about God's perspective on whether or not life begins in the womb.

Finally, remember how the angel Gabriel visited Mary and foretold the conception of Jesus. *"The Holy Spirit will come upon you, and the power of the Most High will overshadow you"* (Luke 1:35 NIV). Hanukkah, now globally celebrated as the Christmas season, became the time period God chose for this encounter.

Based on this fact, can I offer you a piece of advice? Take time during the busy holidays to genuinely encounter Jesus. He truly is the reason for the season. And as you choose to seek Him, He will often release to you key revelation that will bring to birth His covenant purposes for your life.

God wants you to know His timing. He wants to redeem the time for you and for your world. It's time to recover His covenantal cycles of time! It all begins with sanctifying your time to Him. We'll lead you in a prayer in a moment. But now let's discover the roots of Hebraic timing. For this we have to look to the skies.

THE CELESTIAL TIME CLOCK

Some dimensions of God's time clock can only be discerned through observing the celestial realms. In fact, Hebrew timing is based on celestial timing. From creation, God intended the skies above to convey what might be described as "divine messaging" to humanity. And His social media account is pretty vast. As the world turns…

> *Then God said, "Let there be lights in the expanse of the heavens to separate the day from the night, and they shall serve as signs and for seasons, and for days and years"* (Genesis 1:14 NASB).

Ever play a game of pool? Games are won or lost based on the precision of your aim, your angles, and your use of force. With this at heart, it is beyond our capacity to comprehend how our Creator set comets, moons, planets and stars in motion billions of years ago to precisely convey His divine messaging to each successive generation of humanity on earth, even to the very end of days.

Our Creator God is the Ancient of Days. He is much more brilliant, much more glorious, and much more precise through eons than our minds can possibly comprehend.

THE X ECLIPSE

...I will pour out My Spirit on all flesh; your sons and daughters shall prophesy.... The sun shall be turned into darkness, and the moon into blood, before the coming of the great and awesome day of the Lord (Joel 2:28,31 NKJV).

We've covered how, one week before Passover 2024, Iranian missiles were thwarted in the skies above Israel. Two weeks before Passover 2024, on April 8, a dramatic sign appeared in the skies above the United States. A massive solar eclipse made its way from Texas to New England.

The pathway of the 2024 solar eclipse actually intersected with the pathway of a previous solar eclipse in 2018. From an aerial view, the pathways formed a dramatic X over the United States.

Everywhere the eclipse passed over, the brightness of day succumbed within minutes to the darkness of midnight. Including Little Egypt, the region in southern Illinois where the pathways of the two solar eclipses actually intersected. X literally marked the spot.

What is God saying? Remember the Exodus miracle began when God passed over Egypt in a midnight hour, shaking Pharaoh's land to the core and delivering His covenant people. Is Little Egypt parabolic of a shaking in America? An American exodus?

Let's add to the mystery. The X eclipse was immediately preceded by an earthquake that rocked the East Coast. Tremors were felt from Maine to Washington, DC. New York City shook violently. The epicenter of the quake was none other than Whitehouse Station, New Jersey. To make epic events even more epic, Whitehouse Station is just three miles from Donald Trump's Bedminster golf club. In fact, Trump's course was considered by geologists part of the epicenter.

The X Eclipse. Little Egypt. Passover Exodus. Trump-quake shakes East Coast from Whitehouse Station. You can't make this stuff up. Seriously.

Did I mention that the magnitude of the quake registered at 4.8 on the Richter scale? Which meant that the magnitude of the eclipse precisely marked the very date of the April 8 eclipse.

Maybe it's not a coincidence that just three months later an assassin's bullet came within an inch of taking President Trump's life. The enemy literally tried to X out our ex-president. In a true turnaround moment, God's direct intervention not only saved him, but propelled him once again into the nation's highest office.

Can't make this up. No way, no how.

AMERICAN X-OUT

Twenty-eight years before the solar pathways formed an X over the US, prophet Cindy Jacobs saw a vision of an X over our nation. The lines in her vision intersected over Kansas City. Cindy immediately knew that forces of darkness were seeking to X-out America.

Cindy spoke with Dutch Sheets about the prophetic warning. While praying into it, Dutch saw the X transformed into a bridal canopy over the land, with its center pole in Kansas City.

Isaiah 4 conveys God's glory and covenantal protection as a bridal canopy. The Tabernacle of David, with the Ark of the Covenant resting within it, provides you with a great picture. Amos 9:11 conveys the restoration of the Tabernacle of David as a primary catalyst for both Israel's restoration and global revival in the end times. But it can only be secured through a much-needed purging within the body of Christ.

> *When the Lord has washed away the filth of the daughters of Zion and purged the bloodshed of Jerusalem from her midst, by the spirit of judgment and the spirit of burning, then the Lord will create over the entire area of Mount Zion and over her assemblies a cloud by day, and smoke, and the brightness of a flaming fire by night; for over all the glory will be a canopy* (Isaiah 4:4-5 NASB).

Maybe it's no coincidence that a little more than a week after the eclipse, the International House of Prayer in Kansas City came close to shutting down. They actually never did. But allegations of decades of hidden clergy sex abuse brought them to the brink, and led to founder Mike Bickle stepping down.

For more than 24 years the ministry hosted 24-7 worship and prayer, forerunning the restoration of the Tabernacle of David. A focus on the end times was at the very core of their ministry expression, seeking to advance God's Kingdom and counter the antichrist agenda on earth. Mobilizing prayer for Israel was a key component to this call. But covenant with God was compromised at a staggering level, and took a horrific toll—on a personal and global level.

Antichrist is anti-covenant. And nothing will get you out of God's timing and purpose for your life like breaking your covenant commitments in the Lord. Beloved, you cannot defeat what you embrace.

Many ministries have simply failed to confront breaches of covenant within their own houses and territories. The gates of sabotage have never been fully shut. Meanwhile Jesus remains a patient yet unyielding Judge. He's proven capable in both His unbiased analysis and thorough execution of justice. For this reason, for many leaders resisting long term to God's call to repentance, hidden sin is now being publicly exposed.

All that said—if a primary 24-7 worship and prayer ministry has essentially been X-ed out, how should we understand God's warning for America? Can the X-out be averted?

PERSONAL CRISIS DURING THE X ECLIPSE

The X Eclipse will forever be remembered in my heart for personal reasons as well. Because on the day of the eclipse, I came face to face with the prospect of my own "end of days." The full scope of a recently discovered health crisis was made clear. Doctors had ordered immediate tests after a previous MRI showed concerns. As a result, I spent April 8 in a medical center, briefly viewing the eclipse in between exhaustive bone scans and a CT scan.

Thank God all scans were clear! The core health concern was soon resolved by a surgical procedure. The recovery alone took more than a month.

But the Lord was making a point. The enemy has been seeking to X-out God's covenant people, you and me included. However, the

Lord is establishing His canopy of protection! He is restoring His covenant covering, and it is His heart to preserve lives and destinies.

That said, judgment begins at the house of the Lord (1 Peter 4:17). Let's all realize it does not end there. If taken seriously, the implications for the future are staggering. The Armageddon clock is ticking. And God is calling us to fully repent and return to Him (Acts 3:19).

EXODUS MOVEMENT

Prophetically, the 2024 eclipse and its dramatic circumstances convey both promises and warnings for today. Maybe most obviously, the intersection of the end times with real time. Let's also pray for the biblical promise of a long-awaited outpouring of Holy Spirit that concurrents with the eclipse.

Second, the X over our nation intuitively calls to us as if we've failed a test. We've gotten many things wrong. To the extent that the USA may even be in danger of being X-ed out.

It's time to come up higher. Repentance and realignment covenantally with Jesus, divorced from idolatry and abuse, are vital for American freedom to be preserved rather than suffering a radical X-out. The point isn't how. The point is that it could. Even as part of God's severe redemption.

That said, an overarching word of the Lord is this:

> I put the X in Exodus! And I put your Exodus in the X. In this midnight hour you have well seen how earthly shakings, war, and judgment on embedded evil have come even as My sign has passed over your land. The enemy has sought to X you out. Now watch

how I move you through this midnight hour into your promised inheritance.

For I say to you, your turnaround is now at hand! Your role in leading My covenant people has expanded. For I have called you to engage in the birthing of a forerunning move as My Spirit, even the Spirit and power of Elijah, is being poured out. My shakings have shaken your faith. Allow them to refine you. My promise remains secure.

The miracles of Exodus and Acts are being joined to form a global exodus movement from the dominions of darkness that have already begun to encompass your land.

As in the days of Pharaoh, many rulers will arise and many will be pulled down from their thrones. My Throne remains. My resolve remains. My victory remains. And you remain. With a cry that is continually heard before My Throne, "Let My people go!"

WANT REVELATION? SANCTIFY YOUR TIME

So how do we break free from antichrist timing? How do we align our timing with God's timing? Tick tock to the holy clock! As with all other aspects of life with God, sanctifying your time to Him is absolutely vital. Come into covenant with Christ over your timing.

A prophetic experience will give you a hint of the vast potential your covenant commitment can open. In 2007 the Lord gave me a life-changing dream that continues to define our ministry today.

I was walking down a cobblestone path at twilight that came to a crossroads. The path ahead forked into two paths; one veered to the left and the other to the right. Both paths seemed to dead-end at the face of a huge cliff.

Standing at the crossroads, I had come to a place of decision. The choices made now would significantly determine direction for the future, and U-turns were not really an option.

The options of right and left did not symbolize the political world. Instead they represented right versus wrong in direction. The path to the right was seemingly a pathway to a life of ease and provision, a shortcut to what many perceive as the American Dream. In my spirit I knew the personal rewards would seem great, but that the true Kingdom impact would be small.

The Lord showed me that the path that veered left was much more difficult, but led to the fulfillment of His dream for me. This path would have the greatest impact upon society for the Kingdom. I somehow knew that the door to the left was *the door to Daniel 7*.

Thinking at this time of decision, there was a magnetic pull to take the easy way. My path in Christ so far had taken turns that I had never even thought possible. Maybe this was an invitation to life as a "veteran of war" instead of remaining in the battle. Maybe this was actually His will...

Praying at this time of decision, I felt a small tug to turn left. In fact, my feet started walking before my mind was made up! As I walked along the path, still struggling to know if this was God's will for me, the Lord flashed a proverb across my mind: *"There is a way that seems **right** to a man, but its end is the way to **death***" (Proverbs 14:12 ESV).

Maybe you're at a similar point of decision. The Kingdom path is not the path of least resistance—far from it. But it is the path of life.

The Lord also showed me that the path I had perceived as veering left was actually the straight path! In other words the path wasn't warped, but my perspective was. My unhealed, unredeemed perspective made the wrong way look right.

EXCHANGE YOUR TIME FOR HIS SWORD

Close to the door ahead of me, I saw a large sword lying on the cobblestones. The word FAVOR was engraved on the front of the sword, and the number 222 was on the back. Seeing the sword, my first thought was, *This vision is like a video game. Pick up the sword, tap the door, and go through.* Though my strategy was set, the Lord was about to show me that this was not a game.

As I leaned over to pick up the sword, Holy Spirit spoke, "NO." The authority and urgency of the word literally imparted a holy fear. Then, very firmly in my spirit came the words, *"This sword will only be given in exchange for your time."*

I began to understand here what made this path so difficult. God wasn't concerned about redeeming processes on this walk, but redeeming intimacy with Him. He wanted my time.

In this hour, new weapons of war are being released to the body of Christ. The Lord invites you to give your time in exchange for the sword of His Word. To sanctify your time to Jesus, and allow Him to structure and steward it as He desires. Be willing to change course as the Spirit leads you: *"My times are in Your hand"* (Psalm 31:15 NASB).

With His sword in hand, God is opening to us the door to Daniel 7. Daniel was watching by night in Babylon when the Lord began to dramatically unveil His Throne Room activities. He watched in the Spirit and literally prophesied the most significant events of the end times.

If you're like me, you've wanted to move to a corner of the earth where God is moving greatly in order to receive a Throne Room visitation. Certainly not Babylon, or Washington, DC. But here's what's great. As you choose His chosen path regarding time, He will come to your Babylon! As with Gideon, Elijah, and Daniel, He will meet you at your altar of covenant.

That's where our post from 2007 ended. Here's the rest of the story.

In 2014, shortly after publication of our first book, *Crown & Throne*, the Lord highlighted Daniel 7 to me in an incredible way. If for no other reason than the fact I was in the shower at the time, He spoke to me: "Rent Faneuil Hall Boston on July 22, because on 7-22 I am granting your nation a Daniel 7:22 verdict of justice in favor of the saints!"

As soon as I got dressed, I made a beeline for my Bible. Daniel 7 absolutely came alive to me. It is the only chapter in Scripture detailing both the operations of Heaven's Court and the verdicts issuing to impact the earth. Including even the redemption of Christ!

And Daniel 7:21-22 shows how judgment is rendered in favor of the saints, restraining the highest level of forces of darkness and releasing the saints to possess the Kingdom. We have come to call this the "Turnaround Verdict."

PRAYER—MAKE THE EXCHANGE!

Father God, in Jesus' name I consecrate my time—past, present, and future—to you. At my crossroads, I now choose Your path of covenant. Forgive me where I have wasted the times and opportunities You have given me. Forgive me for not putting You first. Order my life, order my day, order my time according to Your will.

Father, I now exchange my time for the sword of Your Word. Grant me a spirit of wisdom and revelation in the knowledge of Jesus (Ephesians 1:17). Mature me, develop my competence to receive and pray Your Word. For Your glory, in Jesus' name!

NOTE

1. Eric H. Cline, *The Battles of Armageddon* (Ann Arbor, MI: University of Michigan Press, 2000); https://bibleinterp.arizona.edu/articles/2001/cli258001; accessed October 15, 2024.

Jon and Jolene receive prayer after picking up Spirit of Elijah mantles by Jordan River with Ed Watts, left, and Jamie Jackson, right.

CHAPTER 5

SPIRIT OF ELIJAH

"What if picking up the mantle is actually not about you in the least?"

—Jolene to Jon, from the chapter

Now let's return to the summit of Armageddon.
Last I checked it was December 9, 2022, and we were gazing out over the Jezreel Valley, praying to fulfill a prophetic action by the Jordan River the very next day. Jolene's vision of a gigantic grandfather clock, hovering over Israel's breadbasket, showed us that a midnight hour was at hand.

The good news is that, as we've learned, Armageddon is a backdrop for the spirit of Elijah.

THE TURNAROUND MANTLE

"Consecrate yourselves as Gideon, and I will give you the mantle of Elijah." On the flight to Israel from Washington, DC, the Lord had given clear marching orders. Just as Gideon repudiated idol worship—in our language he "divorced Baal"—so the Lord desired for us to consecrate ourselves afresh before engaging with Him by the Jordan River.

Jolene and I traveled to Israel with one focus at heart. We came to "up a mantle." I know that sounds perfectly normal to at least a few readers, maybe one or two, with no explanation needed. For the rest—here's a backstory.

Since 2014, Jolene and I have hosted Turnaround gatherings focused on Daniel 7:22, which we like to call God's "turnaround verdict." On July 22, 2022, we were preparing for our annual Turnaround gathering when I had a flash vision. I saw Jolene and myself with a small team standing by the muddy Jordan River. We picked up two Jewish prayer shawls representing a double-portion mantle of the spirit and power of Elijah. I felt the Lord was saying He wanted us to bear witness to the immediate release of this "mantle." It was for our ministry, yes, but especially for the body of Christ.

Elijah, of course, released his prophetic mantle to Elisha by the Jordan River, after his protege sought for *"a double portion"* of his spirit (2 Kings 2:9-11 NASB). The prophet was actually ascending before the Throne at the time, transported by heavenly chariots riding a whirlwind which momentarily connected Heaven and earth. This may sound extreme. But I've seen such a whirlwind portal, representing God's governmental glory. It's an accurate depiction.

Note that the mantle was not released on earth, but fell from Heaven to the earth. This is so important to note. I feel the Lord showed me the reason for this—and this is subjective—is so that the mantle would come down fully cleansed. As holy as Elijah lived, he was still a human being, similar in passions, limitations, and generational challenges to the rest of humanity (James 5:17). The Spirit and power of Elijah came—and comes—from God's Throne.

The mantle transfer empowered Elisha to release exactly twice the number of miracles as Elijah. John the Baptist was mantled with the same anointing, at the very same place, to literally prepare the way of the Lord. As a forerunner for Christ Himself!

The spirit and power of Elijah is released to turn the hearts of the fathers to the children, the children to their fathers, and to turn many sons of the covenant back to the Lord their God (Malachi 4:6, Luke 1:52). The Elijah anointing is a covenant-centric turn-around anointing that repairs hearts, families, churches, economies, and the governments of nations in context with returning to Christ. Every other aspect of awakening and Kingdom advancement largely depends on this one facet. That's probably why we like to call it "the turnaround mantle."

I promise—a further deep dive on this subject is just ahead. But all this said, if you're at all prophetic, you too have probably dreamed at some point of picking up a double-portion Elijah mantle by the Jordan River. For this reason I initially dismissed it entirely, and immediately repented of spiritual pride.

PURSUING THE MANTLE

Thankfully, Jolene prayed about it and soon rescued the vision. But only after, of course, affirming my very clear need to repent of spiritual pride.

Nothing like the power of teamwork! But she made a really good point, which convinced me of the validity of the vision: "What if picking up the mantle is actually not about you in the least? What if that's actually spiritual pride to focus on yourself in doing this? What if God's eyes are actually on all the people He desires to touch through the release of this anointing?"

Good point. Again, the power of teamwork! Upon hearing Jolene's corrective confirmation, I of course, sought to make things right. "Sweetheart, we should go and pick up the mantle immediately." August in Israel—with just a day or two in the desert. Not so bad, right?

Cooler heads again prevailed. It was soon decided we should make the journey privately once our fall ministry tour was over. To avert any potential for misunderstanding, it was one of those assignments we felt best to engage in covertly. And comfortably.

Which made it all the more surprising when our prophetic friend Ed "Wattage" Watts showed up in Israel at exactly the same time! To our total astonishment, it turned out Ed had heard the Lord speaking about a global release of the spirit and power of Elijah as well. He had journeyed to Israel to fast, pray, and write by Mount Carmel.

Out of the mouth of two or three witnesses… (Matthew 18:16, 2 Corinthians 13:1). Can't make this stuff up!

Ed of course joined us to pick up the mantle by the Jordan River. Friends and pastors Jamie and Redonnia Jackson joined us as well, along with worship leaders Michael and Cheryl Tyler.

CHUCK PIERCE PROPHESIES GLOBAL
SHIFT OF THE PROPHETIC

My original goal was to facilitate the prophetic action by picking up the mantle of Elijah on 12-12-2022. After all, Elijah built his altar with 12 stones representing the 12 tribes of Israel. The number 12 also represents apostolic government. Perfect, right?

Sadly, Jamie and Redonnia failed to hear God properly on the date. The fate of the world largely rested on picking up this mantle, but they were already booked on 12-12-2022 for some luxury seaside condo by the Sea of Galilee. Complete with poolside bliss.

So much for "praying the price." It almost led to an Elijah-like confrontation. My internal response was something like, "Okay… and? Cancel the condo!"

But once again cooler heads prevailed. Which means that Jolene wisely admonished me to remain quiet.

To accommodate our friends, we all decided to shift the prophetic action to December 10. Internally I was distressed at the prospect we were all missing God. After all, what significance could December 10 possibly have compared to 12-12-22? I mean, just look at the numbers!

Then Chuck Pierce released a prophecy that the entire prophetic movement would shift on a global level—beginning December 10.

Overall, the word was an astonishing confirmation—that is, except for the date. How could Chuck Pierce of all people get it so right, yet so wrong as well?

Suddenly, it dawned on me that I was the one who was actually missing it. December 10 was God's idea, not mine, even though the other date better fit my own narrative.

Watch out for prophetic presumption. It's a form of pride, and we are all guilty of it. Oftentimes, God requires you to hear and follow completely beyond your frame of reference. Repenting of pride is truly no joke. It allows God to remove the very blinders that keep you most confined. Move with Jesus, in His timing, and you will gain His breakthrough.

Of course I played it off like I knew the date all along. Privately whispering prayers of repentance once again.

THE MIDNIGHT HOUR

As mentioned, we were directed by the Lord to consecrate ourselves as Gideon in order to receive from Him the Elijah mantle I had seen in the vision. So on December 9, we made our way to the Jezreel Valley where the valiant warrior Gideon had consecrated himself and chose his 300 special ops warriors.

Gideon Springs is across the valley from Tel Megiddo. So we had to drive right by the ancient watchman summit anyway. Why not make it a prayer stop first thing in the morning?

Driving by Armageddon. Right. It still sounds surreal, doesn't it?

And from the summit of Tel Megiddo, Jolene was praying into the extraordinary prophecy by Chuck Pierce when she saw her vision.

The imagery of Chuck's "boiling pot" word, with the prophetic movement shifting on December 10, was daunting. Especially from the summit. Jeremiah the prophet saw a similar vision. A boiling pot of water began to pour out over Israel from her northern border (Jeremiah 1:13-16). It represented severe trouble coming from the north. And with the forces of Hezbollah and Iran poised to strike from Israel's northern border, that vision may actually be happening very soon.

While Jolene was praying, three times she heard Holy Spirit say, "I am flipping the numbers from 12-10 to 10 of 12!" In other words, 12-10 or December 10 was the prophetic marker that became ten minutes to midnight. Amazing that on the very date we were directed to pick up the Elijah mantle.

Later we drove to Gideon Springs. And the Lord again encountered Jolene in a profound way. The presence of God suddenly enveloped her. Revelatory instruction came regarding the vision. Israel and America are both entering into a midnight hour. Not the hour of Christ's return, but an hour of challenge our generation has never known. The Lord showed her that many were not prepared to live through the very answers to the prayers we had prayed. To save the nation, for instance. To purify the body of Christ. She saw how great shakings, challenges, and exposure would be unleashed in fulfillment of these prayers. The ten minutes beforehand were given for us to utilize wisely and prepare.

> Israel and America are both entering into a midnight hour.

Gideon was a mighty warrior who saved Israel from many enemies. His journey with God began with a dramatic visitation where the Lord called him to tear down his father's altars to idolatry—to Baal and Asherah—and build an altar of covenant to Him alone. Gideon saw the Lord and exclaimed, "Yahweh shalom!" The Lord is peace (Judges 6:24).

Maybe it wasn't a coincidence that as we consecrated ourselves to the Lord in the same area where Gideon consecrated himself, an overwhelming peace was imparted to Jolene. Quite literally, the tangible Presence of the unseen Spirit enveloped her. Shalom in the midst of war.

Jolene has literally never been the same since. And as with the release of the Elijah anointing, she knew the release of God's shalom was vital for the body of Christ through the midnight hour.

Of course, Gideon received his greatest breakthrough during the midnight hour. Friend, it will be the same with you.

SPIRIT OF ELIJAH—PICKING UP THE MANTLE

On December 10, our team gathered by the Jordan River. Together we picked up the two mantles as one, bearing witness through tears to the promised release of the spirit and power of Elijah. It turned out to be one of the holiest moments of our lives. And with boldness heightened by Chuck's extraordinary confirmation, by the Jordan River we then declared a global shift for the prophetic movement.

Let's briefly explore some life-changing principles from Scripture on the mantle Elijah carried. I'm so excited to share these with you.

Elijah lived and ministered in Israel during the reign of Ahab and Jezebel. At the time Israel was known as the "northern kingdom," and Judah the "southern kingdom." According to Scripture, God considered Ahab the most evil king who had yet ruled (1 Kings 16:30). Ahab established a "house of Baal" as an antichrist worship center tied to his governmental throne. Kind of like setting up a masonic temple in close proximity to the White House. Not a good idea!

Ahab married Jezebel. Even though, according to her name, Jezebel was already married—to a high level principality. Her very name means "married to Baal!"

Bit of advice here. Don't ever marry a woman who is currently married to someone else. Especially if it's a principality. It won't go well for you. Promise.

Something to note now, which we'll explore much more thoroughly later. The Lord gave Elijah a throne or a seat of authority that was above the thrones of Ahab and Jezebel. No man gave it to him, and no man could take it away. It was a throne before the Throne.

Remember how Elijah confronted King Ahab: *"As the Lord God of Israel lives, before whom I stand, there shall not be dew nor rain these years, except at my word!"* (1 Kings 17:1 NKJV). This magnitude of governmental authority can only come from receiving counsel from Heaven's council.

The good news is, you have also been seated with Christ in heavenly places (Ephesians 2:6). Which means that for you, as with Elijah, a whole new realm of possibilities has now opened. We are again in a transition season when the spirit of Elijah is being released. Everything is about to change.

STUDY QUESTIONS AND PRAYER

1. Define the spirit and power of Elijah. What are the primary characteristics? What does it mean to you? How can you benefit?

2. Where is your pathway converging with others? What God-ordained relationships is He now bringing into your life?

3. Jesus promised to mantle or endue His disciples with power from on high. What impartations of God's power are you currently pursuing? How? Why?

4. Describe Gideon's ministry and mandate. How did the Lord move with Gideon to restore Israel? What was required? What was the name Gideon bestowed on God?

5. How have you been affected by presumption—either your own or the presumption of others? What preventative measures can be taken to avoid this trap?

6. How do you see God defining the season we are entering into? Has *End Times in Real Time* helped?

7. In what areas do you desire to see turnarounds in your life? Your family? What does it mean to restore the hearts of parents to their children, and children to their parents? To prepare the way of the Lord?

Father God, You are awesome in Your orchestrations. Please grant me the measure You have ordained of the spirit and power of Elijah. Grant grace to see healings and turnarounds in family relationships. Just as in the days of Elijah, restore our nation back to You. Restore Your covenant. Rescue the harvest. And restore holy fire on the altar.

Jon sounds the shofar October 7, 2023, the final day
of the Feast of Tabernacles, Abilene, TX.

CHAPTER 6

SOUNDING FORTH THE TRUMPET

He is sounding forth the trumpet that shall never call retreat; He is sifting out the hearts of men before His judgment seat…

—"Battle Hymn of the Republic"

The piercing cry of a shofar resounded through the courtyard of Yad Vashem, Israel's Holocaust Memorial on the summit of Mount Herzl. We intuitively moved toward its alarm. A dark brown ram's horn, emblazoned with the words "Lion of Judah," was lifted to Heaven by a resilient Jewish man in a blue denim shirt that covered a weeping heart.

It was May 1, 2023, and our "Spirit of Elijah" tour was on its final day. The sacred memorial was the last official destination of our journey. Earlier in the morning we prayed at the Knesset, followed by an impromptu tour of Ein Kerem, a village at the base of Mount Herzl where John the Baptist was born.

John the Baptist prepared the way for Jesus, Israel's Messiah. He came in the spirit and power of Elijah. And just like Elijah, John was a prophet of fire. For this reason Jesus even referred to him as "the burning and shining lamp."

The last page of the Old Testament culminates with a promise of this coming forerunner. God was going to send Elijah to restore the hearts of the fathers to the children, and the children to the fathers, before *"the great and terrible day of the Lord"* (Malachi 4:5-6 NASB). This day was seen in large measure by John but, as we've shared, according to the Bible its fullness is yet ahead.

Amazingly, the New Testament starts exactly where the Old Testament ends—with the very same prophecy. This continuity of emphasis begs you to seize the vast importance of the subject.

> *...and he will be filled with the Holy Spirit while still in his mother's womb. And he will turn many of the sons of Israel back to the Lord their God. And it is he who will go as a forerunner before Him in the spirit and power of Elijah, to turn the hearts of fathers back to their children, and the disobedient to the attitude of the righteous, to make ready a people prepared for the Lord* (Luke 1:15-17 NASB).

Jesus and John first met at Ein Kerem, translated from Hebrew as "spring of the vineyard." Local tradition holds that their moms got together by the ancient well in the center of town, which gave Ein Kerem its name. When they connected, John was so stirred by Jesus that he *"leapt for joy!"* Immediately both he and his mother Elizabeth were filled with the Holy Spirit, just as prophesied (Luke 1:15, 41-44).

John and Jesus didn't run off to play though, as kids often do. That would have been a little difficult. Instead this connection between them, igniting the exhilaration which they both felt, occurred while they were both still in their mothers' wombs.

"O valley, be raised up! O mountain, be made low. Prepare the way of the Lord!" Jamie Fitt led us in worship at this same ancient well, and our hearts began to burst in glory. It was as though embers from a distant era suddenly became apprehended in our midst. We all felt it together. A forerunner movement was again being birthed to prepare the way of the Lord in our time. What a profound way to culminate the Spirit of Elijah tour.

Our tour buses made their way from the shadow of Mount Herzl to the final destination on its summit. Shofar master Robert Weinger accompanied us through Yad Vashem. A Jewish American who made Aliyah to Israel, Robert had just been notified of a discovery that more of his family had actually perished in the Holocaust.

We viewed violins, torah scrolls, opera lyrics, and storybooks from which starving Jews confined to ghettoes drew upon their own humanity. We hovered over the priceless menorah of a German rabbi and his wife, once defiantly displayed in their window overlooking a Nazi building draped with a giant swastika.

A burning lamp against dictatorship. I yearned to light the flame again. The witness of this lampstand is desperately needed in our time.

Of the six million Jews who succumbed to the Nazi regime, most were deported to concentration camps by railroad. During

> A forerunner movement was again being birthed to prepare the way of the Lord in our time.

Hanukkah 2015, Jolene and I visited Yad Vashem while planning our Glory Train tour for 2016—50 states, mostly by rail. Photographs of families crammed into railroad cattle cars, and plummeted down tracks toward almost certain death haunted me continually. It was the exact antithesis of all we were praying for. You'll see this later in the book.

Suddenly the Lord spoke the following:

> Son of man, *two trains* are again in the earth. My Glory Train is moving to bring freedom, truth, and life. But beware. The Death Train of antichrist dictatorship is again on the move as well. Many nations are already on board!

The enemy desperately wants our generation to forget the Holocaust, to ignore it altogether, even while laying the groundwork for a new holocaust in our day. And back in 2015 when the word came, I immediately "knew" the same authoritarian tactics employed by Hitler were now gaining a resurgence. Mesmerizing, spellbinding deception. Mass propaganda. Seductive elitism. Weaponization of civil institutions. Mass coercion. Confiscation and harnessing of cutting-edge technology toward global conquest. Global dictatorship fueled by the occult.

And, of course, antisemitism at the very core. This warning is already proving heartbreakingly true as in 2024, college campuses nationwide stood for Hamas against Israel and persecuted Jewish students in their midst. Satanic forces hate God's covenant people. We must work together now to derail the enemy's work, before more momentum is gained.

Toward the end of the tour, our group entered the Hall of Names, a vast circular room filled with scrolls of remembrance. *Yad Vashem* in Hebrew means "a memorial and a name." Its sacred mission is to bear witness in Jerusalem to the names of six million Jews who never made it physically to the Promised Land. As with Robert Weinger's relatives, 80 years after the Holocaust more victims are still being discovered.

Finally, light. We moved through a triangular threshold to a giant portico overlooking the mountains of Israel. Against all odds, in 1948 survivors of the Holocaust recaptured this very land and secured it as a nation. Activating volumes of Scripture to suddenly come to fulfillment.

A nation was reborn. And by this, the clearest marker of the end times was set in place for the world to see.

Robert's shofar sounded. But instead of just a few short blasts, the military dirge "Taps" began to pour from his "Lion of Judah" trumpet. No eyes remained dry during the lyrical tribute to Robert's family members, whose passing until now was known only to God.

PROPHETIC WARNING: WAVE OF ANTISEMITISM AGAIN AT HAND

Robert's tribute demanded a response. I felt directed to share a very personal story which we learned about during the class we took at Yad Vashem. Pastor Chris Edmonds, a fellow student, shared the legacy of his father who had led his troops into the notorious Battle of the Bulge. For context, the Nazis were putting Robert's family to death while our friend's father was fighting for their defeat.

The whole company was captured by the Nazis during the battle. I'll let the *Times of Israel's* well-written article take it from here:

The Nazi soldiers made their orders very clear: Jewish American prisoners of war were to be separated from their fellow brothers in arms and sent to an uncertain fate.

But Master Sgt. Roddie Edmonds would have none of that. As the highest-ranking noncommissioned officer held in the German POW camp, he ordered more than 1,000 Americans captives to step forward with him and brazenly pronounced: "We are all Jews here!"

He would not waver, even with a pistol to his head, and his captors eventually backed down.[2]

Seventy years later, the Tennessee native was recognized posthumously with Israel's highest honor, inducted into the "Righteous Among the Nations" at Yad Vashem. The memorial is granted to non-Jews who risked their lives to save Jews during World War II. He's the first American serviceman to earn the honor.

I felt directed to warn our tour group prophetically that a wave of antisemitism was again at hand. It is our honor and obligation to stand courageously with the people God claims as His own by covenant. I felt our own survival might depend on it. In identifying with the Jewish people, in the end Jews and Christians will both be saved.

"I'M A JEW!"

Then I raised my hand, and out of my mouth came a declaration I had never made before. "I'm a Jew!" A few more declared the same. Then the whole tour group raised their hands and pronounced, "I'm a Jew!" With this decree in the courtyard of Yad Vashem, a sacred covenant between us and the Lord was sealed.

Profoundly moved by this dedication, Robert unexpectedly presented his treasured "Lion of Judah" shofar to Jolene and me. We initially refused. As a gift, it was valued at almost $2000, but its true worth was now priceless. Both the moment and the instrument that captured it were way too sacred to be given away.

In the end Robert won. The Lion of Judah won. And through this gift, a prophecy from the beginning of the tour became unexpectedly fulfilled.

WARNING DREAM OF TERRORISM ON TOUR

Twelve days earlier, when our Spirit of Elijah tour started, a series of dreams stirred our tour group. Very clear warnings of terrorism had already been given through dreams from friends back home. Including a word by trusted watchman prophet Lynnie Harlow, who saw explosions and terrorist infiltration coming while we were sleeping in the land.

Lynnie literally saw our hotel room, with a raging fire on the Temple Mount outside the window. In the dream, Jolene was trying in vain to wake me up so we could escape. "It's happening," she kept saying. "It's actually happening!"

Please note Lynnie has been extremely accurate in her prophetic perceptions—over many years. Concern was so high we hosted a special video call to warn all tour attendees. There's more to this story, so tuck it away in your memory for now.

DREAM—PEACEFUL TOUR, PROPHETIC ALARM

After the first day of the tour, our friend Kristin Walch was given a vivid dream. The Lord showed her that no harm would come during our journey through Israel and that all would remain safe. The admonition proved true. The dream then continued in a surprising way.

Kristin saw that on the last day of the tour, the Lord was going to give Jon and Jolene a prophetic alarm. And in her words, the alarm must be released for the body of Christ to advance.

Prophetic alarm given and released. We were comfortable with that. In our ministry, that's kind of what we do. Like a catcher anticipating a fast ball, we signaled back to the Lord our readiness to receive His direction and positioned ourselves for the encounter.

Instead, He threw a curveball.

RECEIVING THE PROPHETIC ALARM

When Kristin received this dream, Yad Vashem was not on our itinerary for the final day of the tour. In fact it wasn't on our itinerary at all. Yad Vashem actually could not fit us in because we had too many people. But the God of Israel loves to trump all chance and circumstance in order to fulfill a word from His mouth.

At the last moment, Yad Vashem was able to fit us in. Robert Weinger was able to accompany us. And as it turned out, the prophetic alarm God wanted to give Jolene and me was not a visitation, a Bible verse, or even a subtle impression. Instead, it was the shofar itself. The very instrument identified in the Bible for sounding an alarm.

Blow a trumpet [shofar] *in Zion, and sound an alarm on My holy mountain!…* (Joel 2:1 NASB).

IMMEDIATE PROPHETIC WARNING—
ENEMIES POISED TO STRIKE!

The context of the Joel 2 alarm is that Eretz Israel, the land of Israel, was being invaded in war. With prophetic downloads from the Lord, we immediately began to sound an alarm on similar threats to Israel in real time. Specifically from Iran.

As chronicled in our previous book *White House Watchmen,* ancient Persia was renamed Iran after Persia approached the Nazis to become part of their alignment of nations. Hitler's leaders venerated the Aryans as the pure white race that will dominate the world. Their bloodline, of course, is from Iran.

So Hitler's leaders issued a demand. Change the name from Persia to Iran—which is Persian for Aryan—and the alignment will be sealed. And today it's like the Iran government inherited the Nazi mantle. The most antisemitic nation in the world.

And receiving the shofar at the Holocaust Museum, called Yad Vashem, it was obvious to see how antisemitism would rise concurrent with war. We just had no idea of the magnitude.

Here's the word the Lord spoke to me:

> Israel, your enemies perceive how you are greatly weakened through your political and religious divisions. Many believe you are weaker now than any other time in your history, and perhaps even your

future. Therefore your enemies are now poised to strike!

And America. Take heed and turn, for you are weakened by the very same reality. And you now face the prospect of the very same destruction. Tick tock to the holy clock. Let Israel be your time clock!

RETURN TO JERUSALEM?

Just two months following, Jolene and I were firmly directed by the Lord to travel from our home in DC back to Israel—with exactly this message.

Every year our ministry friends usually join on July 22 for a special ministry time centered on God's "turnaround verdict" from Daniel 7:22. Through the years we've hosted these gatherings everywhere from Faneuil Hall in Boston to a castle in Colorado Springs to Palmer, Alaska, and Abilene, Texas, and privately even within the State Department and the White House Eisenhower Executive Office Building (EEOB).

But this was the first time we were summoned to Jerusalem. In retrospect, the Lord knew that Israel would soon face unimaginable challenges where His turnaround verdict was desperately needed. Same with the warning we were carrying.

In each gathering, we follow the prophet Daniel's lead and approach Heaven's Court, asking for the Lord to grant His verdict of justice in favor of the saints as recorded in Daniel 7:21-22 (NASB):

> *I kept looking, and that horn was waging war with the saints*
> *and prevailing against them, until the Ancient of Days came*

and judgment was passed in favor of the saints of the Highest One, and the time arrived when the saints took possession of the kingdom.

Note the sequence of the verdict. Daniel kept looking, watching. He kept in focused prayer. He saw how the horn, representing an antichrist force and leaders and armies under its influence, rose up to wage war against God's covenant people. The Ancient of Days, presider of Heaven's Court, rendered judgment against the injustice and for God's covenant people. Suddenly God's people prevailed. The beast set against them was restrained. And through the verdict the "set time" for God's longstanding promise became activated in real time, with the saints immediately released to possess the Kingdom.

When the antichrist force prevailed, the saints were broken, abused, disenfranchised, defeated. But one verdict from Heaven's Court turned things around in a moment. Suddenly these same wounded warriors were liberated to secure their covenant promise.

For this reason, we have come to call Daniel 7:22 the "Turnaround Verdict."

DREAM—WATCH OF THE BREAKER

A prophetic dream made clear the war immediately being faced by Israel. I saw Israel as a valley at twilight. A ram stood midway up a mountain. He moved his head in an aggressive thrust, and then began to intensively scan the entire valley for movement. He was clearly watching the boundaries for enemy activity. This Ram summoned us to keep His vigil with Him. And then the Lord spoke to me, "The Watch of the Breaker has begun!"

For those who not know, a ram is a grown-up lamb. The Ram is the Lamb! And the Ram as Breaker was intent on securing Israel against existential threats. With this at heart, Jolene and I mobilized a "Watch of the Breaker" vigil for July 1-22, with a 7-22 Turnaround Gathering in Jerusalem to culminate.

SHOFAR IN JERUSALEM

We arrived from Washington to Jerusalem a few days before our gathering. Israel is a sacred land filled with meaningful traditions. Over time Jolene and I have developed a few traditions of our own. First night in Jerusalem means dinner at Focaccia on Rabi Akiva Street, savoring flatbread with roasted pepper and olives along with a rich Focaccia salad. We then walk off dinner with a stroll through nearby Mamilla Mall for coffee, usually complemented by a solitary almond croissant.

After a full and delightful evening, we were headed for the elevators when a shofar blast sounded. I figured it was from a tourist trying out a new souvenir. But Jolene turned to me and half-jokingly said, "We're here because of a trumpet blast. Let's follow the sound of the shofar!"

So we did. The culprit was not too hard to find. Tourists were sparse in the heat of July. But a small crowd, comprised primarily of Texans, had gathered right in the middle of the outdoor mall. In the center stood none other than Robert Weinger, showing a pastor from the USA how to make a sound with his new shofar.

Robert had no idea we were coming. Because he lives almost an hour away, at Gilgal by the Jordan River, he rarely visits the mall. But somehow the very man who had gifted us his $2000 shofar in

Robert Weinger sounds the shofar on 7-22, 2023, during gathering at Jerusalem's Succat Hallel. Superimposed with image of 200,000 Israelis marching in protest of judicial overhaul. Prophetic warning was given at gathering that the overwhelming division of Israeli society is provoking Israel's enemies to perceive them as greatly weakened, and war and terror were therefore on the horizon. Illustrative graphic.

fulfillment of a prophetic dream from a friend who conveyed how God was going to give us trumpet warnings that needed to be sounded—warnings which brought us back to Jerusalem almost immediately—that man was suddenly standing before us.

On our first night back. Can't make this stuff up.

The next day we welcomed to Jerusalem fellow team members Perry and Joy Chickonoski and Bob and Laurie Bertelsen. Before the 7-22 gathering we toured the ancient altar of Melchizedek and the Temple Mount. It was humbling to visit the very ground where God promised Solomon, *"If My people who are called by My Name will humble themselves, and pray and seek My face, and turn from their wicked ways, then I will hear from heaven, and will forgive their sin and heal their land"* (2 Chronicles 7:14 NKJV). Our plea before God's Throne—grant this today!

As if in response, when we approached the Al Aqsa Mosque, fireworks started streaming into the air to the immediate north, the immediate east, and the immediate south. Actual explosions were bursting in air.

Was this a terror strike? As six Americans trapped on top of the Temple Mount, would we make it through?

It turned out the fireworks were part of Palestinian celebrations for the last day of school. Little did we know that just a few months later, armed Iranian rockets would literally stream over the same sacred mountain as a solemn act of war.

7-22 JERUSALEM—WHILE 200,000 PROTEST AT KNESSET

Robert Weinger joined us on July 22 for the Daniel 7:22 gathering called "Turnaround Jerusalem," hosted at Succat Hallel by mentors and friends Rick and Patricia Ridings. They are heroes in prayer. We sought God's face together. We told the story about receiving the trumpet. We prophesied Christ's warning about how Israel's enemies perceive the nation as excessively weakened due to the political division and are poised to strike. And we warned how Israel is a time clock for America.

Finally, we declared God's covenantal decree of turnaround. Daniel 7:21-22. Where the enemy is waging war against the saints and prevailing, God is rendering judgment in favor of the saints, restraining the beast, and releasing the saints to possess the kingdom.

Out the window things didn't look so good. That very night the Israeli Knesset became surrounded by more than 200,000 people protesting the far right's attempt at judicial overhaul.

Also that very night, Prime Minister Benjamin Netanyahu's life was actually spared. A few days earlier, he was commanded to wear a heart monitor. The Prime Minister was told that if it ever goes off, he has five minutes to get to the hospital before succumbing. And on the evening of 7-22, while a crowd of 200,000 was protesting and we were praying, Benjamin Netanyahu's alarm went off. Thank God he heeded its warning. We should do the same.

AWAKENING TO WAR

On October 7, 2023, we awoke to war. The leaders of the Spirit of Elijah Tour—including Ed Watts, Jamie Fitt, Jolene and me—had gathered for a special ministry weekend in Abilene, Texas. It was the first time seeing each other since April. We caught up over home-grilled steak on Thursday night, ministered at a local church on Friday night, and prepared for a special Spirit of Elijah summit all day Saturday. Little did we know the substance of this summit would soon change dramatically.

Hamas in Gaza invaded neighboring towns in Israel. Afterward the IDF would compile videos of the killings, most captured by mobile phones of the terrorists. The sheer brutality of the atrocities, with babies beheaded, men and women violated in front of their families before being killed, and bloodied terrorists blocking roads to mow down escaping motorists was beyond human comprehension. As mentioned, in a matter of hours, the event would become the largest wholesale slaughter of the Jewish people since the Holocaust.

Memories of Israel came flooding back. Spontaneous outdoor worship attracting Jews and Muslims alike. Taking in the view of the Temple Mount from the Mount of Olives nearby. Baptisms by the Jordan. Praying at the Western Wall alongside IDF soldiers. Yad Vashem. Pleading with God for Israel's safety on 7-22.

And warnings of terror that never came to pass. Until now. The surprise attack on October 7 literally became Israel's 9/11.

Later in the year Mossad agents (Israel's secret intelligence service) discovered a gruesome trove of intelligence in a tunnel under a Gaza hospital. Among their discoveries—the attack against Israel on October 7 was originally scheduled to launch in mid-April, at the end of Passover. Precisely during our Spirit of Elijah tour. Remember Lynnie Harlow's prophetic warning dream. It was sobering to realize war could have erupted right as we were in the land. This could have been our plight.

As the Abilene summit progressed, Ed Watts shared about a word he had received on January 20, 2023. The Lord showed him that on the 50th anniversary of the Yom Kippur War, a "glory war" over inheritance would begin.

October 7 marked the 50th anniversary.

Jolene and I shared about our recent journey to Jerusalem, including releasing the "trumpet warning" on 7-22 of impending war. We also shared a strong word the Lord gave me for America during the flight over. The trumpet is sounding, and God is declaring to America, "Come up higher."

During the service, Ed Watts pointed me to a Jewish religious calendar. October 7 on the religious calendar was actually the 22nd day of Tishri, the seventh month. On the Hebrew calendar it was literally 7-22.

STUDY QUESTIONS AND PRAYER

1. Has the Lord been giving you warnings of challenges ahead? Course corrections? Ask Him to!

2. What journeys have you taken where the Lord has dramatically impacted your life? What are your takeaways?

3. How are you recording the prophetic words God is giving you? We suggest writing them and storing them so they are easily accessible.

4. Have you ever received an answer to prayer directly related to petitioning Heaven's Court? What challenges were resolved?

5. How have you been affected by Israel's war? How have you been praying for the hostages and for the victims of abuse?

6. Do you believe antisemitism is a major problem where you live? Do you believe America as a nation is vulnerable? How do you think the president should intervene?

7. What does it mean for you to keep watch over a nation?

Father God, please grant me grace to receive from You clear trumpet warnings for the present and future. Help me to pray into the warnings and steward them correctly. Help me, Lord, to keep watch. In fact, keep watch with me and through me, in Jesus' name.

And, Lord, I ask that You send me on journeys of discovery with You—beginning with the one I am on right now! Encounter my heart with Your heart. Connect me with those of like, precious faith. And grant Your protection and provision along the way. In Jesus' name, amen.

NOTE

2.   "Israel honors GI who told the Nazis, 'We are all Jews,'" *Times of Israel,* December 2, 2015.

SECTION 3

COME UP HIGHER

The X Eclipse—I put the X in Exodus! Illustrative graphic.

CHAPTER 7

Chapter Topics: Come up Higher | October 7 | 9-11-01 | National Leaders, Exposure of Abuse | Cindy Jacobs X-out Word | Crisis of Covenant | Exiting the X | Restore the Fallen Tabernacle

COME UP HIGHER— EXITING THE X

"Gather My godly ones to Me, those who have made a covenant with Me by sacrifice"

(Psalm 50:5 NASB).

"The commitment of our fathers is the calling of our time."

—President George W. Bush, 9/11 Prayer Service

The journey chronicled so far explores some of the most vital aspects of the end times recorded in the Bible, in real time. From the summit of Tel Megiddo, the "Armageddon clock" conveyed a midnight hour for Israel and America, with war breaking out ten months later almost to the day. A global release of the spirit and power of Elijah was astonishingly confirmed by the hand of God.

Remember what you've learned. Armageddon is a backdrop for the spirit and power of Elijah. The best is yet to come!

That said, when a cherished shofar was gifted to us at Yad Vashem, we sensed the Spirit of God compelling us to sound an alarm. Not just over war, but over a new wave of global antisemitism. It defies understanding how the savage attack by Hamas could unleash a vicious tide of Jew-hatred on liberal college campuses across the US, with America's most esteemed universities leading the charge.

In the midst of these occurrences, the X Eclipse over the 2024 election year brought a renewed focus on a longstanding prophetic warning by Cindy Jacobs. Attempts of dark forces to X-out our nation have proven immediate and hauntingly prescient. Nuclear threats by Russia reached an unprecedented level, exceeding even the Cold War. Two separate assassination attempts nearly X-ed out candidate Donald Trump as America approached the "crisis elections." Voter fraud and manipulation by foreign powers again exacerbated tensions over election results.

Jesus remains your real-time Redeemer and soon-coming King!

On another front, the exposure of horrendous sin by trusted leaders in the body of Christ left many believers feeling disenfranchised and demoralized, struggling in their faith. Not coincidentally, Kansas City, identified as the convergence point of the X, became the epicenter of both the exposure and the struggle.

End times in real time. Remember that Hebrew time is cyclical. What we have experienced in a lesser measure will be accelerated in a greater measure in days to come. We will see this in Israel, America, and the world. We will see this in the body of Christ.

By wrestling through these events now with the Lord, you are being strengthened to navigate future challenges. Just remember,

God's love for you never ever dims. Jesus remains your real-time Redeemer and soon-coming King!

That said, the alarm is truly sounding. A trumpet is speaking in real time to you and me. *"Come up here, and I will show you what must take place..."* (Revelation 4:1 NASB).

AMERICA, COME UP HIGHER

Just two days before the October 7 attack in Israel, the Lord spoke to me a dire trumpet warning for our nation to "Come up higher." The warning is based on Revelation 4, with Holy Spirit emphasizing a new position we are summoned to attain—both spiritually, accessing a heavenly realm where we are seated with Christ (Ephesians 2:6), and morally in a clarion call to take the higher ground. Both are essential for the end times.

John ascended. He came up higher. So must we.

As mentioned, Jolene and I were on a flight to Abilene at the time, preparing to minister at the Spirit of Elijah gathering. As you will see, the phrase was accompanied by literal alarms, sounding in our proximity over many days. Obviously, neither of us had any idea the real-time significance that was about to play out on a global basis. From our October 6 posting, verbatim:

> En route to Dallas yesterday, the Lord interrupted my mid-flight reading with a very clear word. I simply heard Him say, "America, come up higher."
>
> Earlier in the morning it became very obvious to both Jolene and me that God's alarm was still sounding a warning. As most of you know, we've prophesied

about this since spontaneously receiving a shofar this April at Yad Vashem, the Jewish holocaust memorial in Jerusalem.

That said, within the past week we have literally been surrounded by alarms sounding. Praying over a building in Youngstown, OH, when alarms went off across the entire city. Personal phone alarms that sounded (nationwide as a test) even when the alarm was turned off.

And yesterday, just before four in the morning, THE FIRE ALARM WENT OFF—on the top floor of our DC condominium. "An emergency has been detected in the building. Please evacuate immediately. Do not use the elevators…"

The race to the bottom at 4 am was itself a cause for alarm. Thank God it turned out to be nothing. But surrounded by alarms the past few days, I knew the Lord was making a point…

Then on the plane the Holy Spirit spoke, "America, come up higher." Immediately I remembered the Scripture from Revelation 4.

"After these things I looked, and behold, a door standing open in heaven, and the first voice which I had heard, like the sound of a trumpet speaking with me, said, 'Come up here [higher], and I will show you what must take place after these things.' Immediately I was in the Spirit; and behold, a throne…" (Rev. 4:1-2 NASB).

Wow. Come up higher. Suddenly it all made sense. There was both a warning and a window conveyed by

His word. To this all I could do is bow my head and say, "Yes Lord." I know you agree.

The great news is a DOOR IS OPENING for you and me to move in the Spirit, stand in Heaven's council, and receive His real-time word. But there's also a clear warning. An alarm is sounding a clear warning over America. We are facing an unprecedented challenge the most attentive of us can barely perceive. To preserve our freedom we must take the higher ground. Come up higher.

Alarms sounded continually. Over days. A severe warning word was given of unprecedented challenges ahead. The experience reminded me of another prophetic alarm that sounded just before the terrorist strikes on September 11, 2001. The phrase "Call 911" was highlighted to a friend in a dream, and we found ourselves praying over it while viewing the Twin Towers for the very last time.

Here's a thought to ponder. On the eve of October 7, arguably Israel's darkest hour, why was the Holy Spirit emphasizing America? Why was He sounding a trumpet call over our own need to come up higher?

ISRAEL'S 9/11

It is said that October 7 was Israel's 9/11. Late on October 7, heartbreaking images from Israel began to surface online, validating this perception. A traffic jam frozen in time, with scores of shot-out cars and lifeless drivers still clinging to their steering wheels. A precious family huddled together as their bomb shelter was set on fire. Drone footage revealing the unimaginable destruction of Kibbutz Be'eri, a community largely known for Palestinian advocacy. A video loop showing hostage Noa Argamani pleading for help as her abductor raced her away to Gaza.

"Don't kill me!" The video of Noa became a symbol for all of Israel's hostages. By God's grace, she was among a brave few finally rescued by the Israel Defense Forces (IDF). Noa's mother passed from cancer shortly after, but in a poignant answer to prayer they were able to reunite for three precious weeks beforehand.

"Mom! I did it!" FaceTime videos by Hamas terrorists recorded their own ecstatic conversations with their mothers on the day of the attack. Many were posted online. With unrestrained pride, they bragged not only about murdering Jews but also carrying out horrendous sexual abuse against their victims.

Tears and prayers flowed freely at the Spirit of Elijah Summit as so much of what we and others warned about came to pass before our eyes. The fact that the atrocities occurred on Tishri 22, or 7-22, the final day of the Feast of Tabernacles, haunted our prayer times.

We reminded the Lord of His promise in Jerusalem of a Daniel 7:22 turnaround. We sought Him wholeheartedly to take what the enemy means for evil and turn it for good.

TUMBLING FROM THE WATCHMAN'S WALL

Major prayer moments soon began to respond with calls to prayer. The International House of Prayer Kansas City (IHOPKC) community, led by Mike Bickle, was among the first to mobilize global intercession for Israel. With connections spanning around the globe, a formidable prayer army was activated.

These efforts moved me deeply, as corporate prayer for Israel was part of a legacy I had helped to forge for the house of prayer. During my final year there, I had the honor of partnering with the late Jim Maher to birth the Israel Mandate, an aspect of the movement that had been prophesied more than a decade beforehand but never fully cultivated.

One continual prayer dominated the meetings. From Isaiah 62:

> *For Zion's sake I will not hold My peace, and for Jerusalem's sake I will not rest, until her righteousness shines as bright-ness, and **her salvation as a lamp that burns**. ...And as the bridegroom rejoices over the bride, so shall your God rejoice over you. **I have set watchmen on your walls, O Jerusalem; they shall never hold their peace**... (Isaiah 62:1,5-6 NKJV).*

Protecting Israel as a watchman was a primary motivation for joining the prayer movement. In 2000, one year before 9-11-01, the Lord gave me a commissioning vision. I saw three fighter jets converging and entering into formation over New York. These fighter jets then shot across to Israel to fight for the covenant nation in her most desperate hour.

Prophetically, these three jets represented three separate prayer movements that God wanted to align together for this cause. Due to the urgency, we invested our lives in helping to cultivate each expression of the prayer movement. Then we went to Israel and fell in love.

By the time the attack against Israel broke out, it seemed the movements were finally aligned, and watchmen for Israel were now securely on the wall. But the prayer vigil for Israel soon became trag-ically upended. As shared previously, the exposure of clergy sexual abuse came virtually concurrently with Israel's war.

It was actually on October 7 that initial contact was made between Jane Doe's husband and Mike Bickle to open the dialogue. A brief meeting was requested. Things did not go well. An advocacy group made up of pillars of IHOPKC leadership surrounded Jane Doe and her husband, standing with them to confront the allegations of clergy sex abuse. Over a six-month period, a hidden legacy of covenant breaking, spanning the prayer movement's existence, began to be uncovered.

Disbelief, grief, and anger over betrayal overwhelmed countless thousands globally. And in Israel's most desperate hour, prayer warriors looking to the prayer movement for leadership began to tumble from the watchman's wall. Ourselves included.

It was as though October 7 had become a second 9/11. At least for a prayer movement created to resource Israel in prayer.

RIGHT VALUES, WRONG ACTIONS

Intercession. Holiness. Offerings for the poor. Prophetic ministry. The 24-7 prayer movement's acronym defined its core values. From the beginning, leaders emphasized the mandate of continually enthroning Jesus and mobilizing prayer through the greatest endtimes adversities prophesied in the Bible until Jesus returns. With the Israel Mandate, praying for Israel and the Jewish people through the end times became an essential part of this focus.

Which again makes it all the more extraordinary that, at the exact moment Israel faced her most perilous hour, and needed prayer the most, IHOPKC was nearly X-ed out. Not primarily because of external challenges, but because of hidden compromise within.

"...he will be delivered through the cleanness of your hands" (Job 22:30 NASB1995). Intercession by godly leaders truly unleashes great power. But who will be delivered if our own hands are stained?

The exposure was heartbreaking to Jolene and me personally. Mike Bickle was a mentor to me in the forerunner calling. His Jesus-centric messages unearthed many scriptural truths that had seemingly eluded the broader body of Christ. First and foremost being the power of a global, 24-7 prayer movement sourced from the Amos 9:11 restoration of the Tabernacle of David.

A close second was the end-times unveiling of Jesus Christ as Bridegroom, King, and Judge. From the words of John the Baptist, *"He who has the bride is the bridegroom; but the friend of the bridegroom, who stands and hears him, rejoices greatly because of the bridegroom's voice"* (John 3:29 NKJV). The clear message: the men and women redeemed by Jesus belong to Him alone, purchased at an unimaginably great cost. Protect them. Pray for them. Mentor and heal them. But do not take advantage of them.

With the exposure of clergy sexual abuse, memories of my midnight visitation from the Lord came flooding back. Weeping on my faded blue couch when my midnight vigil was suddenly met with Christ's own vigil over His compromised bride. And I knew in the deepest way possible His anguish over covenant breaking, abuse, and betrayal within His body.

That vigil continues. Relentlessly.

A CRISIS OF COVENANT

Sexual abuse is abhorrent to God. Leaders in the body of Christ who practice sexual abuse must be held to account. It should be obvious to all how compromised covenants lead to compromised intimacy with God and compromised authority over our respective spheres.

But these consequences are marginal compared to the immense pain suffered by victims. More than any church or house of prayer, our bodies are first the temples of the Holy Spirit. Trauma inflicted through sin—sexual abuse especially—affects people at the very core of their being.

Of course Jesus can bring healing. Forgiveness is key. But even after life-changing ministry, the anguish of past experiences can sometimes resurface throughout a victim's life.

If you are a survivor of clergy sex abuse, please consider two suggestions. First, speaking with authorities assures you that your story goes on record. This will help you, and may help other victims. Second, working with a trusted, effective Christian counselor can both accelerate your healing process and enrich aspects of your life you may not have realized were even affected.

It's important to note that within a short period, many more national leaders were implicated for clergy sexual abuse. Global figureheads such as Robert Morris, T.D. Jakes, Brian Houston, Stephen Lawson, and many other evangelical pastors stepped down amidst this wave of exposure. Many Catholic dioceses were forced to file for bankruptcy as priests and bishops became exposed. Reports emerged from various movements and alliances, but all shared a common thread. Victims had gained courage to come out of the shadows.

In the entertainment world, Sean "Diddy" Combs was arrested after a comprehensive FBI investigation documented years of sex trafficking and abuse, with Hollywood A-listers involved. Let's be clear. Judgment begins at the House of God. But it by no means ends there.

So if the near X-out of the Kansas City prayer movement is parabolic for the nation, what have we learned? From our very core to the highest levels of leadership, the body of Christ is suffering from a crisis of covenant, the severity of which cannot be overstated. Corporately we have wounded the hearts of an entire generation. We have compromised our right to lead. We have compromised our seat of covenant.

Second, we have learned that the most dangerous source of the X is not so much the big devil out there, but the hidden sin and sabotage *from within*. Just as a cancerous lesion must be dealt with to protect the body, unless the corruption is properly dealt with, it is poised to imperil the body from the inside out.

Third, gaining healing and deliverance from present and generational bondages is no longer an option for leaders. It is an imperative.

Again, let's shut the gates of sabotage. The Lord is mandating that *we move beyond the X of our own destruction.*

EXITING THE X

Maybe it's not a coincidence that special forces train relentlessly to "get off the X." Taking their lead, let's define the X as a convergence point where forces targeting your destruction perceive a vulnerable position of access and a vulnerable time of access to take you down. How do you escape? Here are a few questions to ask yourself: Where does your internal compromise create an X for the enemy to target or take advantage of you? Where have you given him legal access to imperil your life? Your family? How is the enemy trying to leverage you?

If you're a victim of abuse, how does the Lord desire to lead you and protect you from immediate vulnerability? What steps can you prepare to take?

In combat, certain behavior patterns on the X make you extremely vulnerable. First is remaining stationary. Sedentary targets tend to fall the easiest. Moving targets are much harder to take down! That's why it's drilled into the core of special operators to keep moving. You should too.

The enemy's fight against you can sometimes feel paralyzing. As special operators in the Spirit, you must train yourself to move beyond the paralysis caused by fear, disorientation, and disappointment. Even with yourself. Pray. Then take action. The Bible instructs you to *"Flee sexual immorality"* (1 Corinthians 6:18 NKJV), and the same precept applies to every form of temptation, sin, addiction, corruption, occult activity and abuse. Get off the X!

Not coincidentally, when moving from the X, soldiers are trained to *always move to higher ground.* You must do the same. Take the moral high ground. Don't just get off the X—*come up higher.*

And once off the X, *do not return.* Your enemy is very strategic in his ways. Remember that after the devil tempted Jesus, *"he left Him until an opportune time"* (Luke 4:13 NASB). Don't give the devil any more opportune times!

Let's sum this up. In spiritual conflict as well as natural warfare, when you come under attack or temptation, focus on two overarching goals. Your first goal is to immediately "get off the X" so that your life—and your family's life—are preserved. Spiritually you accomplish this goal primarily through prayer and spiritual warfare, decisive action, wholehearted repentance, continued communication, and accountability.

Second—do not return to the X! Instead, your long-term goal should be to "get the X off of you." Resolve now to shut the gates of sabotage in your life. Gain healing and deliverance, even from generational bondages. Take new ground. Come up higher.

THE PROPHETIC MOVEMENT MUST COME UP HIGHER

A month after the October 7 strikes and subsequent exposure within the Kansas City movement, Cindy Jacobs convened the 2023 roundtable of the Apostolic Council of Prophetic Elders (ACPE). It was our 24th year of gathering annually. Cindy opened with a message to the prophets, which you by now are all too familiar with:

> And the Lord is saying to His people, COME UP HIGHER!

In the midst of conversation, the true scope of the challenges became clear. Weeping immediately followed. The Lord is continuing to confront His highest level prophets with a clear warning. What has been tolerated can no longer be tolerated. We must come up higher. *We must regain basic biblical morality.* The prophetic community first.

A year beforehand, in November 2022, the ACPE roundtable sought the Lord for a word for 2023. Psalm 23 was a popular verse. But along with many other prophets, Jolene and I received Jeremiah 23 for 2023. We were relieved to find a number of other ACPE prophets had received the same passage as well. A year ahead of the crisis, a corporate prophetic directive emerged calling for a much-needed course correction.

Reading the passage made me wonder what the prophetic roundtable of Jeremiah's day looked like when his word was introduced. Probably a lot like ours. Hit the deck! Highlights of Jeremiah 23 (NASB) follow:

> 1 *"Woe to the shepherds who are causing the sheep of My pasture to perish and are scattering them!" declares the Lord. 2*

…*"You have scattered My flock and driven them away, and have not been concerned about them; behold, I am going to* **call you to account** *for the evil of your deeds…."*

9 *As for the prophets: My heart is broken within me, all my bones tremble….*

11 *"For both prophet and priest are defiled; even* **in My house** *I have found their wickedness," declares the Lord.*

13 *"Moreover, among the prophets of Samaria I saw an offensive thing:* **they prophesied by Baal** *and led My people Israel astray.*

14 *Also among the prophets of Jerusalem I have seen a horrible thing:* **the committing of adultery and walking in deceit;** *and they strengthen the hands of evildoers….*

16 *…they tell a vision of their own imagination, not from the mouth of the Lord.*

17 *They keep saying to those who despise Me, 'The Lord has said, "You will have peace"'; and as for everyone who walks in the stubbornness of his own heart, they say, 'Disaster will not come on you.'*

18 **But who has stood in the council of the Lord,** *that he should see and hear His word? Who has paid attention to His word and listened?*

21 *I did not send these prophets, but they ran. I did not speak to them, but they prophesied.*

22 **But if they had stood in My council,** *then they would have announced My words to My people, and would have* **turned them back** *from their evil way and from the evil of their deeds."*

Note Jeremiah's emphasis in the last sentence. Accessing God's turnaround anointing, the grace to release repentance and turn a covenant nation back to Him depends on genuinely standing in the council of the Lord with clean hands and a pure heart. That's how Elijah did it. That's how David did it. So must we.

X-OUT: AMERICA'S 9/11

October 7 was Israel's 9/11. But it was a second "9/11 call" to America as well, especially to the body of Christ. The trumpet blast has been conveying a very clear mandate. Come Up Higher. Because many end-time movements birthed in former seasons are now endangered of being X-ed out.

With this at heart, let's explore the original trumpet message sounded by the Lord on 9-11-01, as a potential X-out of our nation suddenly awakened America to a new reality. Our story begins four years before-hand, in a castle, when the original X-out word was first released.

In 1997, Mike and Cindy Jacobs gathered the top-tiered leaders of the prayer movement to the Glen Eyrie Castle in Colorado Springs for a private strategic roundtable. Cindy introduced the warning word about the X-out of our nation for the very first time. She also shared the prophetic perception by Dutch Sheets that the X could be transformed into a bridal canopy—representing God's covenant covering being recovered and restored to the land.

A posterboard map of Cindy's vision was by her side, with red yarn forming the X. Seattle was connected to Miami and San Diego to New York City. The X converged over Kansas City.

Some prophetic words carry no weight. Cindy's word hit the room with such gravitational force that travailing prayer became the only option. Cries and groanings formed a corporate symphony that crescendoed, diminished, and surged again for almost an hour. By the Spirit of God, the main hall of the castle had turned into a house of prayer, a Presence-saturated portal to the end times.

At a point of breakthrough, the Spirit of God orchestrated a prophetic action to demonstrate what He desires to bring forth. Cindy felt led to launch a procession, circling the hall counterclockwise to symbolize the reversal of the X and the curses it represented. I recall freemasonry being strongly emphasized as one of the curses needing a divine reversal. But we literally walked out the turnaround the Lord desired to grant our nation.

Healing pioneers John and Paula Sandford were asked to take the lead, representing the mothers and fathers of the movement. Joining behind them were the youngest faces in the crowd, myself included. As both a next-generation leader and a descendant of the Pilgrims, my presence bore witness to America's covenantal legacy with God.

"The curse is only lifted," Cindy exclaimed, "as God turns the hearts of the fathers to the children, and the hearts of the children to the fathers!"

X marked the spot. And the spot was moving. It was time to move with it. We together lifted the posterboard display of our X-ed out nation and began circling the Great Hall. The crowd of leaders fell in behind. Loud cries echoed throughout the hall for the curse to be reversed and covenant with Christ restored.

As the procession started, I somehow knew the vision being demonstrated by this prophetic action was about to become a lifelong pursuit.

As the old adage goes: God loves you, and Cindy Jacobs has a plan for your life.

A NAME, ERASED

Can a nation be X-ed out? Israel was. God's covenant covering was completely removed and, for thousands of years, the country simply ceased to exist. It wasn't until 1948, after the Holocaust, that Israel became the first nation ever to be literally born again!

The Bible makes clear that movements of the body of Christ can be X-ed out too. In Revelation, John the apostle conveyed a sobering warning that the church of Sardis faced an impending X-out:

> *...I know your deeds, that you have a name that you are alive, and yet you are dead. Be constantly alert, and strengthen the things that remain, which were about to die; for I have not found your deeds completed in the sight of My God. So remember what you have received and heard; and keep it, and repent...* (Revelation 3:1-3 NASB).

Could it be that America is like Sardis today? Is our reputation greater than our true substance? Are we squandering our inheritance, trading our liberty and blessing for open defiance of God's heart?

> *Then if you are not alert, I will come like a thief, and you will not know at what hour I will come to you. But you have a few people in* [America—I mean] *Sardis who have not soiled their garments; and they will walk with Me in white, for they are worthy. The one who overcomes will be clothed the same way...**and I will not erase his name** from the book of life...* (Revelation 3:3-5 NASB).

There it is. The missing ones. Blank spaces on the unfurled scroll where people, churches, ministries, and even nations were once inscribed. Invited to greatness in Christ, many were seduced away to the extent they actually chose their own X-out.

I saw this process once in a vision. A prophetic word was written on the title page of a Bible, with two names signed beneath it. I saw the hand of the Lord erase one of the names and write another in its place. The Lord then spoke to me that America was in danger of forfeiting her covenant destiny and that He could easily raise up another to nation fulfill what He had called us to accomplish.

CALL 911: RECOVERING THE COVENANT COVERING

Cindy's X-out warning proved hauntingly prescient. The date 9-11-01 is memorialized as a pivot point when the nation and world forever changed. Five years after she shared her vision of the X over America, terrorists hijacked commercial airlines and plunged them into the greatest symbols of American dominance. The Twin Towers of the World Trade Center fell to the earth, seemingly in slow motion. The Western Wall of the Pentagon exploded on impact.

This subject is intensely personal for me. Jolene and I now live right across from the Pentagon. I grew up with summer excursions to the World Trade Center while visiting my grandparents. It is clear to me the incident was a trumpet warning, divulging our enemies' pursuit of even greater destruction, which they seek to unleash. This treachery comes both from the outside and from within.

A primary goal is to X-out America. Our goal must be to see the Lord recover His covenant covering.

> *In that day I shall raise up and restore the fallen tabernacle (booth) of David, and wall up its breaches [in the city walls]; I will also raise up and restore its ruins and rebuild it as it was in the days of old* (Amos 9:11 Amplified Bible).

Amos 9:11 promises that David's legacy will be resurrected and repaired in the end times. What was that legacy? David realigned his sphere in covenant with God. He pitched a tent and invited lovers of God to experience His glory. Worship and prayer ascended night and day. Lives were transformed.

Eerily, the Scripture reference itself seems to allude to the pivotal date 9-11. And did you notice that the passage actually prophesies into events taking place *in a single day?* One 24-hour period day, the overarching span of the last days.

Further, the opening sentence of Amos 9 brings sobering context to the events prophesied to occur: *"Strike the pillar capitals so that the thresholds will shake, and break them on the heads of them all!"* (Amos 9:1 NASB).

What?

On 9-11 our capitals became the primary targets that jihadists chose to strike. The World Trade Center in NYC represents the capital of our financial world. The Pentagon in Washington, DC represents both the capital of our military and the capitol of our nation. And when the capitals were struck, our nation and world shook.

Context is important. The word *capitals* in the passage actually refers to the crowning portion of pillars in architecture. Capitals of pillars multiply support to the structures they are upholding. The capitals of the societal pillars supporting our nation actually function the very same way.

AUGUST DREAM—CALL 911

Maybe that's the reason the Twin Towers always reminded me of two giant pillars. I saw them for the very last time in late August 2001, just a few weeks before the terror strikes. Dutch Sheets and Will Ford were leading a prayer journey through the northeast called the Kettle Tour, which I had the privilege of joining while still on staff in Kansas City.

As we neared New York City, Dutch's wife, Ceci, conveyed an astonishing dream. She suddenly discovered she was pregnant. Then immediately the baby inside her grew to full term. Ceci found herself completely alone just as her newly discovered child was about to be born.

"Call 911! Call 911!" She cried out. "The experts are needed. There's nobody to help me birth my baby. Call 911!"

Clearly the life of a child was at stake. First and foremost, calling 911 means to *call for help in an emergency*. Train now to lean into Jesus from the outset of the challenges you are facing. Learn His ways. Gain His guidance and protection. It may even mean the difference between life and death.

While listening to Ceci relay her dream, Dutch immediately felt directed to Psalm 91:1 (NKJV). It's a great passage. *"He who dwells in the secret place of the Most High shall abide under the shadow of the Almighty."* That's what you receive when you call 911!

I immediately associated the dream with Amos 9:11, birthing the restoration of the Tabernacle of David. We were literally gazing at the Twin Towers above the New York City skyline at the very moment we were discussing various interpretations of the dream.

Yet none of us perceived the end-time crisis about to unfold in real time, right before our eyes.

Call 911. As it turned out, Holy Spirit was giving us more than a Scripture reference, He was giving us the actual date of the emergency. We just didn't press in enough to recognize it.

BIRTH PANGS AND PROTECTION

Just as Ceci's dream conveys, birth pangs are coming. In Matthew 24 Jesus warned that societal contractions would come more frequently as the end times progressed. The good news is that these expressions of travail would show that the birthing of His movement, even leading to His return, is drawing close.

The missing element in the dream—which Ceci called for—was a protective covering, experts who would provide protection and care needed to grant mom and child a safe birth.

Amidst the rubble and ruin of 9-11-01, I believe God's global mandate to restore the Tabernacle of David was birthed and released. After the towers fell, many 24-7 houses of prayer accelerated to global prominence as forerunning expressions.

Looking back at the prayer journey in August 2001, it's not a coincidence the primary prophetic message declared in every city we visited in the northeast was focused on repentance. I can still hear Dutch Sheets thundering these words from Acts 3:19, forever embedded in my heart:

> Repent and return, so that your sins may be washed
> away, in order that times of refreshing may come from
> the presence of the Lord!

TWO TRUMPET CALLS

Two trumpet calls are resounding to you today to redeem both Israel and America from the X. The first—Call 911. The second—Come up higher.

The first trumpet or alarm was sounded on 9-11-01 as Islamist jihadists sought to "strike the capitals," putting their X on the World Trade Center and the Pentagon. The call to recover God's covenant covering was nationally and globally released.

The second trumpet was sounded on October 7, Israel's 9/11, in the midst of a savage attack by the Islamist jihadist group Hamas. On the same date, in a manner resembling the sons of Eli at Shiloh, major breaches of covenant began to be exposed. The trend continued nationally.

Remember the prophets saw Kansas City as parabolic for the nation. The sin exposed rivaled the sins of Eli and his sons at Shiloh, where God's tabernacle first dwelt. God's governmental glory departed and the Ark of the Covenant was sent into captivity from there. In the next chapter, we will explore how David rescued the Ark, after it was sent into captivity from Shiloh, and recovered God's covenant covering.

But now, let me prophesy. God wants to restore His glory to Shiloh. He wants to recover His covenant covering across our nation. In addition, He wants to restore His glory to you personally, as the centerpiece of your life. Let's take genuine ownership of our sins and repent. Let's call 911 and seek His help. Maybe what was meant for evil can finally turn for good, with God's highest blessing restored and our sons and daughters preserved.

The Lord is not afraid to tear down our structures to bring a course correction. He is compelling you and me to gain the higher ground so that many of His long-term promises can actually be fulfilled.

When the Lord has washed away the filth of the daughters of Zion, and purged the bloodshed of Jerusalem from her midst… then over Zion and all her assemblies… the glory will be a [bridal] *canopy* (Isaiah 4:4-5 NASB).

We've seen the crisis. We are gaining God's purging. Now let's redeem the vast, broken potential of His original intent.

STUDY QUESTIONS AND PRAYER

1. Where do you need to "get off the X" and take higher ground? What are you seeking to gain?

2. What real-life experiences have served as trumpet calls in your life? What about prophetic experiences with the Lord? What is God saying through them?

3. How have you personally been affected by betrayal? How have you recovered?

4. What does "Call 911" mean to you? Do you perceive God's covenant covering in your life? What areas of your life is the Lord in process of rebuilding?

5. Who are you praying for to "get off the X"?

6. How is the Lord leading you to pray for Israel and the USA in this hour? For your city?

7. Has the Lord ever spoken to you about living in the end times? From your perspective, how do current events show this? How are you praying?

Father God, I thank You for Your protective care and covering over my life, my family, and my spheres. Thank You for the clear leading of the Spirit of God in my life. Please show me the higher ground You are calling me to attain in this hour. We bless the various expressions of the apostolic movement, the prophetic movement, and the prayer movement in our nation. We ask that You bring these all to healing, maturity and synergy with You. As a nation and as movements, help us to attain Your rescue from the X. In Jesus' name.

A father and young son stand in prayer at the Western Wall.

CHAPTER 8

TESHUVAH

"History can never be changed, but it can be healed."—Dutch Sheets, *An Appeal to Heaven*

In the midst of America's crisis of covenant, many believers in the nation have become critical of prophetic movements in our nation. Why didn't any of the prophets perceive the sins of so many leaders, the abuse, and call them out? Why didn't they warn the movements?

Or did they?

I want to address the issue by sharing a personal prophetic experience in which the Lord called both the IHOPKC movement and the broader body of Christ to repentance. To be clear, the Lord was not specific to me about the sins. But He was supernaturally specific about the call.

May you be filled with hope as you discover how it all plays into the redemptive drama of the end times.

DREAM—LIGHT THE LAMP AND PROCLAIM TESHUVAH

In January 2018, the Lord gave me a warning dream about the movement. It proved to be prescient. I saw a major conference with few in attendance. Permission was granted for a hidden intercessor who worked at the house of prayer to open the gathering.

Her name, Cathy, means "purity." She appeared on the right-center side of the stage, her curly gray hair shining against a black curtain. All eyes became riveted on her. She looked across the sparse crowd.

Then Cathy lit a candle and then held it up. She simply said one simple word, tears filling her eyes,

"Teshuvah."

In the dream, a prolonged moment of silence followed, with tears flowing freely. Again, only one word was said, "Teshuvah." Cathy turned around and disappeared from the stage, leaving the candle to burn on the podium.

Upon awakening I immediately rehearsed the details of the dream, scrambling not to forget. What was the Hebrew word? It sounded like Yeshua, but with a "T."

Teshuvah sounded like a Hebrew word, but like most Hebrew words, I had no idea of its meaning. So I immediately consulted with my Rabbi. Rabbi Google. Maybe you've interfaced with him too. Not the most personable, but very capable of providing accurate information quickly.

What I discovered startled me even more. Because "Teshuvah" conveys the Hebrew meaning of repentance. Returning. And turnaround. Essentially, this one word defines the very focus the Lord has been infusing into our lives over the previous decade.

In short—come up higher.

"In the Jewish tradition, repentance is called teshuvah," according to the website My Jewish Learning. "A Hebrew word translated as 'returning.'" The article continues, "One of the Hebrew words for sin is *chet*, which in Hebrew means 'to go astray.' Thus the idea of repentance in Jewish thought is a return to the path of righteousness."

"Teshuvah" is the embodiment of Acts 3:19, God's call to repent and return, receiving cleansing from our sins, so that a time of refreshing may come from the presence of the Lord.

To sum up the dream, Purity lit a candle and, through tears, called for repentance.

The "Teshuvah" word was submitted privately to the highest levels of leadership. I also released the prophecy on a broad level in our postings, not mentioning any specific prayer movement but emphasizing how we all need to embrace its message.

Teshuvah. Repent and return to covenant with the Lord. Come up higher. I will say prophetically that, in this season, the lamp of the Lord will again light the way. PURITY MUST LIGHT THE WAY.

> Purity lit a candle and, through tears, called for repentance.

TURNAROUND, TRUMPETS, AND THE FALL FEASTS

It was a surprise to discover that "teshuvah" is actually practiced as a sacred calling by Jewish people to start off each new year. Hebraic tradition holds that on Rosh Hashanah, the head of the Jewish new year, God opens the Book of Life and evaluates the lives of each person on earth, as well as businesses, cities, even nations. He then "pencils in" His verdict for the coming year based on their previous conduct.

Maybe it's not a coincidence Rosh Hashanah opens with a series of trumpet blasts. The descriptions of these blasts are hauntingly similar to descriptions of the trumpet blasts in the book of Revelation. The Rosh Hashanah trumpets literally alert those hearing that the head of the year has begun, and it is time to enter into teshuvah. Again, to come up higher.

Maybe it's no coincidence that Christ Himself is returning to the earth in the midst of the trumpet blasts (1 Thessalonians 4:16). Do the fall feasts foretell the return of Christ? It's important to note that Passover and Pentecost have both already found a primary fulfillment in Christ. Rosh Hashanah, Yom Kippur, and Tabernacles remain. And within each celebration you will discover astonishing secrets foretelling the great drama that closes out history.

HEAVEN'S COURT IS OPENED

Between Rosh Hashanah and Yom Kippur, Heaven's Court is opened for His people to approach the Bench and seek the Lord for a better verdict than their actions alone deserve. A common Scripture quoted is, *"Seek the Lord while He may be found; call upon Him while He is near"* (Isaiah 55:6 NASB). Over the ten days the Jewish people engage in teshuvah—repenting and turning—by seeking forgiveness from God and man over hurtful wrongs, making restitution where needed, reconciling, and repairing wounded relationships, and giving alms to the poor.

In Jewish tradition, Yom Kippur is the holiest day of the year. It is the day of national atonement, when the high priest seeks the Lord for atonement for the sins of the nation. Accordingly, at the close of Yom Kippur the Lord takes into heartfelt consideration the teshuvah of His people, of nations, etc. Some "penciled-in" verdicts are erased and rewritten to grant the greater future that was requested. Both blessing and judgment are determined. Some verdicts remain as written. Some names are even erased from the Book of Life altogether. Each verdict is sealed by the close of the holiest day of the year. Then He who judges and makes war initiates their implementation.

You should note that in Jesus' discourse on the end times, He reveals Himself as the "Chief Justice" of this process. Of course, He presides over Heaven's Court even now. And yet upon His return, perhaps over the days of awe, the execution of His justice on earth will bring eternal blessing and eternal judgment on those living on earth.

But when the Son of Man comes in His glory, and all the angels with Him, then He will sit on His glorious throne. And all the [people of the] *nations will be gathered before Him; and He will separate them from one another, just as the shepherd separates the sheep from the goats....*

Then the King will say to those on His right, "Come, you who are blessed of My Father, inherit the kingdom prepared for you from the foundation of the world. For I was hungry, and you gave Me something to eat.... Truly I say to you, to the extent that you did it for one of the least of these brothers or sisters of Mine, you did it for Me."

Then He will also say to those on His left, "Depart from Me, you accursed people, into the eternal fire which has been prepared for the devil and his angels; for I was hungry, and you gave Me nothing to eat.... Truly I say to you, to the extent that you did not do it for one of the least of these, you did not do it for Me, either." These will go away into eternal punishment, but the righteous into eternal life (Matthew 25:31-46 NASB).

Lesson to be learned—best to engage in teshuvah now.

SEVEN STEPS TO TESHUVAH

Let's learn from our forefathers. We encourage you to embrace teshuvah as a lifestyle. And a good way to start the year—both the Hebraic new year especially—is to intentionally practice teshuvah over the days of awe through seven actions, which are relatively self-explanatory:

1. Self-examination.

"The spirit of a person is the lamp of the Lord, searching the innermost parts of his being" (Proverbs 20:27 NASB). Commune with the Lord over the previous year. You might even review your life, month by month. Ask the Lord to highlight areas where you are being called to come up higher.

2. Receive God's forgiveness.

"Lord, forgive me. Cleanse me!" Ask the Lord to forgive you for areas where you may have violated your relationship with Him. Even unknowingly. Ask Jesus to make you aware of what needs to be repented. Ask Him to cleanse you of all unrighteousness.

David's plea is a great invocation to pray:

Create in me a clean heart, God, and renew a steadfast spirit within me. Do not cast me away from Your presence, and do not take Your Holy Spirit from me. Restore to me the joy of Your salvation, and sustain me with a willing spirit (Psalm 51:10-12 NASB).

By denying the enemy access to your bloodline, you are denying him access to your future. So if you haven't done so before, you should also repent for generational sins, including all idolatry or occult activity in your family line. Plead the blood of Jesus, and renounce all generational vows or pacts that may have given the enemy legal authority to your bloodline. Sometimes it's best to work with a counselor or a seasoned, trusted intercessor on this whole process. *"Confess your faults to one another, and pray for one another that ye may be healed..."* (James 5:16 KJV).

3. Forgive those who have wronged you.

"Lord, I forgive...." Sometimes these are the hardest words to say. And the challenge is not going to go away. Jesus warned that as the birth pangs of the end times draw more frequent, so will society's spiral into depravity. Which means it will become even harder to keep your heart unburdened from unforgiveness.

It's best to practice now. Jesus' kind warning also remains that those who forgive will be forgiven.

For if you forgive other people when they sin against you, your heavenly Father will also forgive you. But if you do not forgive others their sins, your Father will not forgive your sins (Matthew 6:14-15 NIV).

Want a better future? Make an honest evaluation of your heart. Where has anger over an offense supplanted His peace? Take time to speak your forgiveness out loud. Ask Him to heal and restore your heart. Ask Him to show His love to those who offended you. Sometimes it's best to work with a counselor or a very trusted friend.

4. Repent of unfulfilled vows from your past.

"Lord please forgive me for the vows and promises from my past which I did not fulfill. Help me to make restitution where appropriate." Here's a hidden point for repentance that's rarely addressed in the Christian world. But it is front and center during the Jewish season of teshuvah. Ask the Lord to review all vows or promises you made over the years that you failed to complete. Fasting. Prayer. Giving. Commitments to your family. Commitments to others. Ask Jesus to forgive you for not fulfilling your vows, and request that He release you entirely from all past obligations so that you may start afresh. Let the blood of Jesus be your plea. Note He may still require you to fulfill the vows and promises you have made as proof of your repentance. No matter what, come up higher and set a new course.

And in the tradition of Jewish teshuvah, consider making restitution wherever appropriate.

5. Reconcile.

Reconcile with people who may have hurt you, and people whom you may have hurt. You've forgiven them. Now put your forgiveness into practice.

6. Give alms.

Extending your heart and your finances to those in need. Where you have withheld your finances from God and man—by not tithing and not giving offerings—take time to repent and return from your sin. Because where your treasure is, that's where your heart is.

Again you might want to recover the blessing promised by making restitution. And no matter what, let your repentance be proven by your deeds.

7. Ask the Lord for a better verdict.

A better ruling than your actions alone deserve! Approach the Lord as your Judge, and present your case in humility before Him. Remind Him of the future He promised you. Show Him how you have entered into teshuvah and changed your ways. Plead the blood of Jesus as atonement for your sins. Ask Him to render His verdict of justice in your favor, restraining resisting forces and releasing you to possess your covenantal inheritance to advance the Kingdom (Daniel 7:22).

A NOTE ON FORGIVENESS

Offenses you are dealing with are yours to either foster or forgive. By choosing not to forgive, you actually grant incredible power to those who wounded you to continue inflicting their pain. When you choose to forgive the people or institutions that harmed you and release them into the hands of the Lord, you forbid them anymore authority to control your life. You will regain your peace.

Further, your release of forgiveness is by no means a validation their wrongful behavior against you—as if the hurtful action was deserved. Quite the opposite actually. Nor is it an admission of powerlessness—as if you were too weak or insignificant to leverage against them the justified consequences of their actions.

Instead, you are a son or daughter of God. In the transaction of forgiveness you stand in the stature of Christ Himself—your own heart has been forever freed by His gift of cleansing, forgiveness, and justification by His own blood. Even when you feel like a victim, you are actually royalty. And you are forgiving those who hurt you from His own seat of authority.

What I've personally found is that it's important to move beyond the obligation to forgive and actually encounter God's love for the person I am forgiving. He still loves them too. Therefore His actions toward them will always encourage their redemption—even if a severe redemption is what's necessary.

Forgiving and committing the offending party into Jesus' hands releases Him to bring about His justice in their lives, His way. Often it unleashes the testimony of a genuinely transformed life. Sometimes God must choose to release greater discipline. But the point is that your action to forgive actually activates the intervention of His justice, not the other way around. *"Vengeance is Mine, I will repay,' says the Lord"* (Romans 12:19 NKJV).

Releasing forgiveness is also key for your shift from a mentality of victimhood into your true identity. You are an overcomer in Christ. Don't deny the Lord the opportunity to manifest this extraordinary aspect of His investment in your life.

Teshuvah. Be free. Let purity light your candle and prepare the way for a better future.

OPERATION DAYS OF TESHUVAH

"Operation Days of Teshuvah has commenced!" Before dawn on October 26, 2024, fighter jets from Israel screamed through the skies above Tehran and other Iranian cities, demolishing air defense infrastructure and missile factories throughout the land. Their provocative strike was in response to Iran's launch of 180 cruise missiles a few weeks beforehand. Unlike the previous attack on April 13, these missiles took only 12 minutes from their launch in Iran to their targets across Israel. In a way similar to April 13, almost all strikes against Israel were thwarted. But the brazen attack demanded a response.

American media correctly interpreted "Days of Teshuvah" as days of repentance, admittedly an odd name for a high-altitude, high-risk military operation with global implications. Perhaps Netanyahu and colleagues were providing a limited strike to show capabilities without endangering the public in hopes that Iran would embrace "teshuvah" and repent of their aggression.

But the secondary definition of teshuvah resonates with the strike even more. Because "Days of Teshuvah" also means Days of Turnaround. And one way or another, Israel is determined such a turnaround will be gained.

Turnaround. Doesn't this resonate as well for America? For your life? Let Operation Days of Teshuvah now commence!

KING DAVID—MAKE COVENANT GREAT AGAIN!

King David can mentor you and me in this holy quest. He became the living epitome of both aspects of teshuvah during his reign. Of all the biblical giants, the legendary king is the only one singled out as a man after God's own heart (1 Samuel 13:14). He took down Goliath and turned his nation back to God, all the while penning the greatest psalms of worship the world has ever recorded.

As with many leaders today, David also made great mistakes. Dramatically. Publicly. Recklessly. Endangering his family, his nation, and especially his own heart. But unlike many leaders today, he consistently embraced the repentance expression of teshuvah. He took responsibility for his sins before both God and his people. He learned to be forgiven and to forgive.

And by his actions, David even prevented an X-out of his nation. Instead he saw the Lord restore His bridal canopy of glory and create a generational altar of teshuvah that still impacts our world today.

You have to hand it to David. Very few can say they have actually lived out the commitments of their youth. But remarkably, the covenant David made with God as a young shepherd directed the entire course of his life. A major focus of his covenant was to establish the tabernacle for His presence. Psalm 132 forever memorializes this:

> Remember, Lord, in David's behalf, all his affliction; how he swore to the Lord and vowed to the Mighty One of Jacob...I will not give sleep to my eyes, or slumber to my eyelids, until I find...a dwelling place for the Mighty One of Jacob (Psalm 132:1-5 NASB).

When David became king of Israel, his promise to the Lord became his first priority. The Ark of the Covenant, representing God's covenant with His nation and people, was sent from Shiloh into captivity by the prophet Samuel. Why? Because God's own priesthood had succumbed to idolatry and abuse.

The window opened for restoration. As mentioned, David rescued the Ark from captivity and restored it to Jerusalem, realigning his nation's covenant with God. David desired for Israel's government, security, culture, law, education, and commerce to all be sourced from Israel's covenantal relationship with the Lord.

Finally, David then erected a tabernacle for this sacred seat of covenant and established 24-7 worship to continually host the presence of God. With this action, Israel was launched into her greatest hour. The boundaries of the land became supernaturally protected, allowing the accumulation of generational wealth. Government and culture flourished. Perpetual innovation caused the economy to thrive.

A PERSONAL X-OUT

But in the midst of prosperity, key decisions nearly took David down. At a time the kings of the region went to war, the renown warrior-king decided to stay home. And a battle of a different kind erupted from the upper level of his palace.

The king caught a glimpse of his neighbor, Bathsheba, as she bathed. And this beautiful woman, married to one of his military leaders, became the illicit passion of his heart. David used his stature to gain Bathsheba's affection, ultimately committing adultery with her. She soon conceived a child.

The king knew Bathsheba's baby bump would spark great controversy. Undoubtedly they had been seen together. Discerning what occurred would not be difficult, especially as her husband Uriah remained at war.

Time to execute a strategic solution. Bring the military leader home! Unite the birds and the bees, add a little honey, and David would soon be off the hook. Except that Uriah refused to sleep with his wife, knowing his troops were still engaged in combat.

A final, dire solution was then implemented. He ordered Bathsheba's husband to the front lines of an impossible battle, specifically so he would be killed.

Adultery. Betrayal. Cover-ups. Murder. David?

It's important to note that "Bathsheba" or Bat Sheva means "Daughter of the Oath." Her very name represents the covenant relationship between God and His people. David sought and received forgiveness. But from the moment Bathsheba was taken, severe consequences never departed his generational line.

WEAPONIZED GOVERNMENT AND THE X-OUT OF ISRAEL

The Bible says that in the days of David, satan stood up against Israel (1 Chronicles 21:1). To my knowledge, it is the only passage in Scripture that so clearly conveys such a direct, targeted assault to X-out the covenant land, with satan identified as the initiator. How satan began his assault is extremely telling. He targeted Israel by targeting David, the leader of Israel.

Clearly the implication is that if the enemy of mankind could X-out David, he could then access Israel to take the nation down. Still to this day, it's one of the enemy's most strategic moves.

Why was the land such a threat to satan? Israel under King David was more than a nation, *it was a freedom movement*. And this movement was fueled by God's manifest presence, hosted night and day in the center of Israel's capital city. BLESSED is the nation whose God is the Lord!

Provoking David to compromise his covenant with God opened the door for satan to take him down, and in the process, imperil his entire sphere of authority. David's plight helps explain the warfare in the spirit over both Israel and America today and especially over leaders of movements within our lands. By provoking them to compromise, satan sought to X-out their entire spheres.

Friend, we cannot excuse compromise. However we must also recognize that our leaders are being targeted by a ruthless enemy. And the spiritual conflict can many times be both hidden and overwhelming in magnitude. Very few realize the true price Christian leaders often have to pay. It's why so many pulpits have been vacated.

And it's why facilitating prayer shields for these leaders is so vitally important.

What was the temptation? Enacting a census. It sounds innocent enough. But as you will see, through the census David was tempted to essentially weaponize government toward political ends. You will see why this gave David the open door in a moment. But the principle itself carries massive implications for today.

Leaders weaponize government first to subvert the balance of power that holds them in check and accountable to God and the people. Secondarily, the government overreach is utilized to control, suppress, and subjugate the people.

Sound familiar? It should. And until we deal with the spiritual entities behind these machinations, our efforts will have little effect.

A THRONE BEHIND THE THRONE

In His day, Jesus even suffered the indignation of satan's temptation. The Son of David was taken to a high mountain and shown *"all the kingdoms of the world, and their glory."* The next action words were so telling. *"All these things I will give You, if You fall down and worship me"* (Matthew 4:8-9 NASB).

Sit on your throne, Jesus. Rule. Just break covenant with Your Father by bowing Your knee to me.

Let's bottom-line satan's goal. The core temptation is to enter into covenant with occult powers to fulfill desires what we don't believe God will actually grant us. More money. Sex. Power. Influence. Satan knew that by co-opting the leader, he would then gain legal right to rule over the seat of authority occupied by the leader. To essentially become "the throne behind the throne," the prevailing spiritual influence directing the entire course of the sphere.

Again, satan still tempts rulers in this same manner today. Very successfully, I might add. In case you believe that backroom occult ceremonies initiating successful leaders into satan's rulership are too far-fetched for our modern world, you might check out the inner workings of Freemasonry today. Don't bow the knee!

YOUR END-TIMES MANDATE

Satan's formula is the exact antithesis of what King David actually demonstrated when he restored the Ark of the Covenant, pitched his tent, worshiped God, and ruled with the Lord from His seat of covenant. David established his sphere of authority in covenant with the one true God, by making a place from which He is welcome to rule.

Please learn this lesson. No matter what your calling or pursuits, make this your end-time mandate today: *Establish your life and your rulership in covenant with Jesus Christ, divorced from all idolatry.*

The advice King David and I just gave you is worth its weight in gold.

COVENANTS ESTABLISH THRONES OF AUTHORITY

Remember, God is enthroned on the praises of His people, right? Psalm 22:3 (NASB) makes it clear: *"You are holy, You who are enthroned upon the praises of Israel."* In other words, your worship invites God's presence into your heart, your life and family, and your spheres of authority. Not just to dwell but also to rule.

Here's a big point though. Your worship alone does not establish a throne for God. Thrones are established by covenant. Your worship is an expression of your covenant. Violating God's covenant imperils your intimacy with Him and His intervention on your behalf.

As our friend Chris Mitchell Jr. pointed out to us, this principle is exemplified by the Ark of the Covenant. The Ark contained the original "ketubah" or marital covenant between God and His covenant people, known today as the Ten Commandments. But first and foremost this "law" was a covenantal agreement with God, entered into by both parties in the same manner as a groom and his bride. I will be your God, and you will be My people!

Remember, covenant with God establishes a throne for Him to rest on and rule from. To better understand this, let's take a look at the golden cover—or covering—of the Ark of the Covenant. Above the covenant itself, the Lord instructed His people to fashion a throne for His presence to rest on, called "the mercy seat." It is surrounded by two cherubim, bowing before the seat or throne while covering it with their outstretched wings.

This beautiful, symbolic expression mirrors the very Throne of God as described in the Bible. And it is a clear picture of the reality that covenant establishes a seat of authority for the Lord to rest on and rule from. Your covenant with God establishes this throne. Your worship invites Him to rest on the throne that your covenant has established.

And if your covenant with God is violated, 24-7 worship can ascend night and day but a time will come when He remains at a distance.

GOVERNMENT OVERREACH—
END-TIMES SUBJUGATION

Let's now put this in perspective for the end times. As mentioned, a term often used today for the trap David fell into is government "overreach," which is the weaponization of government toward political ends.

"The consolidation of power at the federal level in the guise of public safety is a national trend and should be guarded against at all costs," writes Jack Carr, author and former Navy SEAL in his Introduction for his first book *The Terminal List*.[3] "This erosion of rights, however incremental, is the slow death of freedom. We have reached a point where the power of the federal government is such that *they can essentially target anyone of their choosing.*"

Jack Carr continues, "The fundamental value of freedom is what sets us apart from the rest of the world. We are citizens, not subjects, and we must stay ever vigilant that we remain so."

Maybe now you can better perceive exactly how satan arose against King David. Because it's the same way he is tempting our leaders today. He arose against David by giving the impression of coming alongside him to strengthen his leadership over the kingdom. "Do this for your own good."

You must understand the entity, satan, from a governmental perspective. He was a ruler in the government of God when he sought to overtake the Throne. Since his fall, he has always sought to supplant God from government and instigate his own government in its place. Both rulers and systems. In response, the Lord moved decisively in David's time, and He is going to do so now.

Here's another key. According to Scripture, the antichrist is the embodiment of satan himself in human form. In other words, the spiritual entity that aimed to take down Israel by taking down David is going to possess a human embodiment. He is going to overtake nations—by overtaking the thrones of nations. And his ultimate quest is to rule the world from the Temple Mount.

Talk about government overreach. Most of the world will be mandated to either worship his image or face extreme punishment. Scripture says you could lose your right to buy and sell. You could even be martyred.

Again...far-fetched? Just look back to the Nazis and the Holocaust. Or look now to the government of China today, utilizing a "social credit score" enforced by the mass surveillance of their population. Regular church attendance is already being punished with severe restrictions on both economic advancement and freedom to travel. Because their all-seeing eye watches you.

Better keep your social credit score up. Bow your knee to me. Then all this can be yours.

VIRTUAL IMPOSSIBILITIES

Why a census—what are the dangers? Then and now, the data on a nation's population provides clarity on overarching trends as well as profiles, preferences, and actions of individuals. Government surveillance then essentially becomes a perpetual census.

By the way, the capability of mass invasive surveillance is about to come to a whole new level. There is currently no way to hide from the "all-seeing eye" of many technologies now being developed. Living off the grid will soon give new meaning to the phrase "a virtual impossibility."

According to *Defense News*, 6G wireless will soon become a major catalyst. "The Pentagon's Future Generation Wireless Technology Office has shifted its focus to preparing the Defense Department for the next wave of network innovation," according to an online article. "That work is increasingly important for the U.S., which is racing against China to shape the next iteration of wireless telecommunications, known as 6G."[4]

One of the prime features of 6G is its capacity to expand Integrated Sensing and Communication (ISAC), a technology that uses radio signals to "sense the physical world and collect data on an object's position, velocity, size, shape, and more." Mobile phones will soon be capable not only for communication but also for the spatial location of objects via radio signals. Even behind closed doors.

The good news is that the same technologies will rapidly improve capacities for the betterment of humankind. It will provide greater precision in remote surgery, cancer diagnosis, locating hidden objects, hostage rescues, and so much more. But it also has the capacity to be inherently invasive.

Note that China is competing feverishly with the US to harness 6G. Increasing exponentially their capacities of mass surveillance and control in the process.

Another coming virtual impossibility is evading the mandate to bow to the image of the antichrist. Note that John did not say the beast would physically confront each person. People would instead bow to *his image*.

The Greek word for "image" is *eikon* or icon. Any representation—a statue, a photo—would probably suffice in fulfilling the Scripture. But you should know that holographic technology has become so advanced that you may soon be engaging with visual entertainment in 3D—with normal glasses, according to the Princeton University website, and in time even no glasses.[5] So lifelike it will seem to be happening right before your eyes.

A holographic image of the beast could literally become the apparition that you interact with over one of the most important decisions of your life.

X-OUT AT THE THRESHING FLOOR

Let's return to David. Satan arose against Israel. The King of Israel fell by aligning with satan in a seemingly innocent pursuit. God forbade David to number his population. David defied Him simply by taking a census.

The pursuit seems innocent until the potential of such a census is explored. Like when the beast of Revelation numbers the global population in a way that evaluates the loyalty of each individual. Fail the test and your life and livelihood are endangered.

God disciplined David by sending a plague upon the very population he was numbering. The plague was actually released by an angel of the Lord, on assignment from the Throne. It's important to note the book of Revelation prophesies similar judgments will impact the earth through the end times. Let these stories mentor you for what's ahead.

The angel made a dramatic entrance in Jerusalem, hovering over a hill above the City of David so he could be clearly seen by all of the residents. Appropriately, a threshing floor at the top of the hill became the X that marked their destruction. All Israel was actually on the threshing floor at that moment. Especially King David. The people watched, terrified.

TESHUVAH AT THE
THRESHING FLOOR

David fell before God and, against all protocols of his kingship, took anguished responsibility for his sin. He wholeheartedly sought God's forgiveness, even asking for the hand of judgment to be on him and his family instead of the multitudes surrounding him. "What have these sheep done?" The king begged.

Both God and the king knew the answer. "Nothing."

Now that's teshuvah in action. The Lord is speaking to His leaders especially through this parabolic event. Jesus admonished us that the good shepherd lays down his life for the sheep. However, *false shepherds lay down the lives of their sheep for themselves.* The choices of leaders always bring consequences for those entrusted to their care—either for good or for evil. Maybe the repercussions won't be so dramatic. But they will be present. And leaders will absolutely be held accountable to Him.

Be like David. Take responsibility. Repent. Even publicly.

When King David humbled himself before God and his people, his prayer was dramatically answered. By taking responsibility and seeking forgiveness, he literally preserved his people from destruction.

THE X BECOMES A COVENANT COVERING

David was then summoned to the threshing floor over which the angel hovered—the geographic X itself. Again it was a mountain above all of Jerusalem's hills. Figuratively and literally, King David was summoned to come up higher.

David built an altar on the X of impending destruction. The angel sheathed his sword. *Fire fell from Heaven,* marking the restoration of God's covenant blessing to His land and people. Astonishingly, the threshing floor became an altar of mercy.

A generation later, David's son Solomon built a dwelling place for the God of Israel on this same ground. You and I know it today as the Temple Mount. His father's altar became its centerpiece.

At Solomon's dedication ceremony, *fire from Heaven again struck the altar.* The glory of the Lord filled the Temple. Where X once marked the spot of their destruction, God's governmental glory literally became a bridal canopy for His people.

And it was on this ground that God promised Solomon that *"if My people who are called by My name will humble themselves and pray"* just as David did a generation earlier, and *"seek My face, and **turn** from their wicked ways, I will...forgive their sin and heal their land"* (2 Chronicles 7:14 NKJV).

If My people will *turn,* I will heal. You already know the Hebrew word. Teshuvah. The threshing floor of judgment became a generational altar of repentance, mercy, and healing. All because David as king took responsibility for his sin.

Beloved, your threshing floor can be transformed to an altar of mercy and forgiveness as well. Healing can still spring forth. And as David restored God's covenant covering, so can you. Maybe not over your nation yet, but certainly over your own life. Over your household. Over your spheres of authority.

Amos 9:11 prophetically conveys how David's very legacy will be offered to leaders, lands, and peoples in the end times. Repairing covenant and hosting God's presence in this manner is a prototype for us all. It's time to gain the next phase of His promised restoration.

LAST DAYS—X AGAIN MARKS THE SPOT

In the last days, X again marks the spot as the Temple Mount once more becomes a threshing floor for harvest. This time not just for Israel, or even the Mideast, but for all the nations of the earth.

The trumpet will soon sound for Jesus, Son of David, to close out the era. He will move from Heaven's gate to the east gate of the summit where His bloodline forefather cut covenant. Much like the angel who hovered over the threshing floor, every eye will behold Him, perhaps on a global level. The severe plague of antichrist dictatorship will fall. Jesus the Messiah will unseat and remove the most wicked leader in the history of mankind and take His rightful seat in the house of covenant dedicated to His glory.

All Israel will finally see Him as He is and will be saved. Vast multitudes from the nations will also bow the knee as they experience His deliverance.

Again, Hebrew time is cyclical. So it's no coincidence that X once more marks the spot where His end-times threshing reaches its greatest, most cataclysmic culmination. The result will be redemption.

Mercy. Even so, Lord, come!

STUDY QUESTIONS AND PRAYER

1. How have you personally been affected by recent challenges in the body of Christ? In your opinion, are leaders following God's call to repentance or teshu-vah? What progress do you see?

2. Have you ever struggled with forgiveness? With feelings of being undervalued or marginalized, or even violated? What positive actions would make you feel cherished or more appreciated?

3. David's journey shows the potential for your journey. What stood out? What fresh vision or fresh hope was sparked? What warnings became clear?

4. How are you planning on implementing the seven steps to teshuvah? Which step means the most to you? Which is the most challenging?

5. Have you ever seen the Lord bring mercy where judgment was impending? How did things turn out long term?

6. What aspects of government overreach concern you right now? Where are these aspects tethered to idolatry? How are you praying?

7. How are you establishing a covenant covering over your life? Over your family? Over your spheres of authority?

Father God, help me to enter into teshuvah as a lifestyle. Grant me breakthrough in my partnership with You. Just as with King David, I desire to protect, defend, and serve those entrusted to my care. Lead me not into temptation but deliver me from evil. Help me to see and recognize evil when it presents itself. Help me to overcome evil with good!

And where breaches have occurred, help me to forgive, so that I can be forgiven.

Lord, please realign our national government in covenant with You as a beachhead against antichrist idolatry, government overreach, and the weaponization of departments of government against our citizens.

Lord, redeem us from the X-out! Transform the X into Your covenant covering across the land. Restore movements in the body of Christ that have been reduced to barely burning flames. Bring the course corrections needed to thrive in You once again. In Jesus' name, amen.

NOTES

3. Jack Carr, *The Terminal List* (Miami, FL: Atria, 2020).

4. Courtney Albon, "Pentagon readies for 6G, the next wave of wireless network tech," Defense News, September 13, 2024; https://www.defensenews.com/pentagon/2024/09/13/pentagon-readies-for-6g-the-next-of-wave-of-wireless-network-tech/; accessed October 16, 2024.

5. Julia Schwarz, "Holographic displays offer a glimpse into an immersive future," Princeton University, April 22, 2024; https://engineering.princeton.edu/news/2024/04/22/holographic-displays-offer-glimpse-immersive-future; accessed October 16, 2024.

Jon and Jolene's wedding menorah at the Arch of Titus,
Rome, Italy. God is rescuing His lampstands!

CHAPTER 9

RESCUING YOUR LAMPSTAND

*"Don't let my love grow cold. I'm calling out,
light the fire again! Don't let my vision die.
I'm calling out, light the fire again!"*

— "Light the Fire Again" lyrics, Brian Doerksen

"The Year 2025 is the Year of the Lampstand—*the rescued lamp-stand*, says the Lord!"

I awakened to these words on a crisp autumn morning at a cabin on the summit of a small mountain overlooking the Allegheny River. We had just traveled from DC to visit Jolene's mom. At 88, Mom Phyllis still loves to live on the mountain independently, at least for half the year. She calls it her slice of Heaven on earth.

I should probably not mention that Mom Phyllis also loves to joke about tripping over rocks in her yard, with nobody to help her but the bears. Her humor can be truly terrifying at times. And it runs in the family.

No growlers this morning, thankfully. Just a hovering fog. We had left DC for a weekend visit, but in the spirit I was still struggling against what felt like a cloud of reinforced resistance lingering from our nation's capital. It finally broke after praying. Then a word from Heaven beamed down into this slice of Heaven on earth and ignited my heart.

I'm pretty sure it will ignite yours too. In time at least. Right now you may not even understand the biblical imagery of a lampstand. We'll explore this more fully in a moment. But for now, just know it has everything to do with the fire of love, of passion. A mystery to be savored.

"The year 2025 is the 'Year of the Lampstand'—*the rescued lampstand,* says the Lord. You have well seen that the spirit of Elijah is again in the land. For from the outset of 2025 I am inaugurating a *new burning lamp movement.* I am engaging My body to rekindle once-blazing torches, which have now been reduced to barely burning embers. Some have been dimmed due to neglect. Many have been diminished due to the severe resistance you have suffered from your enemy. But the Lord says in this season, from region to region I am resetting your lampstands and relighting the flame!"

Jesus is on the move to rescue your lampstand of love and devotion to Him. For all who have struggled through the previous chapters of your lives—or even the previous chapters of this book—Jolene and I are excited to finally bring you great news. His eyes are on the lampstand of your heart. Of your love. Your prayer life. The brightness of your being.

By no means can we say the midnight hour is spent. But according to Jesus, in the end times the midnight hour actually releases His invitation to light the fire and become burning lamps again (Matthew 25). Again, more on this in a moment. For now, it's good news that the wattage within you has caught the eye of God Himself. He wants you to burn brightly again. And He is going to help you rescue your lampstand.

RESCUING THE FIRE OF FIRST LOVE

Scripturally, what is God referring to when He speaks about your lampstand? And why does it need rescuing? Let's start with a few basics to familiarize you. Then you will receive ten proven steps to recover your fire, even through difficulties being faced. Finally you will gain an overall perspective that will both astonish you and inspire you to become His burning lamp through the end times.

Let's begin with John's classic experience with the lampstands from the book of Revelation. After a quick analysis you'll be surprised how relevant it is to your world today:

> ...*The One who holds the seven stars in His right hand, the One who walks among the seven golden lampstands, says this: "I know your deeds and your labor and perseverance, and that you cannot tolerate evil people, and you have put those who call themselves apostles to the test, and they are not, and you found them to be false; and you have perseverance and have endured on account of My name, and have not become weary. But I have this against you, that you have left your first love. Therefore, remember from where you have fallen, and repent, and do the deeds you did at first; or else I am coming to you and I will remove your lampstand from its place—unless you repent"* (Revelation 2:1-5 NASB).

Remove the lampstand—what?

You may have heard of God's fire. Maybe you've experienced it. But you might not have even known that you possessed a lampstand, or even needed a lampstand, let alone that God was threatening to take it away!

But I bet you recognize fully the season of life John describes, because it so describes what we have just chronicled. A time of resistance that makes laboring for the Kingdom difficult, requiring great perseverance. A time of struggle to discern godly leaders in the midst of great hypocrisy and betrayal. A time when standing in sincerity for the name of Jesus can initiate marginalization, abuse, and even lethal persecution.

Maybe not where you're living. At least not so much. But Washington, DC has proven to be an alternate reality altogether.

And in the midst of these severe trials, who can blame them— or really us—for becoming more guarded or even cynical? For not feeling so passionate, tender, trusting or responsive toward God and our fellow man? For not burning so brightly, even as a form of self-protection?

For losing our first love?

John's lampstand passage conveys the hallmark challenges we are facing right now. All believers will face them at a heightened level as the days progress. End times in real time. Or maybe more accurately, end times in real life.

Here's a litmus test for you. If you've lost your exuberance for encountering Jesus in prayer, for reading the Word, and for relating to the men and women He wants you to impact, you might be struggling in your first-love devotion.

I'm not talking about experiencing an occasional lapse or needing a break. That's normal. But when the lack of passion remains constant, when unforgiveness privately swells in your heart, and your personal relationship with Jesus no longer seems intuitively imperative, you might be in danger of losing your first love.

You might already have.

BREAKING UP WITH JESUS

Like the day Jolene broke up with Jesus. Literally. Shortly after rededicating her life to Christ, she went through a season very similar to what John the apostle describes. Jesus had mandated a radical change in her lifestyle. Among other things—no clubbing, for instance.

No clubbing? Jolene has always been very self-sufficient. But she is also very social and remains a stunning sight on any dance floor. A running joke was that the only club she was allowed to enter was Price Club.

True story. You might not remember Price Club, but it was one of the original warehouse shopping chains that later got overtaken by Costco. Most Friday nights Jolene sojourned to Price Club for appetizers, followed by a $1.50 combo meal featuring a hot dog and a diet coke. She kind of considered these excursions to be date nights with Jesus. They would always include a lingering stroll through the merchandise.

You have to understand, Jesus was—and remains—Jolene's first love. Her Bridegroom with a capital "B," if you will. She learned to relate to Him out of the depths of her heart. She leaned into Him for basic provision as well as for healing from emotional wounds, from generational cycles of bondage, and from betrayal. She clung to Him relentlessly for truth. She learned to hear His voice.

But Jolene still longed for companionship. Turning the yearning into a prayer, she sought the Lord for a godly husband. Some of the leadings she felt were from the Lord proved to be dead ends. One day, circumstances overwhelmed her heart. In frustration, clubbing with Jesus was about to come to an end.

As she had done with many prospective suitors in the past, Jolene spoke kindly but directly to Jesus Christ, her first love, the Savior of the world. She was clear, firm, and immediate.

"Jesus, I'm breaking up with You."

The reply from the Throne was equally clear, firm, and immediate. Almost like Jesus knew what was about to come and had already fashioned a reply.

"That's okay, Jolene. I'll still call you."

True story. Ultimately they reconciled. I'm not sure what happened to Jolene's lampstand at the time, but the Lord absolutely came through with one by the end of her journey. That said, what I love about Jolene, and I'm sure what Jesus finds totally endearing as well, is how she relates to Him in absolute honesty and transparency while moving through her trials. Maybe it's why He always comes through for her.

RESCUING YOUR LAMPSTAND—SEVEN KEYS

Honest dialogue is vitally key to regaining your holy fire. Which is actually one of the primary keys to regain your first-love devotion to Jesus. Let's take a break from Jolene's story to explore these principles together.

1. Welcome His love.

"Jesus, thank You that You love me." Start your time with Him by speaking these words to the Lord, out loud so your own heart and spirit hear them as well. I know this may seem like the opposite of what you should do. Praising your way through difficult times is usually suggested as the first solution for rekindling your fire. But your striving to perform probably won't obtain for you the immediate connection with Him you need.

God is love. Love conquers all. Your faith works by love. If you want to annihilate the antichrist agenda, you must first choose love.

Your welcoming of His love activates your faith. Start with your reminder of who you are to Him. Desired, cherished in your uniqueness, worth His attention and care. Because you are.

You'll find focused worship and prayer flows much more naturally. By the way, we learned this secret from our ministry friend Martin Frankena. We are passing on to you what has since enriched our lives so much.

2. Drop your guard.

"Jesus, this is what's going on." Open up to Jesus about your struggles. Be honest and real. You can trust Him fully with your secrets and your true feelings. And let Him know you are opening your heart to Him, unguarded. Ask Him to remove any hindrances and show you what they are, as needed. This first step is actually incredibly effective. And it's entirely scriptural: *"Casting all your care upon Him, for He cares for you"* (1 Peter 5:7 NKJV).

We strongly suggest making time for a full conversation, just as you would for a friend in the natural. You might consider changing the location of your talk if it helps you stay focused.

3. Ask Jesus to restore your fire.

"Jesus, rescue my lampstand! Please help me restore holy fire for You." Ask Him specifically to restore your desire to connect with Him in prayer, to read His Word, etc. Be sensitive to His Spirit in reply. He may bring to mind areas where He would like to intervene, but where your repentance is necessary to open the door.

"Rescue my lampstand. Restore holy fire." This prayer is so powerful to pray, not just for yourself but for others. So many are struggling. Ask the Lord to restore their lampstands and reignite their flame of holy fire!

Please ask for Israel too. You know the prayer.

> *For Zion's sake I will not hold My peace, and for Jerusalem's sake I will not rest, until her righteousness shines as brightness and her salvation as a lamp that burns* (Isaiah 62:1 NKJV).

4. Renew your covenant.

"Lord, I give my life to You. I renew my covenant commitment to You!" Jesus gave His own body and blood for you so that you could be together forever. Covenant renewal unlocks the potential for every aspect of restoration, provision, and protection in your life.

> *The covenant that I have made with you, you shall not forget, nor shall you fear other gods. But the Lord your God you shall fear; and He will deliver you from the hand of all your enemies* (2 Kings 17:38-39 NKJV).

Here's a secret. In Christ's Kingdom the greatest levels of intimate fellowship with Him, as well as demonstration of authority from His hand, are reserved for those in right covenant alignment with Him. Make every effort.

5. Gain a fresh revelation of Jesus.

"Lord, reveal Yourself to me!" By God's design, a primary way passion is ignited is by the unveiling of beauty. Ask the Lord to put Himself across your path again, to reveal Himself to you in a way that touches your heart. Pray Ephesians 1:17 daily. "God of our Lord Jesus Christ, Father of glory, grant me a spirit of wisdom and revelation in the knowledge of Jesus Christ. That my spiritual eyes, the eyes of my understanding, may be enlightened or made full of light…."

Remember that distraction makes your eyes dim. A singular focus on Jesus, especially while engaging in your prayer time with Him, releases Heaven's fire into your being. He promises that *"…if therefore thine eye be single, thy whole body shall be full of light"* (Matthew 6:22 KJV).

That's what you're after, isn't it? So put down the phone. Forsake the distractions. Gain holy fire.

6. Disengage to re-engage.

"Help me cut ties with my past." Remember the ancient declaration, "forsaking all others, and clinging only to you"? It's that way with Jesus. Ask the Lord to cleanse you and break all ungodly ties with entities from your past, especially where a covenant relationship is involved. This includes ties with former lovers or spouses, with family members and friends, pastors and bosses, with organizations such as churches, networks, businesses or occupations, and even with houses or lands or cities. Ask Him to dethrone and restrain all principalities and powers working through these ties. Take authority as directed, in Jesus' name.

And of course, ask the Lord to bless all godly ties. Your work with Jesus here is to disengage from ties that control, drain, and cause pain. Blessing the godly ties empowers His original intent for these relationships.

One more important step. Ask the Lord to remove you, at least temporarily, from standing in the gap with your intercessory prayer projects. Longstanding ones especially. Take a break from the intensity. Ask Him to restrengthen your human spirit to re-engage in His season for breakthrough. Ask Him to re-center your human spirit before His Throne and within your own being. Disengage to re-engage with fresh vision and strength!

7. First-love devotion requires first-love deeds.

"Lord, help me to do the deeds I did at first." In Revelation, through Revelation 3, Jesus mandated this aspect of our renewal. Returning to first-love devotion requires returning to first-love deeds. Why? Probably because our actions are always attached to our motivations. The Bible puts it this way—faith without works or corresponding action is dead.

What are some of the "first-love actions" you should return to? Start with a daily devotional time with worship, prayer, and reading the Word. Return to giving, to investing in God and man. To loving and serving others.

How did the Lord once move with you to bless others? Write down the ways. These are all actionable pathways of return, which will help keep your fire burning hot long term.

One more quick question. How did the Lord exhilarate your heart in the early days? Maybe through a good book, an album, a nature trail, or a sunrise over the ocean. Maybe a revival message. Take time to awaken these memories. Maybe even go on location. Dare to meet Jesus in the space of your exhilaration once again!

> **First-love devotion requires first-love deeds.**

CONTENDING FOR YOUR PRAYER LIFE

If someone put your child in danger, every warfare prayer in the Book would suddenly become unleashed through your mouth. You would pray through until breakthrough, even if you don't consciously know what that means. You would thunder in tongues. And Heaven and earth would move accordingly.

You sometimes must contend for your prayer life like you would contend for the life of a loved one. The Lord showed me this principle during a time of severe spiritual warfare. Try as I might, I literally couldn't find Him. I couldn't even find my own heart. Out of the storm, the voice of the Lord finally thundered—YOUR PRAYER LIFE IS UNDER ATTACK. PRAY FOR YOUR PRAYER LIFE!

Did you know occultists are taught to curse the prayer lives of believers? It's true. By disengaging you from prayer, they are disengaging you from your most vital source of power. A personal relationship with Him.

I prayed. And to my great surprise, my desire and capacity to pray bounced back so quickly it was stunning. Yours will too. Pray for your prayer life! Interact with Jesus over it. Ask the Lord to fully restore all that He intends for your intimacy and authority in Him. Ask Him to take out all spiritual warfare against you, known or unknown. Take authority over demonic forces targeting your prayer life, breaking all curses through the blood of Jesus and commanding these forces to be disengaged from you. Break the power of all curses and counter-curses. Command the full restoration of everything they were attempting to steal. And more. Nothing can separate you from the love of God. In all these things, you are more than a conqueror through Jesus Christ.

TONGUES OF HOLY FIRE

Here's a great secret to accessing God's holy fire. It's important to remember the ancient flames from which your prayer language has been imparted. When Holy Spirit fell at Pentecost, the very glory of the Lord manifested as tongues of fire. If you want to access this holy fire, pray in tongues!

And take time to listen as you pray. In the Spirit you are speaking mysteries. Some of my most vital revelation comes in conjunction with a flow of breakthrough prayer in tongues. As Paul the apostle wrote, *"He that speaketh in an unknown tongue edifieth himself…. Let him that speaketh in an unknown tongue pray that he may interpret. …I will pray with the spirit, and I will pray with the understanding…"* (1 Corinthians 14:4,13,15 KJV).

JESUS COMES THROUGH FOR JOLENE

Let's now return to Price Club. Jolene broke up with Jesus—and then thankfully reconciled.

She then renewed her covenant commitment. My wife totally meant it when she gave her heart again to the Lord, without reserve. She followed through, even turning her frustration into intercession for her future wedding. Her continual prayer—"Lord, please show up!"

Jolene even purchased a wedding ring, representing her consecration to Jesus as her Bridegroom and to the husband He wanted for her. As you know already, the Lord in turn gave her a sacred promise. It came in the form of a letter in the mail. A formal invitation to her own wedding.

Say what? Who gets an invitation to their own wedding? From the very hand of the Lord! The delivery came in a dream, of course. A beautiful wedding invitation was laying on a table. When Jolene looked closer, she discovered it was an invitation to her marriage ceremony. She couldn't make out the name of the groom, the location of the wedding, or the year the ceremony would be held. The only thing clear in the invitation was her own name.

And a date. December 20. It was the only part of the invitation she could remember.

Seven long years passed before this promised introduction to her future husband even occurred. Talk about endurance. But Jolene remained absolutely faithful to her consecration. And to her Price Club dates.

Something astonishing happened when I proposed to Jolene. Well, many astonishing things happened actually. The first being that she actually said yes! And before I even put her engagement ring on her finger, she put one on mine. She removed the ring she purchased to mark her consecration to Jesus seven years beforehand, and she put it on my ring finger. Against all odds it was a perfect fit!

You know the rest of our story. December 20, 2003, happened to be the first day of Hanukkah. We purchased a special menorah in honor of the occasion, even fashioning our unity candle ceremony around it. Our wedding started with worship. In the midst of worship our unity candle literally ignited! In front of everybody. God Himself lit the flame on the first day of Hanukkah, as we were singing "glory, glory, send your glory!"

And can I tell you—our fire has been burning ever since.

Yes, there was a brief breakup. With Jesus, I mean. But you can see Christ's long-term faithfulness to a woman He treats as His bride. Decades later Jolene is married to the suitor Jesus had desired for her all along, and our journey together eventually led to fulfilling a very vibrant ministry calling as well.

"That's okay. I'll still call you." Jesus, sarcastic? Maybe. But He also gave her a hope for the future that became dramatically, awesomely, and even hilariously fulfilled.

It is still amazing to see how, in response to seven years of prayer, the Lord showed up at our wedding in such a poignant way. On the first day of Hanukkah! Not only did He give us a lampstand, but He literally lit our flame.

The great moral of the story—breaking up with Jesus doesn't really work! But the more important takeaway is this. Jesus genuinely understands what you're going through. He wants you to relate to Him honestly, without a filter. And as you and He process life together, He is capable beyond measure of both fulfilling the desire of your heart and the destiny He created for you. Above all else He can help you recover your life and love with Him.

THE BIGGEST CRISIS
OF THE END TIMES

You might ask what this has to do with the end times. Let Jesus Himself bring the answer. Matthew 24 records His most comprehensive message on the end times, commonly known as the Olivet Discourse. False Christs. Wars and rumors of war. False prophets and betrayal. Lawlessness. The Abomination of Desolation. Martyrdom of believers. The antichrist.

Oh—and the love of many will grow cold.

Remember, God's love is pictured as a holy flame. Fire brings not only light but warmth, right? Conversely, the void of genuine fire causes hearts to grow cold.

The void of His love also welcomes spiritual darkness. So it is no coincidence Jesus identified the crisis of the lampstand—the loss of first love—as a primary calamity of the end times. And it's one you and I must overcome in our personal lives, even in the midst of testings and trials. He will always stay true to your heart in love. Let's stay true to His.

Finally, it's no coincidence that Isaiah compelled us to pray for Zion and Jerusalem until her righteousness shines like brightness and her salvation like a lamp that burns! Further, remember how Jesus called John the Baptist "the burning and shining lamp." The spirit of Elijah is truly the fire of God's end-times lampstands as well. Restoring the hearts of parents to their children, children to their parents, and restoring a nation lost in darkness back to the Lord their God.

That's love. And that's why, amidst gross darkness, Holy Spirit is compelling us all to arise and shine.

BURNING LAMPS IN THE END TIMES

Let's shift gears now. It's time to discover a broader perspective of the end times related to God's burning lamps.

Before John heard a trumpet blast to come up here, to come higher, the shofar first sounded for the author of Revelation to write on a scroll what he was going to experience. The Lord was about to engage the seven churches of Asia Minor in a way that would set a standard for the body of Christ—around the globe and through the ages. John's account:

> *I was in the Spirit on the Lord's day, and I heard behind me a loud voice like the sound of a trumpet, saying, "Write on a scroll what you see, and send it to the seven churches: to Ephesus, Smyrna, Pergamum, Thyatira, Sardis, Philadelphia, and Laodicea." Then I turned to see the voice that was speaking with me. And after turning I saw seven golden lampstands; and in the middle of the lampstands I saw one like a son of man.... As for the mystery of the seven stars which you saw in My right hand, and the seven golden lampstands: the seven stars are the angels of the seven churches, and the seven lampstands are the seven churches* (Revelation 1:10-13,20 NASB).

Jesus showed John that the seven churches before His Throne are the seven lampstands. To a Gentile or non-Jewish person, this may not mean so much. But to a Jew like John, the vision probably provoked both awe and profound heartbreak. Why?

For the sake of biblical continuity, the seven golden lampstands before God's Throne are more accurately translated as menorahs. They are very much like the Hanukkiah menorah God lit during our wedding. The Hebrew word "menorah" simply means "to shine."

Leviticus 6:13 (NIV) describes how the *"fire must be kept burning on the altar continuously; it must not go out."*

FIRE—SYMBOL OF COVENANT LOVE

Let there be light! God has always either established His covenant or reaffirmed His covenant with fire. And from Abraham's time forward, the fire on the menorah has always been a symbol of His covenant love. A burning lamp appeared before Abraham, moving in a figure 8 as God cut covenant for His land and people Israel. Moses encountered God's fire as well. Let My people go! God spoke to him out of a burning bush, commissioning him to deliver His people from Egyptian bondage.

And the imagery of the burning bush, with the tips of its branches ablaze, became the symbol of the menorah.

As recounted, fire fell from Heaven when David repented before God, affirming the restoration of His covenant blessing once again. Fire then fell at Solomon's dedication of the Temple—on the exact same altar. Fire fell for Elijah at his plea. All Israel turned back to God.

And of course, fire fell at Pentecost, sealing the covenant made through the death, burial, and resurrection of Jesus Christ for all mankind.

Solomon described God's love as a holy fire: *"Set me as a seal upon your heart, as a seal upon your arm; for love is as strong as death, jealousy as cruel as the grave; Its flames are flames of fire, a most vehement flame"* (Song of Songs 8:6 NKJV).

Since the days of Exodus, Jewish lampstands or menorahs have hosted holy fire to provide light for His chosen dwelling places—the

Tabernacle of Moses in the wilderness, the Tabernacle at Shiloh, the Tabernacle of David in Jerusalem, and of course, the first and second Temples.

The burning lamp or menorah first became the iconic symbol of Israel in ancient times. It remains Israel's primary symbol today. Yet during John's day, the sacred flame was extinguished and the menorah plundered as destruction overtook the Temple. Close friends and family were either slaughtered or scattered in what became known as the Jewish diaspora.

And Israel literally ceased to exist as a nation.

JOHN'S HEARTBREAK—CHURCH, HEED HIS WARNING!

The Arch of Titus in Rome may give you a visual of this tragedy. Built as a monument to Rome's conquest of Israel, the Arch displays a diorama showing defeated Jewish slaves entering Rome, carrying the Temple menorah on their shoulders.

Whereas Jerusalem once shined as a spiritual epicenter for the region, Roman leaders sought to portray Rome as both the new epicenter of spiritual life as well as the epicenter of global governance. Constantine built his empire on this foundation. He christianized the global empire but divorced Christianity from the covenantal roots of our faith, specifically because they were tied to the Jewish people.

As the Arch depicts, diaspora Jews entered Europe through the gates of Rome under the razor-sharp shadow of antisemitic hatred. Though Jewish communities prospered, this undercurrent was passed on from generation to generation until the horrific climax of the

Holocaust. Meanwhile, many have speculated that the Temple menorah remains in the Vatican treasury today.

Through the Throne Room experience granted to John, Jesus warned him that the seven churches he so dearly loved were now closing in on a similar fate as the Temple. Jesus showed him how the warnings given and the realignments mandated must be heeded. Otherwise, the consequences could be equally as dire. Even their lampstands could be removed.

The warning proved true. As of today, the seven original lampstand churches of Asia Minor (now Turkey), so foundational to early apostolic Christianity, have all been extinguished.

But a window may be opening for change. As you know, beginning in 2025 the Lord of hosts is all about rescuing His lampstands. We are praying for a burning lamp movement to again sweep the Mediterranean region. Rome, Italy, Greece and Turkey. Malta and Crete. Wouldn't be awesome to see the seven original "lampstand churches" become reignited once again!

RELIGHTING THE FIRE—THE MYSTERY OF HANUKKAH

Long before Rome's aggression, during the period between the Old and New Testaments, Greece and Syria joined together to conquer the Temple Mount in Israel and overtake the Temple. Led by ruthless dictator Antiochus Epiphanes, an altar of idolatry to Baal/Zeus was even set up in the Holy of Holies. Antiochus ordered the sacrifice of a pig, abhorrent to Jews, on the altar.

And the holy fire blazing 24-7 on God's menorah was extinguished.

To the humiliation of all, Antiochus reigned over the Temple. Maybe it's not a surprise that Bible scholars consider him a prototype of the antichrist. Undoubtedly he was fueled by an antichrist spirit. The prophet Daniel saw this coming and warned about the Abomination of Desolation being set up in the holy Temple (Daniel chapters 11 and 12).

Remember—by now you will probably quote it to me faster than I can quote it to you—Hebrew time is cyclical. Therefore Jesus likely looked back to Antiochus when He warned about the antichrist as a future "Abomination of Desolation standing in the holy place..." (Matthew 24:15-16).

At the time, the Greco-Syrian army occupying the Temple Mount was the strongest in the known world. But against all odds, a ragtag commando unit of warrior priests known as the Maccabees broke through the line and recaptured the Temple. Led by Judah Maccabee, they relit the menorah to reconsecrate the Temple to the Lord. They restored covenant. They welcomed back God's holy presence.

The Maccabees had only enough oil for the fire to burn one day. But miraculously, the oil kept flowing—and burning—for eight days straight! As you know, Jewish people celebrate these miracles to this day through the Festival of Lights, also known as Hanukkah.

SIGN OF THE BURNING LAMP— COMPLETE THE TURNAROUND!

Astonishingly, an Israeli prophet named Zechariah actually prophesied this miracle hundreds of years beforehand. As recorded in Zechariah 4, the prophet awakened to a vision of a lampstand—a menorah made of gold, standing between Heaven and earth. Oil was supernaturally pouring into the menorah so it could burn perpetually.

The meaning of the vision? God's going to complete what He started, even if it means multiplying oil supernaturally. Not by might nor by power but by My Spirit, says the Lord of hosts!

What does this mean for you? If the Maccabees can face down the strongest armies in the known world, you can face down the spiritual battles in your sphere and win as well. You and I can retake our desolate heritages and reconsecrate them to the Lord. The Spirit of God is ready and willing to be welcomed back in as covenant with Christ is restored. Not by might nor power but by His Spirit!

Dare to enlist in this sacred order of warrior priests. Restore the lampstand. Relight the flame. *Be a Maccabee!*

VISION—JESUS RECOVERING THE LAMPSTAND

Though I've had many prophetic experiences, to my knowledge Jesus Himself has only appeared to me twice in the 30 years I've been walking with Him. The first time was in 2002, when as you know, Jesus visited me on my faded blue couch. My heart became forever united with His in an agonizing prayer watch over His compromised bride.

The second time was in January 2014, when I awoke to a vision during a time of severe spiritual conflict in Washington, DC. Decisions by the White House nationally and internationally seemed in open defiance of God. Knowing the vulnerability this put our nation in, we literally spent ourselves in agonizing prayer. But the turnaround never came.

In the vision, Jesus appeared, dressed in a deep red robe, holding a menorah with a flame that was greatly diminished. This flickering menorah was the only light that illuminated Him. I knew the menorah represented both our ministry and the true state of my heart.

In my vision, Jesus cradled the menorah in His hands, very close to His heart, *and then wept into it.* As His tears and breath fell upon the fire, the lamp literally began to blaze.

The vision of Jesus cradling our menorah was first to Jolene and me, rescuing our personal lampstand of first-love devotion to Him. He cares far more deeply about our personal relationship with Him than we could ever imagine. He wants our affection to shine!

And like a lover's gaze toward her beloved, *that shining brightens His own countenance.*

And there is no doubt the vision was also conveying Holy Spirit's continuing work in Washington, DC and many other regions. In the language given through this chapter, He was rescuing the lampstands over entire regions. Tending the light against the darkness that was in danger of flickering out.

Jesus Himself is willing to partner with you in rescuing your lampstand. He will hold it close and tend it with such care. All that the lampstand represents—passion and intimacy with Him, Throne Room access and ministry effectiveness, even regional breakthrough—He is desiring to preserve. He's making every opportunity available to you and me for this preservation.

STUDY QUESTIONS AND PRAYER

1. Do you feel a genuine passion for Jesus? Were there times earlier in your life when your desire for God was greater? What changed?

2. How has the Lord made His love real to you?

3. Do you feel the lampstand of your heart needs rescuing? Does the fire need rekindling? How brightly do you desire to shine?

4. Do you feel that present responsibilities are overwhelming you? Is it hard to rest, to revitalize? What does it mean for you to disengage to re-engage?

5. Have you ever "broken up with Jesus"? What happened next?

6. First-love devotion requires first-love deeds. What are some of them to you? What actions does Jesus desire for you to return to?

7. What does it mean for you to "be a Maccabee"? What areas of your life and world do you sense the Lord desiring to reconsecrate and restore?

Father God, with all my heart please now restore my lamp-stand of love and devotion to You. Help me to become a burning lamp once again! I ask that You watch over, protect, and defend this dimension of my life and ministry, even as You cultivate the flame. On my part, I choose to return by embracing again the "first-love deeds" that mean so much to You and to me. I love You!

And, Lord, You are warning Your church that the fire could indeed go out. The lampstand is vulnerable to being removed. Help me also to "be a Maccabee" as a catalyst of restoration. Help me to welcome You in once again and complete the work that had such a great beginning. In Jesus' name, amen.

Soaring eagle, Homer, Alaska.

CHAPTER 10

Chapter Topics: Before His Face | Entering His Realm | Receiving End Time Revelation | Intimacy & Authority God in Real Time | Caring for Your Human Spirit | Secure Your Seat | Council of God

COME UP HIGHER—BEFORE HIS FACE

"Come up here [higher], *and I will show things which must* [shortly] *take place..."* (Revelation 4:1 NKJV).

You've taken to heart God's summons to come up higher. If you're like me, your knees have been glued to the floor and your face bowed low for much of this section. That has totally been my posture writing it. Remember, repentance and turning opens the door to times of refreshing from His presence. That's great news. Your lampstand is now being rescued and relit. Hidden aspects of His glory are about to be revealed.

May you and I now gain a similar testimony to John in the book of Revelation: *"Having turned I saw..."* (Revelation 1:12 NKJV).

You've come up higher. You've turned. Jesus is now in process of realigning your life, your world, and even the lampstand of your devotional life for the hour now at hand. He is granting you new vision. Not by might nor by power but by His Spirit! It's now time to come before His face.

Note: A few sections of this chapter have been sourced from our first book, *Crown & Throne*.

RECEIVING END-TIMES REVELATION

Let's begin by clarifying a passage that's been before you this entire section. Let me draw your attention to two passages of Revelation, beginning with the very first verse.

> *The Revelation of Jesus Christ, which God gave Him to show to His bond-servants, the things which **must soon take place*** (Revelation 1:1 NASB).

> *After these things I looked, and behold, a door standing open in heaven, and the first voice which I had heard, like the sound of a trumpet speaking with me, said, "Come up here, and I will show you **what must take place** after these things." Immediately I was in the Spirit; and behold, a throne was standing in heaven, and someone was sitting on the throne* (Revelation 4:1-2 NASB).

Revelation speaks to every era of the church, but it ddresses foremost the final crescendo of the end times. Yet from the opening verse, the Spirit of God sets the expectation that the revelations being given are first in real time. "Things which must soon take place."

End times in real time. Again and again, the Lord shows His willingness—really His eagerness—to share His secrets with His friends.

So let's combine aspects of these two mighty Scriptures, by applying just one word from the first verse to the second. The carryover brings a prevailing theme into John's whole experience.

> *Come up higher, and I will show you what must **soon** take place!* (Revelation 1:1, 4:1).

Come up higher. Let me show you what must soon take place. Holy Spirit has again and again resounded the phrase in the depths of my being while writing this book. It defines your promise, your invitation from Him today as you seek Him.

BEFORE HIS FACE

Here's a secret promise for you from God's Word, which we will examine both here and in the next chapter. Luke 10:1 records how Jesus sent His disciples to prepare the way for His entry into each city He was about to visit. Most look at this verse as a good model for citywide evangelism. But there's a secret facet to the Scripture that very few have ever perceived. Even most Bible translators.

> From the NASB: *Now after this the Lord appointed seventy-two others, and sent them in pairs ahead of Him to every city and place where He Himself was going to come.*

> From the NIV: *After this the Lord appointed seventy-two others and sent them two by two ahead of him to every town and place where he was about to go.*

> From the NKJV: *After these things the Lord appointed seventy others also, and sent them two by two **before His face** into every city and place where He Himself was about to go.*

The New King James Version conveys an action the other two translations seem to entirely miss. Before Jesus sent His disciples into the city, *He first sent them before His face.*

Which rendition is the most accurate? The Greek word used in the passage is *prosopon,* which means "countenance, appearance, or face." The verse is most precisely translated "before His face."

Send is an apostolic word. In fact, Luke records the Greek word *apostello* to describe the work Jesus was accomplishing. He commissioned apostles and *sent them* two by two *before His face* into the city. There has been such an emphasis on the latter expression of this apostolic or forerunner calling—being sent into the city.

But the first dimension of this "sending anointing" is to commission God's forerunners before His face. Without this raw encounter of intimacy with Jesus propelling us, the apostolic or forerunner ministry invariably succumbs to power plays and a political spirit.

Perhaps that is why this message is sounding again in this hour. In a world that values high-octane platforms over prayer chambers, this verse usurps most underpinnings of American Christianity today. We're getting better. But let's rediscover the face and heart of Jesus. Let's regain our first-love devotion as our primary identity before Christ.

That's how Elijah was commissioned. Same with John the Baptist, who called himself "the friend of the Bridegroom" or the friend of God. Now we discover the disciples were brought into the same commissioning.

First before His face. And secondarily, into the spheres the Lord sends you. Why? *To prepare the way for His coming.*

Also, you are being commissioned from the face of Jesus to prepare the way of the Lord within the spheres He sends you to.

That, my friend, is the essence of the forerunner calling. And as the end times draw near, it is far more important than we realize.

An interesting side note. When America's early revolutionaries mobilized to make a break from the British Empire, they often gathered at a historic Boston building called Faneuil Hall. For this reason it is known as the cradle of liberty, the womb of the American Revolution.

Faneuil is actually a French derivative of a Jewish name. *Peniel* or *Phanuel* literally means "the face of God." And the patriots of the Revolution were literally sent from before His face to birth a freedom nation.

No king but Jesus!

ELIJAH'S SECRET

Confronting Ahab, Elijah was in no mood for diplomacy. The king of Israel had been seduced by Jezebel, a woman whose very name conveyed her devotion to the principality of Baal. Now that they had married, Jezebel was using her influence to shift Israel's government and religious structure toward idolatry, sin, and corruption. Israel had strayed from God's covenant and was about to pay a very heavy price.

A disclaimer: Any resemblance to America today is entirely *not* coincidental.

God's verdict was proclaimed. "*…As the Lord, the God of Israel lives, before whom I stand, there shall certainly be neither dew nor rain during these years, except by my word*" (1 Kings 17:1 NASB). Drought immediately ensued.

Elijah was bold. Far bolder than me. In our occasional opportunities to represent God's interests before kings and presidents, the intimidation factor has often restrained us from being so direct. For example, if I were Elijah, I would have at least fashioned the conversation around, "No rain nor dew except by *God's* word." But my word? Wow.

It just sounds more humble. And just in case it actually rained, all the left-wing propaganda machines that haunt our territory like dark principalities would have at least quoted me as calling the rain an act of God.

Not Elijah. He left no room for maneuvering. But then, the proof that Elijah was granted this magnitude of authority was demonstrated by exactly three years and six months of neither rain nor dew on the earth.

The secret to Elijah's power was simple but profound: He stood before the Lord. He dwelt before His face. Demonstrations of great authority came from his time before the face of God and standing in His council over the nation of Israel.

Elijah governed from His place before the Throne. In other words, he gained a seat of authority over Israel that no man could grant and no man could take away. When Elijah declared a revolution, God backed him up.

That's how Jesus taught His disciples to pray, *"Thy kingdom come, Thy will be done on earth as it is in heaven."* Though many of us have recited the Lord's Prayer since we were kids, most of us interpreted the passage to mean that we should passively accept whatever comes in life as God's will. In reality, nothing could be further from the truth. Jesus is saying that Heaven is our plumb line for earth. It's up to us to hear and perceive Heaven's desire, then bring this direction to bear upon our world.

What's it like in Heaven? Elijah knew. Isaiah, Jeremiah, the apostle John knew. And many friends of God today know the real-time activities both of God's throne and our world.

You too are invited to become a Throne Room watchman, perceiving God's work in our time and bringing Heaven's desire to earth. Truly it's the adventure of a lifetime.

ACCESSING GOD IN REAL TIME

"Do you feel that? Heaven's power is flowing...right above us!"

On a fall morning, a group of friends gathered together with the express purpose of experiencing the Holy Spirit. I wanted to. Desperately. But try as I might, I just could not reach high enough or strain prayerfully enough to access His surge of power. As others became ecstatic, I became frustrated.

My friend Martin Frankena was unusually patient with me that day. "You're trying too hard, Jon. Relax. God will touch you!"

Deep in my heart I knew He would bring this touch...eventually. I just figured it would be tomorrow, or next year, after I had fasted enough, worshiped enough, prayed enough, and studied enough to actually qualify for the experience.

My prophetic friend countered my thoughts. "Jon, you keep looking to the future, but God isn't future, GOD IS NOW. He is moving in real time. And He wants to be with you now!" With that statement,

> You too are invited to become a Throne Room watchman, perceiving God's work in our time and bringing Heaven's desire to earth.

Martin prayed for me—something very simple like, "Lord, make this real to him." Suddenly I was on the floor, overcome by the Holy Spirit and wondering what suddenly went right.

Please understand that Holy Spirit is not some sort of distant relative, hard to access and harder to please. He can be demanding, for sure. But He is eternally available for you. He is a present help in time of need (Psalm 46:1). He is your real-time Redeemer, and soon-coming King!

BY MY SPIRIT

Just as God exhorted His revolutionary friends in biblical times, He is coaching us today. "'...*Not by might nor by power, but by My Spirit,' says the Lord of hosts*" (Zechariah 4:6 NKJV). No matter how noble the cause, the governance of God's Kingdom cannot be attained by our efforts alone. Our pursuit must begin and be brought to completion by His might, in partnership with ours. As we remain before His face, seeking His counsel and being strengthened by His Spirit, He will work through us to manifest His purposes.

That said, manifesting "end times in real time" requires two foundational revelations of the Godhead. First, *God is now*. Second, He wants you to obtain results *by His Spirit* and manifest His Kingdom in your sphere.

All great deliverers in the Bible consistently experienced this reality. In fact, that's how God introduced Himself to Moses from the burning bush. "What is your name?" Moses asked. "Who shall I say sent me?" God stunned Moses when He spoke out of the fire in reply. "YHWH. I AM."

Our Creator's proclamation of His own name conveys that He forever lives in the present. He is not "I was," like the old general whose glory slowly fades away. Even over centuries, His nature, character, beauty and power remain absolutely the same! IAM—the God of eternity, ready to act in the now.

The second foundational revelation is that God wants you to obtain results. He is the God of breakthrough. And friend, truly effective prayer must be sourced from intimacy with the Lord as well as focused on results. Just like in physics or a workout, a lack of results is simply an indicator that adjustments are needed. By evaluating what works right—consistently—we can access the power of these proven scriptural pathways.

ENTERING HIS REALM

Often we associate God's realm with the aspects of His nature we enjoy the most. Lovers of God accurately perceive the Throne of God as a bridal chamber—a place of intimacy, delight, and personal attention (see Song of Solomon 1:4). Prophetic singers relate to the anthem of the ages, where His glory is freshly conveyed through new sounds and songs (see Revelation 5:9). Healers find His goodness, prophets His counsel, innovators His wisdom, and we all find His salvation!

Truly the King's domain is all this and so much more. But first and foremost, it's actually His throne—the nucleus and command post of the universe. Like Elijah, you and I today have an open invitation to stand before the Lord, encounter His majesty, and govern your sphere from this portal.

The big question is how.

When the voice within the trumpet spoke to John to come up higher, *immediately* he was in the Spirit. There's no indication of any striving. That's because the God of "now" was with him from the beginning of his journey.

You can experience this too. Let's discover some proven scriptural pathways to help you consistently enter God's realm. In the process, you will learn about His realm and also explore the spiritual dimensions of your own being.

His love has made the way.

Discipline. Judgment. Breaking the seals. Making war. Taking down rulers. The Lion prevails. Have you ever thought about the fact that the same guy who wrote the entire book of Revelation also gained the most revelation about the love of God? The writer describing Heaven's armies was the same one who described God so simply and profoundly that a child could understand. *"God is love,"* he wrote, *"and the one who remains in love remains in God, and God remains in him"* (1 John 4:16 NASB). Further in the chapter, John goes on to observe, *"We love, because God first loved us"* (1 John 4:19 NASB).

John's greatest revelation of God as love, in word and deed, has actually become the foundation for all of Christianity. John 3:16 (NKJV) says, *"For God so loved the world that He gave His only begotten Son, that whoever believes in Him should not perish but have everlasting life."*

Nothing can separate you from the love of God. Jesus Christ loves you so much He literally did not want to live without you. It is unimaginable, but true. When approaching the Throne, remember that He is the One who both initiated your relationship and summoned you to "Come up higher."

Enter His gates with praise.

You are instructed to *"Enter His gates with thanksgiving* [in your heart], *and into His courts with praise"* (Psalm 100:4 NKJV). Praise fills your heart, drawing you into another dimension—the very courts of the Lord. This psalm describes the process and actually prophesies John's very experience. He was "in the Spirit on the Lord's day," likely in worship, when a gate of Heaven opened into the courts of the Lord.

You can enter through this open door as well, as an act of your will. Genuine praise connects us to God and to the boundless love for Him within our own hearts. The primary way to instantly access the Throne is to praise Him.

You have come to Zion.

While visiting Jerusalem I've ascended to the sacred summit of Mount Zion countless times. The upper room is there. So is the historic Zion gate, pathway into the Jewish Quarter and the Western Wall.

But Zion came alive in a new way to me when our friend Chris Mitchell thundered his favorite passage during a recent message. Chapter 12 in the book of Hebrews is a revelation of heavenly Zion as both the epicenter of God's Throne and your true home. Hebrews shows you that the key to the door is already in your hand.

> *For you have not come to a mountain that can be touched and to a blazing fire, and to darkness and gloom and whirl-wind.... And so terrible was the sight, that Moses said, "I am terrified and trembling." But* **you have come** *to Mount Zion and to the city of the living God, the heavenly Jerusalem, and to myriads of angels, to the general assembly and church of the*

firstborn who are enrolled in heaven, and to God, the Judge of all, and to the spirits of the righteous made perfect, and to Jesus, the mediator of a new covenant, and to the sprinkled blood, which speaks better than the blood of Abel (Hebrews 12:18,21-24 NASB).

Note that Paul in Hebrews says, *"you have come."* The deal is already done. So how do you get to where you already are? How do you get "there"?

First by faith.

By reading Revelation or the prophets, it is clear God can sovereignly bring you into His realm through dreams and visions, trances and translations, visionary encounters and more. I love them. But He has also granted you access before the Throne as an act of your own will. The Bible says to enter His gates with praise. Obedience in faith unlocks those gates. He commands you to come boldly before the Throne of grace. The blood of Jesus grants you access. Your response in obedience activates it.

To come before God's Throne as an act of my will, I generally start my daily prayer time something like this:

Father, thank You for Your love for me. Thank You for inviting me to join with You. As an act of my will, I now release my human spirit to be seated with You in heavenly places in Christ Jesus. Synergize me with Your heart, Lord. Synergize me with Your Throne and the real-time activities before Your Throne. Synergize me with the move of Holy Spirit from Heaven to earth. Synergize me also with Your angelic hosts. Grant me a spirit of wisdom and revelation in the knowledge of Jesus. Lord, let me hear Your voice! In Jesus' name, amen.

CREATED TO COMMUNE

Speaking of which, the throne of your heart and spirit is another dimension of the King's domain we need to explore. In the same manner that God's Throne is the nucleus of the universe, the nucleus of your own being has also been designed to be a throne for God to rest on!

Maybe you've read about this great mystery—*"Christ in you, the hope of glory"* (Colossians 1:27 NASB). In the Old Testament, God hinted at this glory when He declared He would be Immanuel, God with us. Furthermore, He prophesied that *"I dwell in a high and holy place, and also with the contrite and lowly of spirit in order to revive the spirit of the lowly and to revive the heart of the contrite"* (Isaiah 57:15 NASB).

You are a spirit being made in God's image. This expression of the image of God resides within the core of your being, and has been imparted from the core of God's being when He breathed His life into you.

Your human spirit was created to be filled with God and to commune with God—literally to enthrone Him. Your spirit can see, perceive, hear, feel, and speak. Your spirit can become drained or become strong and grow in stature. As the apostle John experienced, your spirit can even soar.

Have you ever "felt" eternity in a sunset or a mountain summit? That's probably your spirit, resonating and responding to beauty. Ever weep with compassion for a person for seemingly no reason at all? Your spirit, in communion with the Lord, knows something that is hidden from your mind.

There's a difference between *being in* the Spirit and being *filled with* the Spirit. To be in the Spirit means that by the power of the

Holy Spirit in agreement with your own will, you have entered His realm. To be filled with the Holy Spirit means that He has entered your realm. See the difference?

Just as a reservoir is filled by a stream, your spirit receives constant communion and strength from the flow of Holy Spirit to you. It's why the Scriptures instruct us to *"be filled with the Spirit, speaking to one another in psalms and hymns and spiritual songs"* (Ephesians 5:18-19 NASB). When you commune with God in this way, you open the faucet for His Spirit to fill you and strengthen you, which, of course, is awesome!

CARING FOR YOUR HUMAN SPIRIT

Your human spirit needs nurture, exercise, and stimulation, just as your mind and body do. Occasionally your spirit even needs a good bath. *"Let's cleanse ourselves of all defilement of flesh and spirit"* (2 Corinthians 7:1 NASB).

It's important to care for your human spirit. How? For the most part, in the same way you care for your body. You need to eat right and avoid foods that defile. Jesus said His words are Spirit and life! This is more true than we know.

Above all else, delight yourself in the Lord. Your spirit is exhilarated in worship and loves to be with God. Prayer brings life, both during your personal communion with the Lord and when receiving prayer from others of like, precious faith. Receiving and sharing affection and appreciation greatly impacts your spirit.

Disobedience and sin quench Holy Spirit and also numb your own spirit. As we all know, this can lead to a downward spiral that's hard to recover from. Eventually, like Adam and Eve, you can feel like you're not even truly alive. Don't waste your life on pursuits that are beneath you!

There are times when Jolene and I go into a territory and feel spiritually drained. We have learned to pray for God to cleanse us of all defilement from the principalities and powers that have gained influence in a region. We often experience this in major cities, and not just because of spiritual warfare. Millions of people are compacted into a relatively small spot of geography along with their passions, anxieties, and pursuits. Especially for the spiritually sensitive, this can be very taxing. No wonder Jesus often escaped the crowds to commune on a mountain with His Father!

Sometimes we feel a check in our spirit about a person, or a conversation, a directive, etc. Not heeding this check can be akin in the natural to walking onto a rotting bridge. You can proceed, but you might not make it across! When you sense a check, it's best to push aside the demands of the immediate and check in with the Lord. He will make His direction clear to you in a timely manner!

You might be asking, what in the world does this have to do with end times in real time, being a spiritual revolutionary, advancing the Kingdom for Jesus? Glad you asked! Caring for your spirit not only enhances your receptivity to the Lord, but it multiplies the strength you need to fight today's spiritual battles. When your spirit withdraws, all that's left is brain and muscles. And whether you're in the boardroom or the pulpit, your own strength and striving won't get you very far!

SECURE YOUR SEAT

Learn to enter His realm, and bring His realm to yours. Practice and grow. Nurture your human spirit and stay filled with Holy Spirit!

Learn to abide. *"This is the word of the Lord to Zerubbabel: saying, 'Not by might nor by power, but by My Spirit,' says the Lord of hosts"* (Zechariah 4:6 NKJV).

The prophet Zechariah was viewing a burning lamp before God's Throne when he prophesied those words. If you're like me, you not only long to become a burning lamp, but you long to behold Throne Room scenes for yourself where Jesus now walks among His lampstands.

Positionally at least, access has been granted. When you became born again, you not only gained eternal life but you inherited a seat of authority before God's eternal Throne. And it's yours to access in real time.

According to Ephesians 2:6-7 (NASB), God the Father *"raised us up with Him, and **seated us with Him** in the heavenly places in Christ Jesus, so that in the ages to come He might show the boundless riches of His grace in kindness toward us in Christ Jesus."*

Remember that thrones or seats of authority are established by covenant. The mercy seat on the Ark is our great example. The Throne which hosts God's presence is directly above the sacred covenant made between Yahweh and His people.

It's the same in our day. The US Constitution, for instance, is a covenant that establishes the seats of authority for all three branches of our government. Business charters establish the authority structure of their corporations. Covenants establish thrones of government.

And when you came into covenant with God through Christ, your seat of access and authority was granted. Your throne is similar to the thrones of the twenty-four elders before the Throne, pictured in Revelation 4. They have been granted seats of authority in close proximity to the throne. Think of the president with his cabinet or a general with his aides. Proximity to the leader is determined by rank, assignment, and affectionate trust gained through earned authority.

It's the same with you.

Earned authority? In our age of entitlement, what was once an essential Christian doctrine has largely been relegated to the sidelines. But Jesus modeled for every believer the call to gain the Father's authority His way.

And not just through the cross. Immediately after Jesus conquered satan in the wilderness, He returned to His hometown of Nazareth and made one of His most consequential moves. The town rabbi invited him to read the Torah portion for the week in the local synagogue. Jesus opened the scrolls, read Isaiah 61, and declared He was the Messiah who would fulfill these sacred verses. *"The Spirit of the Lord God is upon me…"* (Luke 4:18; Isaiah 61:1 NKJV).

He then sat down. As a sign to all, Jesus was released by the Spirit to take His rightful seat of authority, the seat reserved in the synagogue for Messiah. Through the taking of His seat He confirmed His messiahship to the spiritual and the natural world. But the wilderness testing came first.

It's the same with you. As you continue to conquer through your journey, conforming more to the image of Christ, you will be granted a promotion in your rulership as well. Just look at a few of the promises given in Revelation to those who overcome.

Similar to Jesus, John, and Elijah, you will become seated with Christ over your sphere in a new way as you overcome.

One of the most insightful resources on receiving your seat of authority in the Kingdom is Faisal Malick's book *Positioned to Bless.* According to Malick, "Your seat of authority is intricately connected to your eternal purpose, or the divine assignment upon your life."

He accurately notes that "most people never fulfill their assignment because they never sit in their seat of authority."

Friend, whatever challenges are before you, come up higher. Follow Jesus' lead and pass your test to secure your seat. The body of Christ earnestly needs the covenant blessing that will be released through you as a result. Then like Jesus, multitudes of others will be delivered through the purity of your hands!

> *The one who overcomes, I will grant to him to sit with Me on My throne, as I also overcame and sat with My Father on His throne* (Revelation 3:21 NASB).

SEATED WITH COVENANTAL AUTHORITY

As mentioned, this book has been written as a witness to the next phase of release of the spirit and power of Elijah. So let's see how Elijah's legacy relates to your seat of authority. Elijah's ministry to Israel is a great example of how the Lord desires for you to function from your seats.

Elijah was a ruler over Israel, yet no man gave him a throne. Instead, God set him in authority over the nation. In this respect, his calling was similar to Jeremiah.

> *...I have appointed you this day over the nations and over the kingdoms, to root out and to tear down, to destroy and to overthrow, to build and to plant* (Jeremiah 1:9-10 NASB).

God still establishes His seats of governance over nations and kingdoms, or spheres of society. He still grants covenantal authority to root out, tear down, throw down, destroy, build, and plant. The prophet Isaiah conveyed this process another way:

*I have put My words in your mouth and have covered you
with the shadow of My hand, to establish the heavens, to
found the earth, and to say to Zion, "You are My people"* (Isaiah 51:16 NASB).

Note that these seats of rulership are meant to bring the governance of God into every facet of community. They are ultimately meant to bring government in alignment with God's covenant. Isaiah identifies three realms in which the prophet's covenantal authority is to be expressed—the heavens, the earth, and God's covenant land.

In Elijah's day, there were essentially two thrones of governance over Israel operating at the same time. Elijah's throne represented God's covenantal interests. Ahab's throne had become so corrupted by idolatry and covenant breaking that it had essentially been given over to Baal. Much like today's world, this covenant conflict was played out before the eyes of all the nation. Eventually, the throne of Elijah prevailed.

YOUR SEAT OF AUTHORITY

In this end-times movement, many are going to be granted assignments over specific spheres of authority. You will receive a throne of authority as legitimate in Heaven's eyes as any in your nation. As with Elijah, God will relate to you not only personally, but according to the office or sphere of authority He has entrusted to you.

Again, your assignment is to establish your sphere by covenant with God, divorced from idolatry, and empower His justice and freedom in your world. Your covenant with God brings your throne into alignment with His. From this alignment, you then have access to God's boundless authority to impact your sphere. It's a lot easier when God is fighting for you than when you are fighting for yourself—even in His name!

This society-shaking, transformative authority is absolutely dependent on your covenant commitment—not just to God, but also to your sphere of influence. For many believers, this understanding is the missing link to their success. Many love God and are resolute in their commitment to Him, but their covenant commitment to their sphere sometimes remains elusive.

Remember, thrones are established by covenant.

As mentioned, this book has been written as a witness to the next phase of release of the spirit and power of Elijah. So let's see how Elijah's legacy relates to your seat of authority. Elijah's ministry to Israel is a great example of how the Lord desires for you to function from your seat.

From the seat or position of authority Elijah was granted before the Lord, Jezebel was unseated. A widow's son was raised from the dead. A global confederation that threatened the sovereignty of Israel was broken. Fire fell from Heaven and a covenant nation turned back to the Lord their God.

Similar to Elijah, when Esther was seated, Haman was exposed and unseated. A Persian holocaust of the Jewish people was prevented. We need these miracles again in our time.

THE COUNCIL OF GOD

But who has stood in the council of the Lord, that he should *see and hear His word? Who has given heed to His word and listened?* (Jeremiah 23:18 NASB).

Elijah stood before God's throne. Prophetically, as a steward of His covenant for Israel, he was granted access to the council of God. He perceived how the Lord was rendering His verdict and executing His judgment based on His covenant with the land. Backed by Heaven, Elijah then announced this verdict.

The power God displayed in conjunction with His judgments was often unprecedented. Think of the signs that accompanied Elijah's ministry. Rain stopped, and three years later rain began again. Food multiplied; a widow's son was raised. Fire came down from Heaven on an altar he rebuilt. A compromised people turned back to God!

How did Elijah know to do all this? The Lord took council with him over the nation. As He did, God revealed to him both the strategy and timing to turn His people.

God holds council with His angels and even His human friends to determine the course of regions and nations. In this regard the council of God is again similar to the scene in Revelation 4, where the twenty-four elders are pictured as seated before God's throne. They are talking with God and with each other—in other words, holding a council meeting.

YOUR INVITATION

As you mature in governing your sphere, you may also be invited by God to stand in His council. Many consider the council of the Lord to be a prophetic experience available only to a few chosen vessels. It is absolutely true that relatively few in the body of Christ have actually experienced a visionary manifestation of the council of God through a prophetic experience. But I believe the Holy Spirit communicates with many leaders and intercessors about decisions being weighed. That's one of the reasons He compels us to pray!

Again, the primary theme of Jeremiah 23 is actually a rebuke to prophets for not standing in the council of the Lord. Not one of the prophets was rebuked for trying to gain access to God's council where access was prohibited. They were rebuked *only for their absence*.

As covered in Chapter 5, the passage chronicles how many were choosing instead to compromise their calling through unjust gain, adultery, and outright falsehood to promote themselves in the eyes of men. They even fell prey to idolatry and started prophesying by Baal. As Jeremiah noted, *"from the prophets of Jerusalem pollution has gone forth into all the land"* (Jeremiah 23:15 NASB1995).

> **But who has stood in the council of the Lord**, *that he should see and hear His word? ...***But if they had stood in My council**, *then they would have announced My words to My people, and would have turned them back from their evil way and from the evil of their deeds* (Jeremiah 23:18,22 NASB1995).

TURNING GOD'S PEOPLE

According to Jeremiah 23, turning a people back to God literally depends upon standing in the council of God. That's where Elijah received both his strategy and anointing to turn Israel back to Him.

Likewise, as you stand before the Lord and receive His counsel, you too will receive strategies and grace to impact your world. These real-time Throne Room interactions will then determine the course of history, even the end times.

STUDY QUESTIONS AND PRAYER

1. What aspects about God do you cherish the most? What secrets have you learned in His presence? How does He communicate with you on a personal level?

2. Have you ever had a vision of God? A vision of His Throne? A vision from His Throne?

3. Have you ever received revelation from the Lord that plays out in real time? How has He moved to meet you in real time? What's the most recent?

4. Many have struggled with striving to try and please God or to connect with Him. Have you? Has this chapter helped you?

5. Have you ever been significantly touched by the presence of Holy Spirit?

6. What subject grabs your heart the most in prayer? Maybe covering your children, your church, or nation. Where do you see God bring the most consistent results?

7. What does it mean to you that you are seated with Christ in heavenly places? What areas do you feel the Lord has assigned you responsibility in prayer and action?

Father God, thank You for inviting me to come up higher, to know You more, and to live my life centered before Your Throne. Thank You for sending me before Your face! Grant me a spirit of wisdom and revelation in the knowledge of Jesus (Ephesians 1:17).

Lord, help me to strengthen myself in You. Beginning with maintaining consistency in my devotional times. And in these times, show me the people, places, and issues that are on Your heart for breakthrough in real time. Show me spheres of responsibility You are giving me as a watchman. Grant me counsel from Heaven's council. In Jesus' name!

SECTION FOUR

THE HARVEST WARS

Horseman statue, the White House. Illustrative graphic.

CHAPTER 11

THE MIDNIGHT RIDERS:

FORERUNNER MINISTRY IN THE END TIMES

"In Judges, Gideon asks God how to choose his men for battle. The Lord told Gideon to take his men down to the river and drink. The men who flopped down on their bellies and drank like dogs were no good to him. Gideon watched as some of his men knelt down and drank with their heads watching the horizon, spears in hand. Though they were few, they were the men he needed."

—Jack Carr, the *Terminal List*

Living across from the Pentagon is not for the faint of heart. A general once told us he would never live within ten miles of the world's most infamous office building. Why? Because for our enemies, X marks the spot.

Of course, our opposition may not have all the facts. Russian intelligence officers once mistook a small chamber at the epicenter of the Pentagon for a portal to its most top secret and strategic site. They saw hundreds visiting every day. They observed even the highest-ranking generals accessing the portal.

But it wasn't a strategic intelligence facility. It was a hot dog stand.

True story. Hopefully our enemies haven't yet discovered our watchman's perch across the street. I can genuinely report that our nation has turned from our windows. That said, one of our greatest honors here is fulfilling our assignment to pray for our military and intelligence communities.

Likely the highest security clearance site at the Pentagon is located on an underground floor, where a 24-7 watch continues unabated over the entire globe. Data and reports pour in for analysts to prioritize. Eyes in the sky provide visuals of military campaigns, terror strikes, emerging threats, and special ops missions.

All in real time.

Back in 1775, Paul Revere relied on real-time signals intelligence from the upper room of a church to convey the movements of a British invasion of Boston. He then mounted his horse for a midnight ride to broadcast the intelligence he had received. The American military awakened that night to what historians now refer to as a "midnight cry."

Revere's cry started a revolution. As mentioned in the Prologue, a global cycle of rulership by bloodline monarchies began to break that night. And the world would never be the same.

As an aside, we need more real-time intelligence from the upper rooms of our churches. Earth-shaking, epoch-defining, Throne Room revelation can be accessed from Heaven's council as relentless prayer warriors pray Heaven to earth. This will be proven true more and more as the birth pangs intensify.

Note: Many themes in this chapter have been sourced from our book *Midnight Cry*. They have been woven into the tapestry of every book we have authored since, but they are specially relevant for *End Times in Real Time*.

THE MIDNIGHT CRY

As we recounted in Chapter 2, one night during Passover 2017, looking out over Washington, DC, the Lord gave me what I can only call end-time revelation. He spoke to me about a "midnight cry" for this hour of history.

Donald Trump had just moved into the office as president. I had hoped that all would be smooth sailing. But the challenges were already beginning to mount. Further, the Lord spoke to me that by the year 2020, we would see the beginning of what He called "midnight crises." He further stated that how we approached these crises and overcame them would even become a road map for believers in the very last days.

We recounted many of the "midnight crises" that erupted in 2020 in Chapter 2. Looking out the same window now, we see how Israel and America are virtually at war with Iran. With Russia backing the former Persian empire. On the horizon we see the rise of idolatry-empowered globalism, 6G surveillance, capabilities by AI to shut down nations, and so much more.

That to say, the word about midnight crises has proven true. Unmistakably beginning in 2020. By the Spirit of God, we have finally begun to access a new season of midnight turnarounds.

The good news is that through the prophetic experience, I saw a road map for overcoming these "midnight crises" from Jesus' parable in Matthew 25, recounting the journey of the 10 virgins and the Bridegroom. Ever since Cindy Jacobs prophesied I was a "spiritual Paul Revere," I have been focused on the classic end-times passage. But it suddenly caught on fire for me in a new way. Revelation simply leapt off the pages. The following is the sequence:

1. **A midnight crisis—and falling away.** *"When the bridegroom was delaying they all got drowsy and fell asleep...."* The delayed arrival also meant a delayed intervention amid the crises of the end time. The clear insinuation of slumber is withdrawal.

2. **A midnight watch** by a remnant who stay awake, releasing a midnight cry in prayer. Actually this part came by revelation from the Lord. A promise from Holy Spirit that even in the midst of the hardest circumstances, He will have a remnant who will keep faith—and keep watch. A midnight cry by this remnant especially will release His midnight turnaround.

3. **A midnight turnaround.** The midnight cry in prayer gives way to a Daniel 7:22 turnaround. Many of the midnight watchmen will become His "midnight riders" announcing God's turnaround. First because they're the only ones awake.

4. **A midnight cry from midnight riders,** sent to prepare the way of the Lord, announcing God's ultimate new move. Probably like Paul Revere, they will race through villages and cities, holding out their burning and shining lamps, shouting, "Behold the Bridegroom. He's coming. Rise up to meet Him!"

5. **A burning lamp awakening** is released by the midnight cry. "Then all those virgins rose and trimmed their lamps." At the midnight hour the slumber will break. And the bride's lampstand of first-love devotion will be rescued. She will light the fire again. And thereby light up the night.

6. **A midnight procession.** Out of isolation and into the streets, ultimately following God's forerunners to the culmination of the age. But again, revivals will be part of the "dress rehearsals" for the big event. In every case, don't forget the oil!

7. **A midnight wedding.** A destination wedding, actually—Jerusalem! Probably over the fall feasts. And there will definitely be a feast. A few won't make it through the door though. They will have missed the wedding by seeking oil for their lamps instead. It is so important to keep reserves of oil so your lamps can burn through the night.

If you're listening carefully, the voice of the forerunner can be heard even now. Behold the Bridegroom. He is coming! And the Midnight Cry is a summons to a wedding.

This is how the end of the age culminates. With burning lamps released into the streets to follow the Bridegroom to the wedding celebration. The *huppah*—the bridal canopy—of God's glory will be extended over Zion and all her assemblies. Under the canopy, covenant vows will be exchanged. By the close of the end times at least, the body of Christ will have succeeded in making covenant great again.

And isn't it amazing that the bridal party will bring their burning lamps to Zion! Perhaps in fulfillment of the Isaiah 62 cries of the saints through countless generations, for her righteousness to shine like brightness, and her salvation as a burning lamp.

He who has the bride is the Bridegroom. This passion expressed by John the Baptist for his Friend will be dramatically fulfilled.

For this to occur, in a midnight hour, the burning lamps must arise. Again, according to Hebrew understanding time is cyclical. But we already know it's a midnight hour. Actually, ten minutes to midnight or later. Your lampstand has been rescued. It's time for you to shine.

HEAVEN IS READY TO RIDE! TRUMP DREAM

Today's "midnight riders" are being prepared. Heaven is ready to ride! While writing this chapter, our intercessors have been hearing from the Lord again and again about the horses of the Lord being released. They had no idea what I was writing.

Back in May 2016, while Donald Trump was campaigning the first time to become president, the Lord gave me a dream. I saw Trump on the home plate of a baseball diamond, hitting balls to fielders as part of batting practice. Massive storm clouds gathered, and Trump and team were forced off the field into the locker room. Trump deliberately walked alone. The sky got darker than I had ever seen.

I'll let the posting, from May 21, 2016, take it from here:

> We were leaving the field after batting practice.
> I heard and felt the ground shake. Looking up I
> saw two white horses, strong steeds galloping right
> toward us on the field! One especially was focused
> on me, with a look in his eyes I can only describe as a
> resolve of fierce delight.
>
> My instinct was to get out of the way, but the horses
> were coming so quickly. And before I even could
> move, one horse raced right to me and thrust his
> head into my hands and chest. I intuitively embraced
> him.
>
> At that precise time, Donald Trump was walking by,
> wearing a blue blazer, tan pants and a red hat like
> the one he always wears which says, "Make America
> Great Again." He seemed completely absorbed in
> thought. With the team, but walking alone.
>
> Trump came over, nodded, smiled and said very sim-
> ply, "You gotta keep praying for me." Then I woke up.

I knew the dream overall conveyed a final thrust of victory. Heaven's horses were joining to bring breakthrough.

But I also knew intuitively that the appearance of the horses amidst the dark storm clouds represented a demarcation of a new season associated with the forerunner movement within the end times. The horses of the Lord were being released, even to us.

There is no doubt we are also seeing a gathering storm. For whatever reason Donald Trump remains very important as part of the end-times drama now playing out before our eyes. The dream concluded with a clear admonition to continue praying for President Trump. We should all follow this admonition carefully.

HEAVEN IS READY TO RIDE!
JAMIE JACKSON DREAM

My friend Jamie Jackson also caught a glimpse of Heaven's preparation of midnight riders—at a funeral of all places. Jamie and his wife, Redonnia, pastor a powerful church in the small seaside town of Brunswick, Georgia. Burning Wick, as they like to call it. He had just delivered a brief eulogy when all of the sudden the veil was rolled away, and he saw how Heaven's midnight riders were actually being prepared to ride.

Jamie writes:

> I spent a few moments talking about the road that Jack had traveled over the past few years and that he had traveled it well. As I concluded, I wanted to convey a little of what he's experiencing now. "With all the technology that we currently have, watching our big flat screens in high definition showing the most brilliant detailed colors yet...NONE OF THIS CAN COMPARE to the heavenly realms Jack is seeing today!"

> Once I sat down, the Lord took me into a vision, one like I've never seen. The room I'm in changes and I'm now standing at the gates of Heaven. As I stood before them I was thinking the gates are the size of buildings and that there is nothing that was ever created by man that couldn't fit through these massive gates.

The Lord brought my attention to the opening of these gates, where I saw Jack walking through. I never entered the gates but stood at the opening. Once standing at the gate, the Lord allowed me to peer in.

What I saw was unexpected but confirmed the times and season that we are in. My eyes focused on white horses like I had never seen before. The images of these horses were so clear. And the colors, the sheer whiteness of the horses, was beyond the purest of white known on earth. The details of the muscular build and their manes were like silk, so smooth, with every hair in place.

As I marveled, I saw people everywhere and their only job was to attend to these horses. Some were putting on bridles and others were putting on the saddles. As I continued to gaze I began to try and count the horses, yet the more I counted the more I saw them without number. At this I was then brought back into the funeral home where the service was coming to a conclusion.

As I sat there overwhelmed by what I had just seen, I realized Heaven was now at our gates. The Lord spoke to me these words: HEAVEN IS GETTING READY TO RIDE!

HEAVEN'S RIDERS—JOHN'S VISION IN REVELATION

Now let's peer into an account from Scripture where Heaven's armies are ready to ride. As recounted in the book of Revelation, John was granted the extraordinary privilege of actually viewing a move of God from Heaven's perspective. Transported by the Spirit of God, he saw this end-time move from God's very Throne.

> *And I saw heaven opened, and behold, a white horse, and He who sat on it is called Faithful and True, and in righteousness He judges and wages war. ...And the armies which are in heaven, clothed in fine linen, white and clean, were following Him on white horses* (Revelation 19:11,14 NASB).

Note that Jesus judges and makes war. There's a key progression within this simple statement. God first renders judgment on a matter. He then makes war to *establish* His verdict on earth. In other words, the *verdict* comes before the actual turnaround. We then become announcers and enforcers of Heaven's judgment.

Let's also note that in a midnight hour for God's people, the armies of Heaven are following Jesus from His Throne to earth. Somehow these horses and riders are able to bridge the dimensions to bring Heaven's authority, vitality, and resources to bear upon our world.

Friend, there's more to "rising up to meet the Bridegroom" than we may perceive. The Lord is calling us to come up higher to perceive His Throne and move as He moves. Hear the trumpet, and rise up to meet Him.

Revelation 19:11-14 actually conveys a *spiritual revolution* that is catalyzed by a verdict from Heaven's Court. And in the spirit of Moses or the Maccabees or Paul Revere and his midnight ride, it's time now for a similar revolution that shifts the power base of nations from subjugation to freedom.

The context of this glory procession is powerful. Heaven opens. Jesus and His army descend upon the Mount of Olives, Mount Zion, and the Temple Mount. There they dethrone an antichrist Pharaoh and reclaim rulership of planet Earth.

Note that this is in context with the wedding where He joins His covenant people to Himself.

That said, when the white horses of the Lord appear, know that Heaven's movement is truly at hand. And we have the privilege of synergizing with Jesus and His new move!

THE END-TIMES FORERUNNER MOVEMENT

Not only does the Bible culminate with a spiritual revolution, but the journey of God's people from slavery to freedom begins with a spiritual revolution. According to Exodus 12:12, God waged war against the gods of Egypt and the government of Egypt to begin a freedom movement during Moses' day. Passover. Deliverance from Pharaoh as the Red Sea parted. A covenant of marriage in the wilderness. And finally, the Promised Land.

This freedom movement set a precedent for the nations. And it provides a template for the "Moses Movement" prophesied for today. Remember, God put the "X" in Exodus. And prophetically, 2025 marks the inauguration of His freedom movement. The Lord has shown many, ourselves included, that this movement will marry the miracles of Exodus with the miracles of Acts.

Revolution and glory, as Cindy Jacobs described it. A glory revolution!

ANGEL OF THE LORD

So let's follow a midnight ride that our forefathers in the faith pioneered. The midnight exodus out of Egypt and into the Covenant Land. Vital lessons must be learned from their freedom journey. We're going to engage from the vantage point of the Angel of the Lord, the true leader of this exodus movement.

The Angel of the Lord led Moses and his people out of Egypt and through the afflictions of the wilderness. He then partnered with Joshua to lead God's people into possession of the Promised Land. And ironically, that's when the greatest crisis ensued.

Judges 2 records an astounding prophetic directive delivered to all of Israel—by the Angel of the Lord. It was essentially His "State of the Union Address." To my knowledge it is the only time in the Bible where an angel of the Lord tangibly appears to audibly address an entire nation.

Note that the Angel of the Lord is distinctive from other angels in God's created order. This honor was conveyed even through the typography of the original Hebrew, with the name capitalized. And there's every reason to believe this honor is due. Because scripturally, the "Angel" referred to in these passages can only be either Holy Spirit or the pre-incarnate Christ.

> *Now the Angel of the Lord came up from Gilgal to Bochim. And he said, "I brought you up out of Egypt and led you into the land which I have sworn to your fathers; and I said, 'I will never break My covenant with you, and as for you, you shall make no covenant with the inhabitants of this land; you shall tear down their altars.' But you have not obeyed Me; what is this you have done? Therefore I also said, 'I will not drive them out before you; but they will become as thorns in*

your sides and their gods will be a snare to you.'" When the
Angel of the Lord spoke these words to all the sons of Israel,
the people lifted up their voices and wept. So they named that
place Bochim; and there they sacrificed to the Lord (Judges
2:1-5 NASB1995).

The name *Bochim* means weeping. The movement of the Angel
of the Lord from Gilgal to Bochim conveys the journey of Israel
from the time of circumcision, when God rolled away the reproach
of Egypt, until this day of weeping conveyed through his "state of the
union" address. Note again this was after huge swaths of the Promised
Land were already possessed and inhabited.

The Angel of the Lord appeared in order to bring the tribes of
Israel into the next phase of possessing the land. But He could no
longer move with God's people because they had compromised God's
covenant and even worshiped demonic powers.

Instead of completing the process of possessing the land, the
Angel of the Lord departed. He literally vacated the premises. And
the nation came to ruin.

Please note that idolatry brings desolation. Especially when
the people of God are seduced by it. The Abomination of Desolation recorded in Daniel 7 refers to the antichrist. But as with all
aspects related to the end times, the biblical principle remains the
same. Idolatry is an abomination. And wherever you go, it causes
desolation.

When the spiritual guardianship of the land was rescinded, homeland security immediately failed. Borders suddenly became very
porous. Foreigners, essentially terrorists, began to flood through these
borders to plunder the nation. And the Jewish people became captives in their own Promised Land.

Not surprisingly, Judges 2 is actually a powerful warning to the United States of America and other nations as we move forward. Pride, especially *open defiance of God*, comes before a fall. Israel experienced the consequences of their defiance, and if we're not sincerely deliberate in our repentance and honoring of the Lord, America could experience this same measure of discipline.

I WILL SEND MY ANGEL BEFORE YOU

Though the address by this Angel was unprecedented, the people of Israel were actually very familiar with Him. Again it was this Angel who brought God's people out of bondage under Pharaoh's idolatrous dictatorship. He led them across the waters, through the desert and into the Promised Land. His introduction to Joshua compelled Israel's great general to fall on his face.

God even made a promise to the 12 tribes regarding the Angel. It's worth rehearsing so that you can see the full context of His final address to the people. From Exodus 23:

> *Behold, I am going to send an angel before you to guard you along the way and to bring you into the place which I have prepared. Be on your guard before him and obey his voice; do not be rebellious toward him, for he will not pardon your transgression, since My name is in him. But if you truly obey his voice and do all that I say, then I will be an enemy to your enemies and an adversary to your adversaries* (Exodus 23:20-22 NASB1995).

That's our God! I have long felt this passage is a sacred commissioning for the movements of our day. It is also a promise from the

Lord to many who will read these pages. Beginning now. May the Word of the Lord leap off the page and into your spirit!

For many believers, it's turnaround time. Your personal journey is now becoming a glory procession. God is sending His angels before you to prepare the way, to guard you and protect you, and to bring you to the place He has personally prepared for you to flourish.

Okay. Let's look at the next verse in the passage. This is where things get sobering.

END-TIME IDOLATRY

For My angel will go before you and bring you in to the land of the Amorites, the Hittites, the Perizzites, the Canaanites, the Hivites and the Jebusites; and I will completely destroy them. You shall not worship their gods, nor serve them, nor do according to their deeds; but you shall utterly overthrow them and break their sacred pillars in pieces (Exodus 23:23-24 NASB1995).

God's original charge to the Israelites was to refuse to succumb to idolatry or erect pillars of idolatry in the Promised Land. As you can see by the warning of the Angel of the Lord, they failed massively in this. Yet over generations, He never changed His mind. He held them to the same standard.

One of the greatest lies pushed on the body of Christ today is that the spirit of the age should dictate the standard by which mankind should be evaluated. God's heart is true and His commandments infallible. Neither rock stars nor rock star presidents have the right to redefine what God determines to be sin.

> **Neither rock stars nor rock star presidents have the right to redefine what God determines to be sin.**

As the body of Christ in America, we too have failed in the promised land He has entrusted to us all. It is still staggering to me how many Christians take the subject of idolatry so lightly. It is nothing less than spiritual adultery, striking the very heart of our Bridegroom.

And the idolatry of the end of the age is only going to get darker and more blatant.

Jesus Christ is not the same God as Allah or Buddha or the Queen of Heaven or other gods worshiped in the religions of the world. He stands alone. His life and blood, given on your behalf, prove this to be true. And He alone is worthy and deserving of your devotion.

As it was, the Angel of the Lord evacuated the premises. The covenant land came to ruin as bordering nations plundered Israel's harvest.

THE ANGEL OF THE LORD AND GIDEON

After the Angel of the Lord vacated the land, He did not show up again for an entire generation. But eventually there was a re-emergence. He was dispatched in response to the sincere cries of God's people as they were being overcome, marginalized, subjugated, and abused within their own covenant boundaries.

The Angel of the Lord appeared to Gideon with a signal in the night. Time for turnaround. He was dispatched to literally pick up right where he left off—*restoring homeland security and securing Israel's boundaries.*

In America this is exactly where we are right now. And as with Gideon, beginning in 2025 the Lord is moving in a new way to complete the turnaround He initiated in a former season.

RESTORING COVENANTAL AUTHORITY

Then the Angel of the Lord came and sat under the oak that was in Ophrah... The Angel of the Lord appeared to him and said to him, "The Lord is with you, O valiant warrior."...The Lord looked at him and said, "Go in this your strength and deliver Israel from the hand of Midian. Have I not sent you?" (Judges 6:11-12,14 NASB1995)

What a commission. The same angel who partnered with Moses to rescue God's people from Egypt to the Promised Land, the same angel who partnered with Joshua to possess the land, was now inviting Gideon into the sacred partnership. And they together were about to re-possess the land!

Only one thing stood in the way. Turns out that Gideon's dad was one of the original settlers who completely disobeyed the Lord by building on his land an altar to Baal and Ashtoreh. The open defiance of Gideon's father in erecting his sacred pillar was a primary reason the Angel of the Lord vacated the land in the first place.

Not a coincidence the Lord's first assignment to Gideon was to tear this thing down. Fulfilling the original call given to the people of God to *"break their sacred pillars in pieces"* and opening the door for the Angel of the Lord to return and move in God's covenant land.

Let's put it another way. Gideon's obedience to "divorce Baal" and restore covenant with the Lord were mandated by God to satisfy the standards of Heaven's Court. On a personal level, he dealt with the generational idolatry in his bloodline. On a corporate level, the repudiation of his father's idolatry secured for Gideon *the covenantal authority to deliver the entire nation.*

Again. Only after Gideon divorced Baal was he released to deliver the nation. I cannot emphasize this point enough. It is the same with your sphere of authority.

PREPARING THE LAND

Until this covenant restoration, the Angel of the Lord was forbidden to even move through the land. But Gideon's obedience opened the way for the Angel of the Lord to deliver Israel again. The Angel of the Lord and Gideon, reporting for duty!

Further, Gideon's actions not only prepared him for military victory, they actually *prepared his land for military victory.* The land mourns when defiled by man's sin and disobedience. The ground itself rejoices when repentance brings cleansing and the glory of God again moves upon it.

The perceptive will see the message of the Maccabees within this story. Separation and rededication can launch a new beginning.

SPECIAL OPS PRAYER

Gideon soon overcame Israel's fiercest enemies with a small band of special ops warriors. In fact, Gideon's example has become the prototype of many special ops communities today. Sometimes small teams of highly trained, highly competent warriors are more effective than mighty armies.

Gideon's warriors came to the battleline fully armed. With swords, of course. But also a vast arsenal of secret weapons only special ops warriors are capable of handling. Fiercest ever seen on earth. They stop the enemy right in his tracks.

I'm talking about lamps, of course. Burning lamps.

And at midnight, a cry was heard. Gideon's warriors all became Lamplighters. They lit their lamps and held them high. And at the speed of light the enemy was supernaturally defeated. Further, a revolution was started, a freedom movement that restored the Promised Land to God's covenant people.

Lamplighters. I hope you don't miss the parallel. Or the potential. God is raising up special ops prayer teams today who enter territories covertly, blow up spiritual strongholds, rescue hostages, and return before anyone even knows they were there. Jesus gets all the glory that way. And it's happening now. Many colleagues have also found that the highest level spiritual warfare is consistently met with tangible, lasting results.

CAPITOL TURNAROUND

Our personal record of breakthroughs from "special ops prayer" spans from the White House, Capitol, Pentagon and Department of State to virtually every state in America as well as Israel, England, and other nations. Over and over again we have seen extraordinary initial confirmations followed by long-lasting results.

All our previous books, especially *White House Watchmen,* contain comprehensive documentation of special ops prayer assignments. I'll mention only one more overarching assignment here, patterned after Gideon's amazing breakthrough. Jolene and I collaborated with John Benefiel and Cindy Jacobs, and their respective networks HAPN and RPN, to engage in the largest and most comprehensive repudiation of idolatry in American history. Leaders prayed on-site at every Masonic lodge, abortion clinic, and other known occult altars across the nation, asking God to grant a divorce from Baal and restoration of covenant with Jesus Christ alone.

The initial sign of breakthrough came shortly after we completed the first phase of the initiative. Standing at the Lincoln Memorial on July 4, 2011, national leaders presented to the Lord the on-site repentance He had called us to facilitate nationally. We then presented Him with a Declaration of Covenant, asking for His hand in marriage to America once again. I had the honor of writing the Declaration.

Together we then asked for a confirmation that the Lord had indeed heard us and granted our request. Similar to Gideon with his fleece, we asked for a specific sign. Apostolic leader Rick Ridings had prophesied that the Lord would crack the hard shell of demonic resistance over Washington, DC. He literally saw a nutcracker, cracking a giant-sized nut.

Giant nuts in Washington, DC. The vision immediately resonated. So we asked the Lord to grant this breakthrough as a clear sign. Not only that He had granted the divorce from Baal but also the restoration of His covenant with our land.

Maybe it's not a coincidence that fifty days later to the day, Washington, DC was rocked by an unprecedented earthquake measuring 5.8 on the Richter scale. The Washington Monument, which some would call America's best-known sacred pillar, cracked in the quake. Gargoyles toppled from the National Cathedral. And the headquarters of a certain occultic fraternal order just a mile away from the White House was also impacted. The roof cracked. And the altar, where their highest-level initiates bow their knees to Baal, was damaged.

Can't make this stuff up. Truly.

On a broader scale, we saw how the acceptance of our repentance before the Lord restored the status of our foundational covenants with Him, thereby launching a new season for our capitol. The largest and most comprehensive repudiation of idolatry in American history soon initiated the largest and most comprehensive governmental turnaround in modern American history.

Against all odds, the turnaround continues to this day. No king but Jesus!

REDEFINING THE FORERUNNER CALLING

Jesus is redefining the forerunner ministry in this hour. He's preparing His midnight riders now so they can prepare the way for His expressions on earth. Turnaround. Glory! A freedom movement. A midnight ride to resound a midnight cry.

Because of this, in this hour Jesus is again drawing many of His disciples to Himself for personal renewal. As mentioned in the last chapter, the picture conveyed by Luke is our calling:

> *After these things the Lord appointed seventy others also, and sent them two by two before His face into every city and place where He Himself was about to go* (Luke 10:1 NKJV).

Before His face. Like Gideon in his day, or Samuel or Elijah or John the Baptist in their day, the body of Christ is now in a fore-running season. We are bridging a gap, preparing the way as God inaugurates a new era of history. Beginning in 2025 and beyond, Jesus is sending His forerunners into many cities He is about to visit. Many will soon prophesy, cast out demons, heal the sick, reap the harvest, and multiply the same miracles that defined His own ministry. We're going to see so much of this in coming months and years.

Jesus sent His disciples two by two before His face into every city He was about to visit. Like John the Baptist before them, they were sent to prepare the way. This best describes the primary mission of the forerunner spirit, the spirit and power of Elijah today. But it encompasses many facets.

Remember the midnight riders of Matthew 25 remained awake at midnight when the rest of the world was asleep. They were keeping watch. Directing your lifestyle to receive His divine intelligence is a major aspect of your calling.

And from the days of Gideon to the days of Elijah and John the Baptist to our day, the *forerunner call* is ultimately to prepare the bride for the Bridegroom. In other words, to prepare God's people for His coming. How is this done?

The first priority is restoring covenant. This includes leading people to Jesus, but as covered here it is even more vast. Friend, if you miss this, you miss the greatest purpose of God's midnight cry. And perhaps of the forerunner ministry. Because the door is wide open for nations as well as peoples to enter into covenant with Him.

And we must keep in mind that Heaven's Court will not be satisfied in this process of covenant restoration until the divorcement from Baal—historic and present idolatry—is complete.

It is extraordinary to me how much material on the forerunner anointing exists, yet how little is written about this process of the calling. Yes we are friends of the Bridegroom. That is our identity.

And as friends of the Bridegroom, our highest calling after prayer is to *prepare the way of the Lord.*

Note that in the spirit and power of Elijah, John the Baptist fulfilled this mission to "prepare the way" by immersing multitudes in the Jordan River. Symbolically he brought all Israel into a *mikvah* of God's own creation, for cleansing from their sins and iniquities, or generational sins. They were cleansed to possess their inheritance in the land, and especially to meet their God.

Forerunners lead in the cleansing of God's people. There are two times when *mikvahs* or baptisms were mandated in Jewish society. First, men and women both were mandated to be immersed and cleansed before ascending to God's holy Temple. Second, brides were required to be immersed as preparation for their wedding ceremony. These two aspects come together in the baptism revivals of this hour. We are going to receive a baptism of deliverance, and deliverance in baptisms!

Remember, Purity lights the lamp and prepares the way. Our lamps must continue to shine with an uncorrupted flame. Bringing an anointing of holy conviction, which releases correction and redemptive exposure to our world.

For far too long we've been all thunder and no lightning. Where is the shining of gentle conviction that pierces hearts and makes known the need for Jesus to our world?

Here's a secret. As the glory returns, so the conviction returns.

We must also function as kings and priests (Revelation 5:10). An area where many have gotten into a religious rut is that they've tried to function in the forerunner anointing out of the priestly anointing alone. There is a tremendous shift right now in the spiritual realm as the Lord brings forward His kingship anointing in His people. We will reign on the earth!

Speaking of reigning... The Bible makes clear that Zion and the Temple Mount demarcate the earthly seat of God's chosen Throne. You might have noticed that much of this book has explored a relentless generational quest for rulership by both the enemy and the Lord over Israel, Jerusalem, and the Jewish people. Our God is the God of Israel. Because your authority is derived from His covenant, you must understand God's covenant with His land and people.

And it must be honored.

APOSTOLIC COMMUNITY IN THE MIDNIGHT HOUR

One final subject must be covered. As we approach the midnight hour, the facilitation of home fellowships will grow in importance. Both because of the discretion afforded by home meetings and the deeper bonds of community naturally cultivated.

Many faith communities in Washington, DC have been challenged by what can only be termed religious persecution from opposing forces. This occurred especially during the Trump administration, where administration leaders were harassed and even prayer meetings infiltrated by the radicalized left. The safest spaces became violated. Many friends still deal with trauma inflicted by their abuse.

Since 2014, Jolene and I have led a weekly home fellowship in Washington, DC as an expression of apostolic community. We chose to cultivate a home fellowship rather than a more public forum so that high-level leaders could find a sequestered place to safely connect, without the controversy that so often accompanied their public appearances. And a beautiful thing happened. Almost from the beginning, acquaintances became friends. Friends genuinely became family. Greater privacy allowed for greater opportunities for personal growth, relational connectivity, care and accountability, as well as a greater freedom of expression. Especially in prophetic ministry and breakthrough prayer.

Note we are 100 percent for the local church! And we celebrate the fact that many area churches facilitate home groups for the very reasons cited. Our point is simply that as religious persecution becomes imposed at a greater level throughout America and the world, the need for wholistic home groups or home fellowships will become much greater as well. In a forerunning kind of way, it's best to start now, before the storms fully materialize.

REDEFINING FORERUNNER MINISTRY— TWELVE CHARACTERISTICS

So let's sum up what we've received so far. The following are twelve characteristics that redefine the forerunner ministry in our time. If three or four or all resonate with you, you are probably being drawn into a deeper expression of this calling in your life.

1. *Spirit of Elijah*—Bridegroom prophets cultivating a lifestyle of intimacy with God's heart and His voice, dedicated to purity. Core identity continually sourced in Christ's love. Loyal. Leading the people in covenant restoration.

2. *Kingship Anointing*—set over nations and kingdoms. Growing in authority to governmentally rule in the spiritual realm and influence the earth. Elijah is a

prototype. "No rain nor dew all these years except at my word."

3. *Throne Room Watchman*—as a "son of Issachar," receiving and responding to real-time prophetic revelation. Standing in God's council, receiving divine intelligence, keeping watch. And let's not neglect the watch of the Bridegroom for His bride's return.

4. *Pleading in His Courts*—receiving real-time verdicts from Heaven's Court to release God's justice on earth as in Heaven. Jesus judges and makes war. We interact with Heaven's Court and announce His judgments on earth.

5. *Preparing the Way*—intercession and even strategic level "special ops prayer" for breakthrough, for the restoration of God's glory, and ultimately even for the second coming of Christ. Preparing the heavens, bringing Heaven's alignment to earth.

6. *Preparing the Bride*—restoring covenant where covenant has been breached. Being a guide or mentor. Developing community. Healing and bringing deliverance both personally and corporately. Baptizing God's people.

7. *Restoring Hearts, Families, Nations*—of fathers to their children, children to their fathers, and the sons of the covenant back to the Lord their God. First through turnaround prayer. Generational revival will come!

8. *Ministering Healing and Deliverance from Generational Sins*—part of the same Elijah calling to prepare the

bride by repairing hearts. Zechariah 3 is an incredible model.

9. *Special Ops Warfare*—engaging in covert, strategic-level spiritual warfare, shifting regions and nations by dethroning principalities and powers. With smaller teams modeled after Gideon and his 300 top-tiered warriors.

10. *Apostolic Diplomacy*—providing effective communication of Kingdom solutions and accurate prophetic ministry for leadership within the seven spheres of society. You are called by God to influence the influencers.

11. *Focus on Israel, the Jewish People, the Nations*—standing for God's covenant dream for His land and people to be fully established. Keeping always in mind that we are grafted into their covenant, not the other way around. In reality we must be restored to our own roots!

12. *Apostolic Community*—establishing safe spaces for forerunning communities where relational accountability and collaboration can be organically cultivated. Face to face with God, and through the gates to impact our world!

The Lord is with you, mighty man of valor. The Lord is with you, mighty woman of valor! His angelic hosts are being dispatched to work with you. You may even sense the tangible presence of the Lord and His hosts beside you as you read this. He is aligning you with

Heaven's heart and movement. Nations will come to the brightness of your rising!

Now—grab your burning lamps, mount your horse and let's roll. It's midnight. Time to launch an awakening. Heaven is ready to ride!

STUDY QUESTIONS AND PRAYER

1. Do you consider yourself a forerunner? Are you a pioneer? What aspects of your life reflect this calling?

2. Identify three justice issues that provoke you at a heart level. How is God calling you to address them? To bring change?

3. Do you agree that we are in a midnight hour? How does this impact your life?

4. How is the Lord communicating with you today? Have you ever received a vision or a dream that foretells the future?

5. Do you know of idolatry or occult practices in your family line? Has it affected you? What's your current approach to gaining freedom?

6. Abomination causes desolation. Do you see areas in your life or world that seem to be under a curse? From the chapter, what ways have been identified to bring a turnaround?

7. What is the role of covenant in your life? Where do you see breaches of covenant that need to be repaired?

8. What is the role of apostolic community in your life? Have you found safe spaces to worship the Lord and share your life at a greater level of transparency? Who are your true friends?

Father God, our journey into the forerunner ministry begins with a fresh consecration to You. In covenant with Christ, divorced from idolatry. Help me to live out the commitment to You that I have made. Protect our relationship. Draw me deeper into Your heart and purpose for my life. Help me to tear down the altars that invite desolation instead of blessing. In Jesus' name, amen.

Prayer on a field in upstate New York where Charles
Finney and Daniel Nash walked and prayed.

CHAPTER 12

Chapter Topics: Elijah v Jezebel | Jezebel's Table | Antichrist Globalism | Altar Fire | Securing Israel | Revival in the Muslim World| | Miracle on Capitol Hill | Prayer—Dethroning Jezebel, Securing Seats

THE HARVEST WARS:
OVERCOMING END-TIME IDOLATRY

"This third great awakening is a Great Return, where multitudes disengage from Jezebel's table and return to the Table of the Lord."

—From the chapter

When you make an investment, you want a return. Right? And when you sow a seed you want a harvest. God initiated this principle. But sometimes He must imperil this very process. At least until His conditions are met.

"No rain nor dew all these years, except at my word." Remember that Armageddon is the backdrop for the spirit and power of

Elijah. And when the prophet declared God's judgment to Israel's king, it was likely in the fertile valley below the Megiddo summit. Ahab and Jezebel resided in a palace there, in the nearby village of Jezreel.

Elijah's prophetic decree was nothing less than a declaration of war against the antichrist strongholds represented by Ahab and Jezebel, seeking to overtake God's covenant land. It is the same in the end times. We, like Elijah, are engaged in a Harvest War over nations.

You might question the "antichrist" part. Too dramatic? Probably not when you realize that the name Jezebel means "married to Baal." From Babylonian times until now, the principality Bel or Baal remains essentially the face of the antichrist spirit.

Or perhaps its executor.

Jezebel took her espousal to Baal seriously too. Her efforts included propagating Baal worship, with rites encompassing ritual sex of all varieties, sexual abuse even against children, idolatrous sacrifices and occult invocations, in every high and low place in the land. She recruiting and actively mentored prophets for Baal. And she fundamentally changed the covenant-centric culture of Israel from devotion to the Lord to hard-core idolatry, with their corrupted value systems imposed on the masses.

Again, sound familiar? Hope so.

America is among many nations now in an existential battle for our national sovereignty and for the harvest Jesus died to redeem. Generations are in the balance.

How do we pray? What can we do? Many secrets can be found in this chapter.

GOD'S RESPONSE TO JEZEBEL'S CAMPAIGN

The judgment decreed by Elijah is far more intensive than a superficial reading conveys. Streams are rare in Israel, and virtually all the water for irrigation comes from rain. So when Elijah called for downpours to cease, the encroaching drought dried up the crops and ultimately instigated a regional famine. He crippled the farming community providing sustenance for the people.

The economy plummeted as well. Revenue from regional taxation dried up with the crops.

Why was the judgment so strong? Basically because the arranged marriage between Ahab and Jezebel was equated to an attempt to establish a regional empire—essentially a globalist empire—fueled by antichrist idolatry. The newly claimed capital was in the Jezreel Valley, also known as the Megiddo Valley. Or, of course, Armageddon. It was located in the heart of Israel's harvest fields, the only nation in the world that God Himself claims as His own.

The antichrist spirit is a takeover spirit, set on global dominance. By this I mean taking over the thrones of government, the fields of harvest in all spheres, as well as within human hearts. Seat by seat, resource by resource, and family by family. These days across every nation.

NABOTH AND THE VINEYARD OF PROPHETIC DESTINY

The spirit is ruthless, treacherous and it is relentless. A fact that a neighbor of Ahab and Jezebel named Naboth found out the hard way. Naboth's vineyard basically bordered the royal palace. And the power couple next door wanted to take possession.

Naboth's name in Hebrew means "prophetic words." It comes from the root word *nabi* or prophet. So Naboth's vineyard could accurately be translated as "the vineyard of prophetic destiny." And Jezebel's tireless quest to overtake the vineyards of prophetic destiny accurately defines the harvest wars from Elijah's time until today.

And even to Armageddon.

Naboth died trying to save his farm from Jezebel. Ahab initially approached him, offering the farmer a deal. Naboth's refusal must define our resolve today. Because our inheritance is at stake as well. *"The Lord forbid that I should give you* [Ahab and Jezebel] *the inheritance of my fathers!"* (1 Kings 21:3 NASB).

Jezebel got involved immediately. She wrote to the "influencers" of her day, making up a story about Naboth's unfaithfulness to both God and king. In the Nazi era the manufactured story would have been termed "propaganda"; in our world today, it's called "fake news." She then engaged the legal system of her day to prosecute him for his crimes. Which was relatively easy because she populated the jury with a group the Bible calls "Sons of Belial." Most translators will tell you the phrase simply means "sons of worthlessness." But throughout ancient literature Belial is primarily equated with either the Baal principality or satan himself.

You guessed it. Jezebel hired sons of satan to get the job done. In the uproar that followed, Naboth's life was taken, and Jezebel conveniently claimed ownership of the vineyard.

You may think a sect like this does not exist today. Certainly at least, it would not be embedded within government. You are wrong.

Remember, satan and his fallen angels were leaders in the government of God. They rebelled. And they have sought from Adam's day to corrupt government by seducing and corrupting governmental leaders into following them *in their rebellion.*

That said, one prevalent secret order, originating from the same antichrist idolatry that Jezebel served in her day, remains prevalent. And at the highest levels of the order they openly reveal Lucifer is the "god" they serve. That is the fraternal order of freemasonry.

"Many religions forming one altar to the Great Architect of the Universe" is a primary creed. Only the "Great Architect" is not Jesus. In fact, the name of Jesus is forbidden to be spoken in most lodges. So biblically, their motto actually sums up the quest of antichrist idolatry.

Proof of this pursuit is also found in another foundational principle, engraved on the House of the Temple, just a mile north of the White House: "Freemasonry builds its temples in the hearts of men and among nations."

Targeting hearts, targeting nations in the occult. Establishing covenant at temple altars. Doesn't that sound like the antithesis of the Elijah call? That's no coincidence. "The Craft" has functioned as a forerunning expression for antichrist forces, in the same manner that the spirit of Elijah is functioning to prepare the way of the Lord.

First by turning hearts.

Freemasonry today is nowhere near as influential as it was even a decade ago. Yet occult practices introduced by the Craft have now spread so much they are normative in American life, education, and culture.

Many openly deride a godly patriotism that compels lovers of the God of Israel to stand for His dream for our land, and for the land of the Jewish people. Elijah is a great prototype. Perhaps most don't perceive the alternative offered by the enemy, which is antichrist globalism. Yet it is now gaining widespread acceptance in America and throughout the world.

The confrontation between these two forces largely defines Armageddon—and defines the accompanying harvest wars. Just remember that Armageddon is a backdrop for the spirit of Elijah.

ELIJAH—DETHRONING JEZEBEL

Through the Sons of Belial, Jezebel weaponized the justice system of her day to overtake the vineyard of prophetic destiny, the vineyard of inheritance, the vineyard of covenant harvest. Not long after, Elijah appeared on the scene—confronting the king again, this time right in the middle of Ahab and Jezebel's newly acquired harvest field.

Naboth's unjust arrest and death sentence had triggered the convening of a higher court than their remote-controlled legal system. Heaven's Court become involved. A verdict by the Ancient of Days was set—judgment in favor of the saints, restraining the enemy, and releasing the saints to possess the Kingdom. And Elijah was sent to declare the verdict.

This verdict, presented to the king on the very ground where the crime occurred, *brought down the entire government tied to Ahab and Jezebel.*

Let me remind you that these events all occurred in the shadow of Mount Megiddo. The Jezreel Valley is referenced as the "valley of Armageddon." From the beginning of the Bible through the end times, it's a consistent symbol for the land of Israel.

I feel the Lord showed me that the true battle of Armageddon, described in Revelation 16 as "the war of the great day of God, the Almighty," is directly related to these very issues—on this very ground. In truth, each generation must confront them to perpetuate the covenant freedom ordained by God for our land.

POSSESSING EDOM, POSSESSING NATIONS

Let's switch gears and examine a different aspect of God's harvest wars. And in the process you're going to discover another astonishing mystery embedded within a passage we've already examined. Let's take another look at Amos 9:11 (NKJV):

> On that day I will raise up The **tabernacle** of David, which has fallen down, and repair its damages; I will raise up its ruins, and rebuild it as in the days of old.

Thanks even to this book, so far you're in very familiar territory. Let's go a step beyond:

> "That they may possess the remnant of Edom and all the nations who are called by My name," declares the Lord who does this.
>
> "Behold, days are coming," declares the Lord, "when the plowman will overtake the reaper and the treader of grapes him who sows seed; when the mountains will drip sweet wine and all the hills will be dissolved.
>
> "Also I will restore the captivity of My people Israel, and they will rebuild the ruined cities and live in them; they will also plant vineyards and drink their wine, and make gardens and eat their fruit.
>
> "I will also plant them on their land, and they will not again be rooted out from their land which I have given them," says the Lord your God (Amos 9:12-15 NASB1995).

Tell me the first answer that pops into your mind. What's God's primary intention in restoring the Tabernacle of David? Hosting God's presence in intimacy, right? And that's true. But Amos perceived another one. A big one.

Possessing Edom.

Edom or "Red" became another name for Jacob's twin brother Esau. You might remember that Jacob wrestled him in the womb and came out first, thereby receiving the firstborn blessing.

Esau hated Jacob. He sought to kill him. And the wrath against the sons of Jacob continue today primarily through radical jihadist ideology.

Amos is essentially saying here that hosting God's covenantal presence in the spirit of the Tabernacle of David, even with 24-7 worship and prayer, is an essential end-times catalyst to possess Edom. To overtake and dethrone his dominion.

And in perspective, isn't it interesting that the Lord chose the attack by jihadists on 9-11-01 to trumpet the restoration of the Tabernacle of David! Essentially, He is reminding us that to overcome the weaponized hatred of Edom's descendants, a magnitude of intercession far beyond a weekly prayer meeting will be needed.

And further, possessing Edom is no longer killing them. It's harvesting them. Bringing multitudes of sons and daughters of Abraham to faith in Jesus Christ. Same with "all the nations that are called by My name."

Remember Jolene's vision of the Armageddon clock, set at ten minutes to midnight. In conversation with a high-level government official, we learned that renown minister Derek Prince received a similar vision from the Lord. Shortly before he passed on, he too saw a grandfather clock. The Lord showed him that when the clock struck midnight it would signal a great awakening in the Muslim world!

A Muslim awakening? Absolutely. It's actually happening already. Against all odds, especially in Iran. Pakistan as well.

Could it be that the "grandfather clock" in both Jolene's vision and Derek Prince's vision represents Abraham, the grandfather of Jews, Muslims, and Christians? And that the midnight awakening is an awakening of his offspring? I believe we will soon see a Holy Spirit expression of the "Abraham Accords" pioneering awakening, salvation, reconciliation, and the healing of nations. Many grandsons and granddaughters will be restored to the God of Abraham through Jesus Christ!

SWEET WINE—SONS OF ISRAEL RESTORED TO THEIR LAND

Amos 9 prophesies that, concurrent with this move of the Spirit, fueled by night and day worship, Israel finally becomes settled within the boundaries God gave Jacob's descendants. They are planted in the land He gave them. And the Lord vows that they will never again become uprooted.

One more piece of the passage to explore right now. Amos declares that the mountains will drip with sweet wine. This may not sound like such a big deal to you. But after Israel ceased to exist, and the Muslims began to occupy the land, Israel's vineyards became completely barren. Why? Muslims are forbidden to drink alcohol.

So for literally thousands of years no vineyard was cultivated. Until the Jewish people began to return to the land. They discovered in the scrolls of Jeremiah, Amos, and other prophets that the land would flourish once again with wineries. The vineyards would thrive, to the extent the mountains would literally drip with sweet wine.

Nothing like this happened until 1948, when Israel was reborn. There were no vineyards. Now Israel's wineries are winning international competitions! And biblical prophecy is being fulfilled before our eyes.

TURNING ISRAEL BACK TO GOD—FROM A VINEYARD!

Elijah's quest to turn Israel began with a declaration of drought in the Jezreel Valley, in the shadow of Tel Megiddo. It culminated on a mountain called Carmel with the restoration of rain. Translated, *Carmel* means "the vineyard of God." And by the time Elijah ascended the mountain, the vineyards on the mountain had likely dried up completely.

The prophet gathered representatives from all 12 tribes for a power contest between God and Baal, the prophet of God and the prophets of Baal.

Elijah's only requirement of them was that they pour water on the altar he had built for the Lord. Many interpret this action as God eliminating any doubt of His supremacy, as water obviously quenches fire. The appearance of His fire would then rightly be perceived as supernatural.

But there's an even more important understanding. What's the most precious commodity in a drought?

And he said, "Fill four large jars with water and pour it on the burnt offering and on the wood." And he said, "Do it a second time," so they did it a second time. Then he said, "Do it a third time," so they did it a third time. The water flowed around the altar, and he also filled the trench with water (1 Kings 18:34-35 NASB).

Elijah commanded the people to pour their most precious commodity on the altar he built. Twelve stones. Twelve jars of water. Elijah then prayed a very simple prayer:

Hear me, O Lord, hear me, that this people may know that You are the Lord God, and that You have turned their hearts back to You again (1 Kings 18:37 NKJV).

Then the fire of the Lord fell. The burnt offering and the wood were consumed. The fire even *"licked up the water"* that was in the trench.

When all the people saw it, they fell on their faces; and they said, "The Lord, He is God! The Lord, He is God!" (1 Kings 18:39 NKJV)

What happened next was equally stunning. Elijah climbed to the summit of the mountain and entered into travailing prayer for the restoration of rain. A cloud the size of a man's hand appeared. And the people gained a perpetual flow of the very substance they had poured on the altar.

They sowed water, and reaped the restoration of rain.

And Carmel, the dried-up vineyard on the mountain of God, became a firstfruit of the economic restoration which overtook the land when the drought broke. It is *vital* to understand the government of God mandated covenant restoration with God, divorced from Baal, for the harvest to flourish again and the economy to thrive.

And the Lord is saying that under the influence of the spirit of Elijah, economies will be restrained and economies will be repaired. "For I will throw a wrench into globalist systems and cycles says the Lord, that will damage them beyond repair. And I will provide my prophets with both covenantal authority and creative solutions to turn the economic taskmasters from pharaoh subjugation to unhindered freedom. So meet Me at the summit! And watch the supernatural multiplication that you and I together can release."

DREAM—ARMAGEDDON AND WASHINGTON, DC

Note: Portions of the prophetic experience were shared in our book, *White House Watchmen.*

On Wednesday, April 12, the third day of Passover, I dreamed I was on a high hill overlooking the Promised Land. I saw both our view of Washington, DC and a view of Israel's Jezreel Valley from Tel Megiddo.

Yes, in the dream Washington, DC was superimposed on Armageddon. Honestly that's kind of unsettling. But though a clear warning was conveyed in the dream, the Spirit's primary emphasis was actually good news. It was time to secure the harvest! God was summoning us at Passover to begin taking His Promised Land.

Before we go there, let's focus more specifically on the view. From our prayer perch, Jolene and I actually overlook the seats of authority for all three branches of our government—the White House, Capitol, and Supreme Court. We also see a portion of the Pentagon. So on our prayer calls, your declarations are resounding to the highest seats of power. No king but Jesus!

In the dream, the Jezreel valley was juxtaposed with this view of Washington, DC. Jezreel is the site of countless wars—from the days of Abraham to Gideon, Solomon and beyond. Jezebel was cast down from her tower there. Hosea's bride was restored there. As a child, Jesus grew up overlooking this valley and learned to pray there.

And Revelation bears witness that Har Megiddo or Armageddon will be the site of a cataclysmic battle between good and evil, marking the end of days.

That said, war was not the primary emphasis of the Spirit in this dream. It was harvest.

Note that for the first time in centuries, the previously uninhabited land known as the Jezreel valley now produces the vast majority of the produce for Israel. Jezreel has become Israel's breadbasket—just as the biblical prophets foresaw. More on this in a moment.

CALL TO TAKE THE PROMISED LAND

In the dream, a group of us were strategizing on the next steps to take the Promised Land. The view from the hilltop was so expansive—like we could see from one end to the other.

I knew the "land" we were overlooking represented promises from God to us personally as well as to nations. Harvest, blessing, promotion, increase. We saw personally the ground we are called to take in this "Crown & Throne movement," including the restoration of His glory across the land.

In the dream I could see both opportunities and obstacles both near and far. In other prophetic experiences my vision was limited to what I was shown. But in this prophetic experience, it was as though my vision was only limited by what I chose to focus on!

I looked, I saw.

In this season of training as watchmen, He is giving many believers fresh vision. Some of what you receive will be by God's sovereign choice. But some of what you see by His Spirit will actually be determined by what you choose to focus on. Watchman, what do YOU see?

JEZEBEL

Here's what I saw in my dream as our primary obstacle. A woman in a loose-fitting white robe was resting on a rock in the exact geographic center of the field. She smiled at me, waved, and leaned forward showing her cleavage. Jolene was by my side, and I turned to her and said, "That is witchcraft!"

Here's a clear warning to us all. The primary risk to the advancement of God's movement on earth is still covenant breaking and idolatry. We must pray even for our government leaders in this. Lead us not into temptation, but deliver us from evil!

Keep in mind again that Jezebel was thrust from her tower in Jezreel. Because this was the primary enemy identified in the dream, I believe the Lord desires for this spiritual stronghold to fully come down in this hour. This means the defenses of this principality are disempowered in a way they have not been in decades.

Let's take this ground. LET MY PEOPLE GO!

THE THIRD GREAT AWAKENING IS A GREAT RETURN

"This third great awakening is a great return. When multitudes will disengage from Jezebel's table and return to the Table of the Lord!"

Fourteen years ago, these words came from Heaven with such power and authority it was overwhelming. And through this prophecy, directives came that have defined our ministry focus ever since.

Your sons and daughters are going to return to the Lord. So are your mothers and fathers. In fact entire generations are going to disengage from Jezebel's table and return to the Table of the Lord.

And as a forerunner of this work, you personally have a fresh opportunity to gain freedom from Jezebel's table through teshuvah. Despising the defilement, degradation, control, and covenant-breaking Jezebel seeks to feed you, your family, and your world.

It's the "now time" to return to the purity of unbounded love, covenant love, redemptive love that enriches you, restores your dignity, and draws out of you the true treasures of life.

It's time to return to the Table of the Lord!

THE HIGHEST COURT IN THE KINGDOM

I believe it's for this reason the Lord has continually emphasized receiving communion in this season. Please receive the Table of the Lord every day! Let's remember that the highest Court in the Kingdom of God is the Table of the Lord. You are summoned before the Throne both to receive the "evidence" of your amazing verdict—His very body and blood—and present His "evidence" on behalf of those you are interceding for.

For many especially, it's our sons and daughters we are contending for. You may find our book *Turnaround Tuesday* helpful, as it is a deep dive into strategic prayer for them. But for now, let's let John the Revelator speak again from ancient times and bring real-time clarity to our world.

> *But I have this against you, that you tolerate the woman Jezebel, who calls herself a prophetess, and she teaches and leads My bond-servants astray so that they commit sexual immorality and eat things sacrificed to idols* (Revelation 2:20 NASB).

Jezebel likes to gain for herself the top titles of her sphere. Prophet. Queen, as in Ahab's instance. President. Even King. Because yes, the opportunity to enter into covenant and be "married to Baal" is open to all genders.

But Teacher? As, like, an "influencer" over your children's educational system? That may be a new discovery for many of you. At least until observing the unrelenting efforts of lawmakers and school board officials to sexualize our children through state-mandated curriculum. Or to further "educate" them through the unhinged promotion of occult literature and culture.

K-12 and beyond, it's all there. Remember, Jezebel served Baal. Very clearly, the same principality that fueled Jezebel's idolatry and sexual immorality has sought to take our children captive.

Here's good news. Christ's verdict has already been announced. And at your bidding, Heaven's army is being released to back it up. LET MY CHILDREN GO.

> *But thus says the Lord: "Even the captives of the mighty will be taken away, and the prey of the terrible will be delivered;*

for I will contend with him who contends with you, and I will save your children" (Isaiah 49:25 NKJV).

"THE PROPHETS OF BAAL EAT AT JEZEBEL'S TABLE"

But wait, there's more. You might ask what Jezebel's influence has to do with the weaponization of government systems against its constituents. We the people. To find out, let's check out the original reference in Scripture to "Jezebel's table."

Remember that Jezebel married Ahab to create a transnational alliance tied to the idolatry of Baal worship. She sought to overtake the covenant land. And that's when God set Elijah in authority over Israel, to restore God's people back to Himself and to overcome the overreach of Israel's compromised government. He did so first by proclaiming the drought. When the time came for God's restoration process to be implemented, Elijah again was summoned to address the king: *"Go, present yourself to Ahab, and I will provide rain on the face of the earth"* (1 Kings 18:1 NASB).

In the confrontation—and it was a confrontation—Elijah noted that the prophets of Baal and the prophets of the Asherah *"eat at Jezebel's table"* (1 Kings 18:19 NASB).

Please note this. Jezebel's table was funded by Israel's taxpayers. Jezebel was taking the collective wealth of the hard-working Israeli population and funneling money to sustain the prophets of Baal. And by sustaining these corrupt leaders, even through the famine, Jezebel was sustaining their ideologies and influence over society to continue defiling the generations.

Boom.

So how do you gain the upper hand against Jezebel's table? You can clearly discern the "food" she is serving up. Sexual immorality, food sacrificed to idols. It's time to disengage.

Most of us clearly understand that Jezebel is trying to corrupt us through sexual immorality. But what about "food sacrificed to idols"? What happens when your supply line is actually compromised by idolatry at the highest levels? Sadly this is the case with countless corporations in the private sector, as well as government bureaucracies. And let's be honest—it will likely become even more challenging with the cascading waves of the end times.

Yet God saw the end from the beginning. He has made a way for you to fully disengage. And His methodology of conquest may be surprising to many. Instead of disengaging you from your job or your sphere of influence from overarching idolatry and defilement, He has made a way for you to sanctify your supply line so it is no longer subject to the curse.

> For if the firstfruit is holy, the lump is also holy; and if the root is holy, so are the branches (Romans 11:16 NKJV).

By presenting the firstfruits of your supply line or income to the Lord, you grant Him the right to sanctify your entire supply line. It becomes holy. All the way through the end of days.

Maybe you're familiar with this classic passage on tithes and offerings from Malachi 3. I want you to read it with fresh vision:

> "Would anyone rob God? Yet you are robbing Me! But you say, 'How have we robbed You?' In tithes and offerings. You are cursed with a curse, for you are robbing Me, the entire nation of you! Bring the whole tithe into the storehouse, so that there may be food in My house, and put Me

to the test now in this," says the Lord of armies, "if I do not open for you the windows of heaven and pour out for you a blessing until it overflows. Then I will rebuke the devourer for you, so that it will not destroy the fruit of your ground; nor will the vine in the field prove fruitless to you," says the Lord of armies. "All the nations will call you blessed, for you will be a delightful land," says the Lord of armies" (Malachi 3:8-12 NASB).

Your divine exchange of tithes and offerings is a cyclical expression of your covenant with God. It is received before His very Throne and continually bears witness before the Throne that your heart is with your treasure. In turn, the Lord takes the firstfruits of your supply line and restrains the forces seeking to corrupt and devour it. He opens for you the windows of Heaven, granting you access to fresh innovation and direction from His Spirit.

Further, according to the Bible, your obedience in investing tithes and offerings into the Kingdom actually initiates God's commanded blessing for the entire nation. It's right in the Word.

Living in a watchman's perch overlooking the Pentagon, the Capitol, the White House, the Supreme Court, and many diplomatic and intelligence communities, Jolene and I can say with full assurance, *we need the benefit your obedience secures!*

Let's see Heaven opened and the devourer rebuked from your harvest. Let's see Jezebel dethroned and the encroaching curse of darkness lifted from our nation. Let's partner with Jesus to actually win the harvest wars!

Test Him in this. Try Him. And see how He comes through. You will find that the horizon you sow into will soon be at your doorstep.

> **Test Him in this. Try Him. And see how He comes through. You will find that the horizon you sow into will soon be at your doorstep.**

MIRACLE ON CAPITOL HILL

Through these examples and prophetic experiences, I hope you see how overcoming the influence of Jezebel, by exercising your authority in the spiritual realm by implementing course corrections to restore covenant, is key to winning the Harvest War. Including the war over your own sons and daughters. It's time for your inheritance to be secured!

Let me share with you a final testimony on overcoming the Jezebel spirit—in the highest realms of government. Let me clarify again that the spirit behind Jezebel is actually Baal. Antichrist is anti-covenant, and the Baal principality is absolutely an expression of the antichrist spirit.

Recently Jolene and I received a precious gift from a congressional leader, honoring a miracle turnaround the Lord brought from the floor of the US Congress. In a framed photo, seven congressmen are pictured in the House chamber, praying through a special decree I had written called "Reclaiming Seats of Authority."

Without knowing, I had been interceding on Capitol Hill at the very time these congressional leaders were praying inside. Many within our Lamplighter community and national prayer networks were also praying concurrently.

Then came a turnaround. We'll share about it in a minute.

In a time of challenge, Jesus brought an intervention as only He can. Not just once but twice. And in the face of the great challenges before us, it's refreshing to rehearse these victories in the Lord. Let

Congressman Greg Steube and group praying a decree written
by Jon and Jolene on the floor of the House of Representatives,
January 6, 2023. Immediate turnarounds followed.

your faith expand. We can't complete the turnaround—but if we
engage with Him, He can!

DETHRONING JEZEBEL—RECLAIMING SEATS OF AUTHORITY

The photograph featured in this chapter was taken on January 6, 2023.
Two years after the infamous march to Capitol Hill, House Republicans had found themselves in an all-out brawl just as their majority

term began. The American people were promised breakthrough. But they could not agree on a new House Speaker. Not a good way to start!

I saw by the Spirit how occult forces aligned with the previous Speaker were still claiming the seat of the speakership, wreaking havoc in process. Here's an important principle. When a seat of authority has been occupied by a person compromised by actions the Bible identifies as sin, it is imperative to engage in identificational repentance and ask God to cancel all covenants with forces of darkness, however and wherever access has been allowed (see Isaiah 28).

Otherwise even though the leadership may change, the cycle tends to perpetuate.

In this case we dealt directly with a Jezebel spirit. The Lord inspired us to write a prayer to cleanse and reclaim the seat of the House Speakership, restraining this force of darkness as well as every other demonic entity tied to it, which empowered the resulting chaos. We released the decree on our Wednesday conference call, drove home Thursday, and I made a beeline to Capitol Hill Friday morning to pray through the decree on-site.

Heaven's direction was clear to release both the "turnaround mantle" and the decree on-site on Capitol Hill. Right after we finished, I received a "crayzee" text from a friend. The spiritual warfare decree I had written had been forwarded to congressman Greg Steube of Sarasota, Florida, who had actually gathered other congressional leaders to help him pray it through.

On the House floor.

Fox News showed live video of the prayer time. It turned out the congressional prayer meeting was being held at exactly the moment we were praying outside. Can't make this stuff up. By the next morning the chaos broke. A new Speaker was elected.

Later in the year, Jolene and I were privileged to have dinner with Congressman Steube and his beautiful wife. He told us how—his language—*everything turned* after this prayer. And it kept on turning!

Now maybe this is all just coincidence. An impossibly well-timed coincidence of course. Or maybe the Lord actually released a turnaround movement in the House of Representatives that day, securing His covenant purposes, with key congressional leaders on the inside and intercessors outside the Capitol building and across the nation all bearing witness to what He longed to do!

Kevin McCarthy secured the seat. But turmoil again erupted within the ranks. He was ousted less than a year later. We again engaged in prayer, along with countless others, decreeing that Jesus' covenantal turnaround stands. Against all odds Mike Johnson, a fervent believer in Jesus who genuinely lives his beliefs, was nominated.

If you notice in the decree, we called for God's *Eliakim* to be set into place. That sums up Speaker Johnson's wholehearted pursuit. He was literally born to be House Speaker.

And would you believe…it just so happened that Speaker Johnson had been one of the congressmen recruited to pray and cleanse the seat of the speakership. Really, you can't make this stuff up.

God is demonstrating the power of consecration and covenant. And He is positioning America to complete the turnaround. He is redeeming His harvest in our land.

STUDY QUESTIONS AND PRAYER

1. Where do you perceive the harvest wars in your life? How are you partnering with the Lord to see breakthrough? Maybe praying for your sons and daughters? For the success of your business? Based on this chapter, what further steps can you take?

2. On a national level, where is the enemy seeking to steal the harvest of righteousness in our nation? What fields of destiny do you perceive Jezebel is targeting?

3. Have either you or your family members been involved in secret orders tied to the occult? Have you worked with a counselor to gain healing and deliverance?

4. It's time to disengage from Jezebel's table and return to the Table of the Lord. What "food" does Jezebel serve at her table? Addictions? Sexual immorality? Idolatry? How are you actively disengaging from this compromise?

5. Are you currently committed to tithing? How are you actively claiming the benefits promised in the Word? How are you experiencing them? Consider writing out a personal declaration.

6. Are you praying for your leaders to escape the seduction, control, and occult targeting conveyed by Jezebel? How are you involved in establishing a prayer covering for them?

7. By dealing with demonic strongholds God's way, we are seeing breakthroughs at the highest levels of

government in Washington, DC. But it's still a perilous fight. Will you consider contending along with us for His continued breakthrough?

_____

Jolene and I encourage you to continue to pray as directed by Holy Spirit over your school boards, city councils, state seats, your congressional seats in the House and Senate, the Supreme Court, and of course, the White House. The decree follows. Again—NO KING BUT JESUS!

Dethroning Jezebel, Reclaiming Seats of Authority—Petition Before Heaven's Court, January 6, 2023

Father God, we lift up to You the seat of authority You desire to cleanse and redeem. We bring this seat literally before the Throne of the Ancient of Days, in the highest Court of the Kingdom of God. We ask for Your verdict of justice in favor of the saints. Whereas covenants establish thrones of governance; and whereas our foundational national covenant with You has been restored and upheld by Heaven's Court; therefore this seat belongs to the Lord Jesus Christ by covenant.

We therefore ask that You open the scrolls and review each place in history or present time where sinful actions, decisions, policies, and laws have been created from this seat which defy Your heart and covenant. Forgive the sins that have taken place by those stewarding this seat, including all sexual immorality and abuse, abuse of power, abuse of children, unjust bloodshed, occult sacrifice, betrayal of national interest, etc. Ultimately they are all a betrayal of You. Please forgive these grave injustices. We as witnesses before Your Court remit these sins, and ask that You remit these sins. Through the blood of Jesus, roll away the reproach that has formed over this seat!

We ask that You also review each place in history or present time when covenants with principalities and powers have been established—including with Satan, Baal, Jezebel, antichrist spirits, etc. According to the vision You granted, and even more according to Your Word from Isaiah 28, please annul every covenant with death and hell, with principalities and powers, that has been established over this seat and its rulers.

Covenant with death and hell annulled! Therefore let all precepts of the Divorce Decree from Baal, the Writ of Assistance, and other verdicts from Heaven's Court applying to this case be upheld and immediately enforced by said Court. Let all claims of ownership of this seat by occult powers and human beings aligned with these forces be immediately rescinded, all forces dismissed, in Jesus' name.

And we ask that You release Your angelic hosts to watch over, protect, and defend this Seat and the one You choose to lead from it, in Jesus' name.

Father, we ask that You grant that Your chosen leader for this Seat be summoned by You and chosen by the other leaders responsible for his or her election. Whether man or woman, we ask for an Eliakim. One who will remain loyal to You and Your covenant, and who will be a father or mother to the Nation and to the sphere entrusted, and to the constituents being led. Grant counsel from Heaven's council continually, to lead this nation away from judgment and into the shalom and blessing granted to the nation whose God is the Lord. Verdict hereby received, in Jesus' holy name, amen!

Guardian of the Orphans Statue, Yad Vashem
Holocaust Memorial, Jerusalem, Israel.

CHAPTER 13

END-TIMES TREACHERY AND TRICKERY

"Tricks and treachery are the practice of fools, that don't have brains enough to be honest."
—Benjamin Franklin

"The treachery of demons is nothing compared to the betrayal of an angel."
—Brenna Yovanoff, *The Space Between*

"TRICK OR TREAT!" Driving through local neighborhoods during the fall, it is hard to miss the fact that Halloween is closing in on Christmas both in terms of popularity and also the sheer magnitude of yard displays. The pleasure taken in showcasing blatant evil surrounds us everywhere you look. Even to entice the most innocent among us.

And not just because we live in Washington, DC. It is everywhere across the United States. And frankly, here in our nation's capital most political figures tied to the occult at least maintain some level of discretion, hiding their true alliances from public view.

At least until they seek to impeach, let's say, a sitting president. Even making their announcement of the pursuit intentionally on October 31. It would get even worse if they were to privately threaten said president with treachery, leveraging said president to move out of their way or face consequences. Then finishing the threat with a smile, saying "Trick or Treat."

Most of the above story is recounted in our book *White House Watchmen*. A trusted congressional leader who read our book told us about the side conversation featuring the "trick or treat" threat. I have no reason to doubt this actually happened.

And it exposes a desperate need. Thank God Jolene has heard from the Lord to share keys to discern and overcome treachery and trickery. It's a defining issue of the end times.

The antichrist, for example, will be known for these character qualities.

DISCERNMENT—A BIRTHDAY GIFT IN A DREAM

Jolene here. As I contemplated the chapter I am to share with you, the Lord was very clear on the title. As I was praying one day, the Holy Spirit spoke the phrase "Treachery and Trickery—two of the enemy's greatest strategies in the end times." Of course, this might seem obvious. Especially for Jon and me as we live and minister in Washington, DC. It's always a little treacherous out there!

But the Bible is full of examples of both treachery and trickery, and we can learn greatly from the stories told within the Word. Our hope is that the instruction will help you sharpen your capacities to discern treachery and trickery before the scenarios are played out.

I want to begin with a very impacting dream that I had on the morning of August 15, 2017. I was so impacted by the dream that I woke up immersed in the presence of Holy Spirit. August 15 happens to be my birthday, and I found it very interesting that the Lord gave me this profound dream on that day.

The dream is about discernment. Many friends, including my husband, would say that the gift of discernment is one of my highest giftings. But through the dream the Lord gave me a much-needed upgrade. The Holy Spirit was instructing me personally in the dream on how to grow in discernment, especially for the end times.

Here's the scary part. The dream shows both the rise of a false church within the church, as well as infiltrators within what I will call the true church of Jesus today. Trickery and treachery were exposed throughout. It was obvious that a deliberate infiltration in the church by witches and witchcraft, along with a lack of understanding about it, was one of the key ways the enemy would seek to get over on us during the end times.

DREAM—FALSE CHURCH, TRUE CHURCH

Here is the dream. A large screen is showing two separate church services. The videos are playing side by side simultaneously, with a dividing line between them. As I viewed both services, a teacher is standing beside me and giving me encouragement and instruction throughout. Upon waking I immediately understood this Teacher to be Holy Spirit.

Each video frame is showing a separate church service and the camera is scanning the crowd inside the building. I see a woman whom I know very well, joined with a few of her friends and even a man she is dating. They are standing directly in the middle of the crowd. She somehow knows I am keenly watching her, and wants to draw my attention. The screen shows her quickly flashing a sign with my name on it, then hiding it, then flashing it again, trying to retain my attention. It is like she is inciting me with subliminal messages to focus on her church and her video portrayal.

Major questions—why did she want me to focus on her? Her church? How did she know beforehand I would be watching? What would I have otherwise seen and discerned?

The camera keeps showing screenshot after screenshot of the people inside both churches. Both scenarios are running side by side with a clear dividing line down the middle. I immediately have a distinct knowing that one screen represents the true church, and the other conveys a false church rising up that is working through enticement and trickery.

Interestingly my first reaction is fear of being deceived. My instructor keeps encouraging me that I will definitely know the difference between the two, and not to be afraid. I have been well-trained, and my discernment is keen, and I must trust it in a way that I have been instructed. But I am still a little uneasy because I recognize people on both sides of the split-screen, and some are very close to me.

While examining the crowd on each side, I comment to my teacher, "I hope the church on the left isn't the true church because I recognize people in the crowd that I had previously discerned were not operating in a right spirit."

He quickly replies to me, "You have discerned correctly—*there are infiltrators in the camp!*"

In the next scene I am surveying items on a table that are utilized for rituals in more traditional church services. My instructor continues to encourage me that I continue to see very clearly and it will be easy to know the difference between what is holy and what is unholy or idolatrous. I then wake up.

WHAT DOES THE BIBLE SAY?

I am reminded of many directives in Scripture on discernment. John the beloved warned:

> *Beloved, do not believe every spirit, but test the spirits to see whether they are from God, for many false prophets have gone out into the world. By this you know the Spirit of God: every spirit that confesses that Jesus Christ has come in the flesh is from God; and every spirit that does not confess Jesus is not from God; this is the spirit of the antichrist, which you have heard is coming, and now it is already in the world* (1 John 4:1-3 NASB).

The apostle Paul adds to the subject while addressing the "warfare church" he was overseeing in Ephesus:

> *That we should no longer be children, tossed to and fro and carried about with every wind of doctrine, by the trickery of men, in the cunning craftiness of deceitful plotting* (Ephesians 4:14 NKJV).

And to the Romans:

Now I urge you, brethren note those who cause divisions and offenses, contrary to the doctrine you learned and avoid them. For those who are such do not serve our Lord Jesus Christ, but their own belly, and by smooth words and flattering speech deceive the hearts of the simple (Romans 16:17-18 NKJV).

David learned discernment the hard way, as recorded in Psalm 55: *"...he violates his covenant. His talk is smooth as butter, yet war is in his heart..."* (Psalm 55:20-21 NIV).

I felt immediately the weight of importance the Lord placed on this dream. So I opened my computer to journal it. The screen saver immediately caught my attention. It was a picture of a beautiful fall day with a remote castle high on a hill, with a town encased in fog below. My first thought was that we need to remain in a place of clarity, above the fog!

The time on the screen caught my attention as well. The digital screen was flashing 7:47 continually. It was like the prophetic momentum from the dream continued as I wrote. This kind of experience does not happen to me often, but when it does I know to pay close attention to every detail being conveyed. I was reminded of a 747 jet that brings you to a higher view, way above the clouds. I also sensed the Lord was highlighting Psalm 7:4-7. So I retrieved my Bible to look it up. Psalm 7:6 (NKJV) says:

Arise O Lord, in Your anger; lift Yourself up because of the rage of my enemies; rise up for me to the judgment You have commanded!

When we come up higher and see the true picture of what is going on, we realize that the Lord is arising in a profound way, because of the raging of our enemy. Because of his treachery and trickery to deceive. God not only desires judgment. The language is strong and clear that He is commanding judgment!

The next verse in the psalm declares, *"Let the wickedness of the wicked come to an end, but establish the just..."* (Psalm 7:9 NKJV). This is a season when God is establishing the just! Establishing the true church while exposing and removing the false church.

Both scenarios in my dream are happening all around us. False churches rising up and also infiltrators among the true church. Infiltrators that need to be discerned, and sheep that need to be protected from them. Many in this end-time season are being trained by Holy Spirit to grow in love-saturated discernment regarding what is false on one hand and what has been planted among us to distract and destroy all that is true.

EXPOSING THE BETRAYER

In prayer that same morning, I heard the Lord reiterating to me that He is bringing exposure to those who remain set on intentionally betraying the people of God through their treachery. He grieves over betrayal. He feels it deeply and knows that ultimately it is a betrayal of Him also. I continue to feel His heart to establish the just, and to judge those who are set on wickedness in this time.

Exposing betrayal is always a delicate matter, to say the least. Years ago the Lord taught Jon and me how to partner with Him to release His exposure—by taking communion as a prophetic action. The direction came in the midst of my most powerful prophetic encounter.

COMMUNION— EXPOSING THE BETRAYER

Jolene received this unusual word and assignment regarding the exposure of betrayal during a prophetic experience in August 2017, just before we launched our second Glory Train journey. The public focus of the Glory Train project was seeing the restoration of God's glory. But we also carried a private assignment—all across the continent. The story was first recounted in our book *Midnight Cry*.

The Lord showed Jolene we needed to receive communion at every stop along the way of our tour, declaring that God was covenantally releasing the exposure of systemic, intentional betrayal within the body of Christ and our world.

We carried this focus privately from coast to coast, and then we continued the project publicly with the Lamplighter family.

It is interesting that Hugh Hefner died the very day we completed our national journey, rolling into California. Soon betrayal at the highest levels began to be exposed almost every day, from the backrooms of Washington's most powerful offices to the casting couches of Hollywood's most prominent actors and producers. Harvey Weinstein and Michael Epstein made headlines.

Many victims of sex abuse came out of the shadows afterward. Exposing rape, even pedophilia, by Hollywood producers and actors. Soon after, extraordinary cover-ups of indiscretions by the Clintons, Congressional leaders, and other DC players also began to be exposed. For months following.

As we have already chronicled, in 2024 we have experienced another round of God's redemptive exposure, this time primarily within the body of Christ.

TURNING THE TABLES, EXPOSING THE BETRAYER

The following is Jolene's prophetic experience, in her own words.

I (Jolene) was at my prayer group in Frederick, Maryland, where I had the following experience.

It was early August, right before we started the second tour of the Glory Train. It was a very intense day of prayer and many women showed up on this particular day that usually for one reason or another can't usually come. So we had noted that there were 11 of us that day, which became very important later in this experience.

The prayer group was praying for North Korea at the time but I was silently asking the Lord to heal some pain in my feet that I had been experiencing. I was holding my feet up off the ground when I felt the actual presence of Jesus Himself entering the room. As in most experiences, it is hard to convey what happens in the supernatural but I will do my best.

PROPHETIC EXPERIENCE— JESUS WASHING FEET

In my experience, Jesus lifted my feet up and began to wash them, which was a very humbling experience. Exactly at that time I had the very same sense that Peter had that I should be washing His feet not the other way around. Then in the spirit the entire conversation with Peter, recorded as part of Christ's Last Supper, began to play out with the Lord. When I began to protest, He said "What I am doing you do not understand now, but you will know after this." I have read this account many times but the exact wording of the John 13 scenario played out between me and Jesus. Please read the passage through. Here's how it begins:

> *During supper, the devil having already put into the heart of Judas Iscariot, the son of Simon, to betray Him, Jesus, knowing that the Father had given all things into His hands, and that He had come forth from God and was going back to God, got up from supper and laid His outer garments aside; and He took a towel and tied it around Himself. Then He poured water into the basin, and began washing the disciples' feet...* (John 13:2-5 NASB).

THE LAST SUPPER—COMMUNION

While reading John 13, there also seemed to be a supernatural illumination of the Word as I got to the part where Jesus is sharing communion with His disciples. I then felt led to take communion with the 11 women in the room just like Jesus did at His Last Supper (see Matthew 26:17-40; Mark 14:12-26; Luke 22:7-38). But I also became aware that the same communion that drew the 11 true disciples to Jesus was also what the Lord used to expose Judas as His betrayer.

I love how Luke records this moment:

> *And he took bread, and when he had given thanks, he broke it and gave it to them, saying, "This is my body, which is given for you. Do this in remembrance of me." And likewise the cup after they had eaten, saying, "This cup that is poured out for you is the new covenant in my blood. But behold, the hand of him who betrays me is with me on the table. For the Son of*

Man goes as it has been determined, but woe to that man by whom he is betrayed!" (Luke 22:19-22 ESV)

PROPHETIC ACTION—
EXTENDING THE BREAD

So in a prophetic act I felt to call in all the true disciples of the Lord with communion. To gather, as it were, the 11 faithful disciples to Jesus.

I then felt to also extend the same bread and wine to those who are in the midst of betraying Jesus. I felt Jesus was using me to be His hands and His heart at that time. It was one of the most powerful communions I have ever taken, and I felt a very grave sense that much had shifted in the spirit realm and the betrayal of the enemy even through human agents would begin to be exposed in many situations and in the nation. Some will repent. But there are some betrayers who are sold out infiltrators, committed to the enemy's work.

And I knew the Lord was calling us to receive communion across the nation on the Glory Train. From city to city, this was to be a private witness before Heaven that those sold out to betrayal must now be exposed.

I feel that the most important thing the Lord asked us to do on the Glory Train was to take communion across America with this focus. And to take it exactly the way He told me during my experience at the prayer group. Drawing the 11 faithful to Jesus. And extending the bread to expose those who are intentionally betraying Christ's heart and cause at this time, both in His body and in our nation.

The purging actually begins with us. If we were truthful, each of us has unredeemed pockets of betrayal in our own hearts. Can your

> **The purging actually begins with us.**

loyalty to Jesus be bought or sold? Let's ask God to create in us a clean heart, and renew a right spirit within us.

The Lord showed Jon that the Table of the Lord is the highest Court in the Kingdom of God. Please approach the Bench, seeking the Lord for the willful betrayers to become exposed. Jesus desires to advance us beyond the sabotage the enemy has planned.

TREACHERY OR TRICKERY— WHAT'S THE DIFFERENCE?

Differentiating between treachery and trickery is very important. Trickery is simply employing deception to get a person to believe or take action on something that they otherwise would have discerned. In fact, deception, duplicity, guile, and cunning are all synonyms.

Treachery is obviously much more debilitating than trickery. It involves intimate betrayal that takes advantage of a person's love and trust. In many ways, unrepentant acts of trickery can lead to treachery.

You may wonder why we are differentiating so strongly between treachery and trickery. But trickery can be done by any one person to another, whereas treachery is generally much more intimate. The goal is not just to deceive but to intentionally destroy, generally through a betrayal of trust or covenant commitment, in order to take advantage of the person for selfish gain.

The antichrist, for instance, is identified in the Bible as the ultimate expression of treachery:

By his treachery he will succeed through deceit. He will have an arrogant attitude, and he will destroy many who are unaware of his schemes. He will rise up against the Prince of princes, yet he will be broken apart—but not by human agency (Daniel 8:25 New English Translation).

Trickery may be a careless act, while treachery is a planned deception by someone plotting your destruction while smiling in your face. In Psalm 55, King David puts it this way:

For it is not an enemy who reproaches me; then I could bear it. Nor is it one who hates me who has exalted himself against me, then I could hide myself from him. But it is you, a man my equal, my companion and my familiar friend. We took sweet fellowship together walked in the house of God in the throng (Psalm 55:12-14 NASB1995).

Let me simplify this verse for you. We went to church together. We became friends. I looked to you for advice and direction. By every appearance you loved and served the Lord, but then your betrayal came out of nowhere. Jolene's version!

David then brings out a key for discerning hidden treachery. Covenant-breaking is at the core of the treacherous:

He has put forth his hand against those who were at peace with him; he has broken his covenant. The words of his mouth were smoother than butter, but war was in his heart... (Psalm 55:20-21 NKJV).

...Rouse yourself to punish all of the nations; spare none of those who treacherously plot evil (Psalm 59:5 ESV).

Evil pretenders, even in churches and ministries, treacherously plot evil. They plan out evil, strategizing ways to take advantage of

God's covenant people, and even ensnare them. We're talking far more than just our sin nature slipping up in a weak moment. They plan the malicious evil, playing on the trust of the other in order to deceive. Intent is everything.

As we have shared, a perfect example of treachery is Judas, who walked intimately with Jesus for years. He then betrayed Him with a kiss. It was intimate betrayal at the core. The most intimate of actions.

> *My enemies speak evil of me: "When will he die and his name perish?" And if he comes to see me, he speaks lies; his heart gathers iniquity to itself; when he goes out, he tells it* (Psalm 41:5-6 NKJV).

Let's ponder this statement for a moment. The enemy you consider your friend is speaking evil against you. He is pondering your demise and your ultimate death. And then he is bold enough to come see you and speak lies to your face. This is where the Bible begins to talk about your hardened heart. All those actions have hardened your heart to the point that the Word says your heart gathers the iniquity to itself at that point.

Look out! Because iniquity is a pattern of personal sin or generational sin which defines us, becomes part of us. Iniquity is the darkness that lives inside you, and this Scripture says that your heart begins to gather iniquity to you. Which leads to the next level of sin that the psalm says is the direct cursing of the person by whispering against the person and devising their hurt! They speak death and disease over their "friend"!

This portion of Scripture about betrayal ends in verse 9 (NKJV): *"Even my own familiar friend in whom I trusted, who ate my bread, has lifted up his heel against me."* Again, a direct prophecy about Judas betraying Jesus brings clarity on the intimate betrayal of the ugliest kind. And unfortunately we will see this more and more in the days ahead.

> *Woe to those who devise* [plan] *iniquity, and work out evil on their beds! At morning light they practice it, because it is in the power of their hand. They covet fields and take them by violence, also houses and seize them. So they oppress a man and his house, a man and his inheritance* (Micah 2:1-2 NKJV).

What is the end game in all this? Heightening our discernment is vital not only to differentiate between the true and the false, but to raise up a standard against it, just as the Lord showed me in my dream.

After all, deception is at the very core of the warnings given in the Word of God. Genesis begins with the serpent deceiving Eve, and it ends with false prophets, false christs arising to lead us astray. Their treacherous intent is to steal, kill, and destroy—to drain our time, our resources, and most of all our destinies.

Just like we have conveyed throughout this book, we are in a battle between the Spirit of God and the spirit of the antichrist. We must come up higher, recognize treachery as a threat, and take actions to test and discern the true from the false.

Matthew 24:24 (NKJV) puts it this way:

> *For false christs and false prophets will rise and show great signs and wonders* **to deceive***, if possible, even the elect.*
>
> *The coming of the lawless one is according to the working of Satan, with all power, signs, and lying wonders* (2 Thessalonians 2:9 NKJV).

*You are of your father the devil, and the desires of your father you want to do. He was a murderer from the beginning, **and does not stand in the truth**, because there is no truth in him. When he speaks a lie, he speaks from his own resources, for he is a liar, and the father of it* (John 8:44 NKJV).

DISCERNING DECEPTION

So how do you grow in discerning the treacherous, to protect yourselves and those you care about? That's a good question. Gaining solid training and good solid practice. *"But solid food is for the mature,"* writes the apostle Paul, *"who because of practice have their senses trained to distinguish between good and evil"* (Hebrews 5:14 NASB).

Note that the apostle John warned the Ephesian church of losing their lampstand of first-love devotion. Why were they in this precarious position? Among other reasons, they likely became hardened by the necessary efforts to test the authenticity of fellow church leaders.

I know your deeds and your labor and perseverance, and that you cannot tolerate evil people, and you have put those who call themselves apostles to the test, and they are not, and you found them to be false; and you have perseverance and have endured on account of My name, and have not become weary (Revelation 2:2-3 NASB).

Note Jesus referred to their intolerance of evil people and continuing efforts to persevere in discerning as "deeds." He further commended them for developing standards and investigating to discern true apostles from the false.

That's pretty heavy, right?

But it's needed. Church abuse is skyrocketing. Often the guilty are re-released into their positions without genuinely being restored. And the cycle unfortunately only perpetuates itself.

John the Baptist demanded that those who seek forgiveness must bear the fruit of repentance (Matthew 3:8). Love. Forgive. But do not shy away from testing the long-term fruit of a person's life.

How can you pray? Three Scriptures come to mind. The first, of course, is Psalm 91. Lord, deliver us from the snares of the trapper!

The second Scripture comes from the apostle Paul who was facing down extreme treachery by forces opposed to the gospel. They actually wanted to take his life. Paul wrote a powerful prayer seeking deliverance from unreasonable and wicked or treacherous men. God will answer it on your behalf!

> *Finally, brethren, pray for us, that the word of the Lord may run swiftly and be glorified, just as it is with you, and that **we may be delivered from unreasonable and wicked men**; for not all have faith. But the Lord is faithful, who will **establish you and guard you** from the evil one* (2 Thessalonians 3:1-3 NKJV).

The third Scripture is a secret passage that I've prayed almost every day since discovering it. You must learn to invoke God's covenantal protection over your lives, and this is an incredible promise.

> *The covenant that I have made with you, you shall not forget, nor shall you fear other gods. But the Lord your God you shall fear; and He will deliver you from the hand of all your enemies* (2 Kings 17:38-39 NKJV).

Pray these prayers! You will find God engaging with you not only to discern trickery and treachery but to overcome them.

THE VOICE OF THE VICTIMS— VATICAN ENCOUNTER

Jon here. I want to close with a final story, originally published in our book *White House Watchmen.* It is an astonishing example of how the Lord moves through intercession to expose and overcome treachery. And most of all, how He hears the cries of those who have been victimized.

I was walking a few steps ahead of Jolene as we toured the Vatican Museum, the Sistine Chapel, and Saint Peter's Basilica. She lagged farther and farther behind. When I looked back, she was hardly moving. A fountain of tears was gushing from her eyes. She could barely even talk.

"As we've been walking, Holy Spirit opened my ears," she stammered. "And I heard the screams of the children who were abused by priests. They are echoing through these halls. I cannot get away from them!"

For more than an hour, walking through the halls of the Vatican, Jolene had entered into full-blown travailing prayer for these children. She heard their cries. She could feel their fear and pain, even children through previous ages who had suffered abuse.

The rest of the group had to stop and wait. For good reason. Really, Holy Spirit had taken the lead.

Again and again, I sent friends to walk alongside Jolene to speed her progress. And again and again, Holy Spirit came upon each one with a solemn, overwhelming travail so heavy that they themselves would nearly collapse. None of them were seeking it. Obviously, it was not protocol. And yet it was happening.

In the Sistine Chapel, the intensity of their intercession had dissipated, and my eyes were free to take in the priceless paintings adorning the ceilings and walls.

But when we entered Saint Peter's Basilica, the travail began again with great intensity. A few nuns gathered at a distance, watching. The Vatican police were not far behind. I decided a conversation was in order.

"This woman, she is your wife?" asked a cloistered nun in broken English.

I nodded.

"What then is wrong with your wife. Is she okay?"

"She is having an experience with God," I replied, my mind racing to find common ground. "Kind of like the mystics, the contemplatives who had visitations of Him."

A visitation at Saint Peter's Basilica, that they could understand— and even appreciate. Their countenances brightened.

"Ah, this is like Saint Catherine of Sienna, yes? Or Saint Theresa of Avila?"

"Perhaps, Sister. Jolene is often prone to visionary experiences like them. But probably not like this. While we were walking, the Lord Jesus opened her ears, and she began to hear the cries of children who have been abused by priests. She heard their pleas for help. Nothing like this has ever happened to her."

The two nuns stared back at me, wide-eyed.

"I don't know if this makes any sense."

The Sisters generously suggested we let Jolene and the other women alone until the experience with God subsided. Then it would be time to leave.

About five months later, Pope Francis made a very courageous statement during a Vatican summit to counter child abuse: "Our work has made us realize once again that the gravity of the scourge of the sexual abuse of minors is, and historically has been, a widespread phenomenon in all cultures and societies," he said. "I am reminded of the cruel religious practice, once widespread in certain cultures, of sacrificing human beings—frequently children—in pagan rites."

What he shared next brought tears.

"The echo of the silent cry of the little ones who, instead of finding in them fathers and spiritual guides encountered tormentors, will shake hearts dulled by hypocrisy and by power," Pope Francis exclaimed. "It is our duty to pay close heed to this silent, choked cry."[6]

Intercession permeated the atmosphere and declarations from Heaven paved the way for much-needed repentance. Pope Francis displayed the impact in his own profound, humble words—and even more, his very courageous stand he took. Isn't that what prayer is all about? We don't wrestle against flesh and blood but against powers and principalities. One declaration from Heaven perhaps changed hearts and even the public stand of the pope.

We all must be humbled by the fact that the cries of the victims are still resounding before Heaven's Court. Whether the courts of earth ever hold the perpetrators accountable or not, there is one Judge they will stand before, whose verdict they will by no means be able to evade. Not after death, and not even in this life.

In fact, Exodus 3:7 conveys how God convened a special hearing to hear the cries of His afflicted. He rendered judgment against both the demonic principalities and the governmental authorities who abused His covenant people.

The Ancient of Days "heard their cry" and remembered His covenant. The word *heard* is actually *shema*, a word conveying a courtroom hearing. He held Court and brought the cries and groanings of His people into the hearing. He reviewed each case with great focus and great intentionality. Then He rendered a verdict. The dramatic exodus of His covenant people was initiated.

What should terrify us the most is that the Lord hears the cries of all victims of abuse, even those in the womb. He responds. And in the rendering of God's verdict, *their voice prevails.*

WHO WILL RISE UP FOR ME AGAINST EVILDOERS?

Jolene here again. My deepest desire is that we all grow in discernment in this hour. With the increase in discernment, our prayers can affect great change. From our home, our neighborhood, the nation and sometimes even the Vatican and whole religious structures. After all, Psalm 94:16 (NKJV) asks this question: *"Who will rise up for me against the evildoers? Who will stand up for me against the workers of iniquity?"*

If I could point out my one mandate in ministry, it would be this: raising up an army of people who will stand. My dream I shared in the beginning and my experiences throughout my walk solidify my calling, but the Lord wants to add many more warriors to this end-time army. He is training us each right now. Join us in the fight. Also find other ministries that provide training and join a group that will allow you to come along in their training exercises.

After all, the end times has definitely intersected with REAL TIME. We must be prepared!

STUDY QUESTIONS AND PRAYER

1. Where do you perceive treachery or trickery in your sphere? The church? The political world? How has it affected you?

2. Based on this chapter, what do you feel you can do to counter the treachery? What is stopping you? How is your prayer focus going to change?

3. Have you ever been betrayed? By whom—a loved one or guardian? A spouse? A leader? How has the betrayal affected your outlook? How are you pursuing healing?

4. Have you ever received a warning dream from the Lord? A vision or a prophetic word? How did you respond? How did you pray? Did the warning come to pass?

5. What steps are you now taking to sharpen your discernment?

Father God, thank You for Your overarching protection in my life. Help me now to become a protector, made in Your image. Grant me an increase of the spiritual gift of discernment by Your Holy Spirit. Help me to perceive and overcome hidden treachery, stopping the enemy's work before it is enacted.

And Lord, I ask that You expose and overcome hidden treachery and trickery within our churches, within our school boards, all the way to the corridors of power in Washington, DC. I sign up to stand with You against evildoers. Help me to take action. Help me to pray. Help my prayers to prevail! In Jesus' name, amen.

NOTE

6. "Address of His Holiness Pope Francis at the End of the Eucharistic Concelebration," *Vatican.va;* February 24, 2019; https://www.vatican .va/content/francesco/en/speeches/2019/february/documents/papa -francesco_20190224_incontro-protezioneminori-chiusura.html#:~:text =The%20echo%20of%20the%20silent%20cry%20of%20the,pay%20 close%20heed%20to%20this%20silent%2C%20choked%20cry; accessed October 17, 2024.

Award-winning photo of a tornado hovering over the Colorado
State capital building in Denver, Colorado, June 15, 1988.

CHAPTER 14

TURN THE STORM:

END-TIME PERIL, END-TIME GLORY

"That this Nation, under God, shall have a new birth of freedom."

—Abraham Lincoln, Gettysburg Address,

amid the storm of Civil War

TICK TOCK TO THE HOLY CLOCK! It's midnight on October 7, 2024. Actually, 12:12 am. You could say the book *End Times in Real Time* is being birthed. It certainly still needs some editing, some cleaning up. But as implausible as it seems, the writing process has come down to the final chapter in the midnight hour.

Maybe it's not a coincidence we are midway between Rosh Hashanah and Yom Kippur at this very time. Our pleas of teshuvah remain. May we all—all who read this—receive a better verdict than our actions alone deserve!

Through the transaction of reading, our journey has been woven together with yours. To the extent you allow, it has become yours. You are being enriched by the lessons learned. But please also note that Holy Spirit is imparting to you more than you are currently aware. The spirit and power of Elijah is mantling you for both present realities and for the future.

THE OVERCOMER'S MANTLE

Once again, "to Him who overcomes I will give...." Grades are given according to scholastic achievement. Promotions are gained through hard work, loyalty, and innovation. The highest level of warriors endure the harshest conditions, learn teamwork, push far beyond the peak of their endurance, and attain mastery over skills they never imagined they would need. Now their lives depend on it.

So do yours.

Jolene and I hope this book has equipped you in a similar way. You too are fashioned as an overcomer. To stand at the threshold between success and capitulation, and to gain the victory.

> ...*Run in such a way that you may win* (1 Corinthians 9:24 NASB).

You live in the end times. As promised, it's hard. Even perilous. But when God dreamed your life into being for this very hour, He fashioned no limitations on your potential. He created you to overcome. And He has opened new doors of access to you, both for revelation and authority from His Throne.

You're a lot like Elijah. His name means "The Lord is God." Yet the book of James describes the prophet *"as a man with a nature like ours"* (James 5:17 NASB). Elijah was not really Elijah until he became Elijah. He was a virtual unknown, an overlooked commodity who dared to allow God to refine him, mature him, to provoke him in the privacy of the wilderness until his very nature became a mirror of his name.

And then Elijah suddenly came on the scene.

Can I offer you some advice? Embrace your wilderness seasons. Cling to the Lord through them. Know Him more. Get everything you can get from the training He is investing in you. And do not stop until your nature begins to reflect His nature. Run your race to win and you will gain the mantle.

It will become a defining moment. Your life, your essence will be infused with power from on high to prepare the way of the Lord. Both by creating storms and by turning them.

OCTOBER 7—STORMS ON TWO FRONTS

Two storms are growing exponentially even as I write. A tropical depression has just become a category 5 hurricane, and is now barreling toward the west coast of Florida. Also word just broke that America is coordinating with Israel on a major retaliation against Iran, opening the possibility even of global war.

Last week the darkened skies above the Temple Mount again lit up with bombs bursting in air, actually while we were live-streaming our Turnaround Tuesday broadcast. A fresh barrage of Iranian cruise missiles had been fired.

As with the April barrage, most were intercepted in mid-air. This immense takedown was even more miraculous than the April 14 launch because this time every cruise missile made it from Iran to Israel in only 12 minutes flat.

It is said that American diplomats have been working behind the scenes to prevent an all-out conflict. Of course, many in the communities that direct American policy privately say Iran has crossed a red line and that destroying the nation's nuclear capacities is not just warranted but now mandated. From our watchman's perch over the Pentagon and Washington, DC, it is sobering to realize that Iran's nuclear threshold, which we warned about at Yad Vashem, has seemingly been crossed. And the same enriched uranium now threatening Israel also threatens America.

COVERT OPS FROM THE THRONE

Who was it that wrote about perilous times in the last days? It seems the apostle Paul knew what he was talking about. That said, just because we don't see Israel's attack doesn't mean it's not happening. Israel has proven extraordinarily capable in covert operations.

You know, when it comes down to it, God Himself has also proven very capable at covert operations as well. Jesus' birth in a humble manger was right under King Herod's sight line. Talk about treachery. Herod told the religious authorities he desired to bless the child. In reality he sought to kill him. But God trumped Herod every step of the way. And He is doing so with the Herods of our day as well.

I am also reminded of revivalist Charles Finney's words that "Revival is a divine attack upon society." Just because we don't fully see God's awakening yet does not mean it is not actually here. As in the days of Jesus' birth, the birth of this new movement is already being tracked by those who would like to abolish it.

Or more accurately, abort it.

VISION OF GOD'S GLORY

Ezekiel saw the governmental glory of God. The cyclone rotation of a massive tornado wrapped around a pillar of holy fire that connected the Throne of God to earth. Lightning flashed. Currents of ethereal fire struck with precision. Angelic beings ascended and descended. Heaven's atmosphere pushed through the portal with a force that toppled human beings face-down in holy awe, the way trees fall in a storm.

In the center was a divine Being. Ezekiel describes Him as "one like the Son of Man." The nations are His by inheritance. Peace and war are under His domain. A vast covering extends from His Throne to all who love Him and call on His name.

God called to Ezekiel:

> *Son of man, do you see what they are doing, the great abomi-nations…* [they] *are committing, so that I would be far from My sanctuary?* (Ezekiel 8:6 NASB)

Far from His own sanctuary. Do you feel the heartbreak within these words?

We imagine that we need to strive to persuade God to come. It's exactly the opposite. The Lord yearns to be with His people, to display His majesty and glory. It's our sin that separates us, not His desire. Idolatry is an abomination that causes desolation.

Ezekiel saw the glory of God hovering over the Temple. A graven image was placed defiantly at the gateway of God's governmental threshold, mocking Israel's true King as if the enemy's heinous seduction had actually prevailed. The priests bowed their knee. The prophets became profane. The shepherds abused. The people became defiled.

The covenant had been broken, seeming beyond repair. As the prophet Hosea perceived, God Himself had issued a decree of divorce. Suddenly the glory lifted.

> *I will go away and return to My place until they acknowledge their guilt and seek My face; in their distress they will search for Me* (Hosea 5:15 NASB).

And yet there was a turnaround. It took a while. But when Jesus bore the cross to redeem mankind, a new way forward was opened. Heaven, hell, and earth had no option but to submit!

Jesus went to the Father. Holy Spirit was sent to dwell with God's people once again. And during Shavuot, or Pentecost, the tornadic tempest of God's governmental glory rushed through Jerusalem's streets for the first time in centuries.

But this time the Temple was bypassed. Instead, the Spirit of God came as a mighty rushing wind, with tongues of fire bursting forth, to the upper room where the disciples were gathered to pray. They were filled with the Holy Spirit—the very glory of God.

From the well of glory, tongues of fire burst forth from within each disciple. They spoke in other tongues, as the Spirit gave utterance.

Meanwhile all Jerusalem heard the roar of this supernatural wind. Men and women from every region of the Mideast gathered. *"And they were bewildered because each one of them was hearing them speak in his own tongue"* while the disciples were exercising their newfound prayer language (Acts 2:6). A fisherman named Peter, a vibrant man who had just been restored after stumbling through Jesus' last days, arose to address the crowd.

The church was birthed. And a new era called the end times was inaugurated.

> *But this is what was spoken by the prophet Joel: "And it shall come to pass in the last days, says God, that I will pour out of My Spirit on all flesh; your sons and your daughters shall prophesy, your young men shall see visions, your old men shall dream dreams. And on My menservants and on My maidservants I will pour out My Spirit in those days; and they shall prophesy. I will show wonders in heaven above and signs in the earth beneath: blood and fire and vapor of smoke. The sun shall be turned into darkness, and the moon into blood, before the coming of the great and awesome day of the Lord. And it shall come to pass that whoever calls on the name of the Lord shall be saved" (Acts 2:16-21 NKJV).*

Beloved, never ever forget that the biblical epoch known as the end times was inaugurated in glory. It was birthed in glory—the restoration of the very glory of God. Though the third Person of the Trinity has many times withdrawn, He has never left. And as we move closer to the final hours of this same epoch, the sound of the mighty rushing wind is again drawing close. Like a train on the edge of town, you can discern His proximity. But soon the alarm will be right at your door.

Again—the epoch known as the end times was birthed in glory. And it will crescendo in glory.

But for this to occur, you and I are being called to prepare the way for the restoration of His glory from region to region, and from even nation to nation. In fact, succeeding in this aspect of the forerunner call equips His church for the final thrust—to prepare the way for Christ's coming.

Just don't forget His glory comes as a storm. Mighty rushing winds are hard to control. So don't.

DISCERNING GOD'S MOVE

> The epoch known as the end times was birthed in glory. And it will crescendo in glory.

Most Christians simply don't realize that the manifest glory of God rarely remains stationary on earth. He comes and goes. Revivals flare and wane. But Holy Spirit is never haphazard, random, or reckless. Covenant is always involved, either by alignment or by breaches. To serve as real-time prophets discerning the times, we must understand the movements of the glory of God. Why does He come? Why does He withdraw? How can we compel Him to stay?

Like Ezekiel, we must become Throne Room watchmen. Like Hosea, we must become watchmen of God's covenant. Hopefully the journey we have taken together has taught you and equipped you to grow into a new synergy with Holy Spirit, a partnership from the heart.

For His glory.

So what's ahead? In many ways the future is ours to define together. In this midnight hour, our lamps are burning with fresh fire. It's time to prepare the way. And it's time to see God's glory restored. Our heart right now is simply to invite you to take this journey with us.

Make sure you sign up on our website so we can stay in touch. And let's run together!

THE TURNAROUND ANOINTING

The spirit and power of Elijah is a turnaround anointing. And it's going to define much of God's work through the days ahead. Man's limitations will soon become crystal clear. But God will accomplish what we cannot alone attain. He will complete the turnaround that He initiated.

As covered earlier, the Elijah anointing encompasses two facets of turnaround. The first is what is described in Daniel 7:21-22, as judgment is rendered in favor of the saints and the time comes for the saints to possess the Kingdom. We've covered this facet very thoroughly in our last book, *Turnaround Decrees,* as well as sharing about it here.

As you already know, the second facet of the turnaround anointing is teshuvah. Turning the hearts of the fathers to the children, the children to the fathers, and the sons of the covenant back to the Lord their God. Repent and return, so that your sins may be washed away. Why? So that times of refreshing may come from the presence of the Lord (Acts 3:19).

The word *refreshing* by the way is quite something. On the 2001 prayer journey through the US Northeast, I learned something about this from Dutch Sheets. Really I had no choice because he preached Acts 3:19 in every city we went to, at a very high volume. Sooner or later I was bound to catch on.

The Greek word for *refreshing* is *anapsyxis.* It's a compound word. And it actually means "recovery of breath." Or you could say "the blowing again of the breath of God."

Beloved, the winds of God are about to blow again.

Funny thing about a whirlwind or a tornado. It's a turnaround wind. A revolution. Get caught up in the rotation and you'll invariably come up higher!

WHIRLWINDS OF REVOLUTION— CHUCK PIERCE PROPHECY

Chuck Pierce gave a wild prophecy about whirlwinds and revolution during our 2018 Revolution gathering in Washington, DC:

> Revolution is an interesting word. Because it can mean overthrow. Revolution can have an interesting meaning. It can have a meaning with connotations of rebellion. Our nation without it having revolution in its bloodstream, I don't think we would have ever changed. There's a cry of revolution that's rising up in body of Christ, I'm not sure it's just a governmental cry. Because revolution can have another meaning also. It can mean a WHIRLWIND THAT CREATES A NEW CYCLE.
>
> Revolution says to us there are lots of incredible whirlwinds on the way. And remember Job heard the Lord in the whirlwind. So we're going to have to listen for the Lord in ways we have never listened for Him before…
>
> It's time to break out of conventional ways of thinking. There's a lot of intense conflict, intensity going on. As in Daniel 7 there's this amazing conflict going on in the atmosphere. Ancient of Days is beginning

to come into His position. The enemy is speaking and wearing down the saints. Causing mindsets, ways of thinking to grow weary. Then all the sudden Ancient of Days comes in.

We had to be worn out! Too much understanding of what we wanted. Therefore without us being worn out, we won't be able to see the Ancient of Days make His judgment. We are now in process to see new decrees come into position. It came from a wearing-down season of thought processes.

This is what's hard with DC. We have to see a GLORY STRUCTURE get established. Something representing His people established in the city. So wine forming after 7 years pressed out, we can go into fields we've never gone into before.

Wine forming seven years pressed out. Not quite sure what that means. But we are actively seeking to see a "throne of glory" established in Washington, DC. The fact that Chuck even prophesied into 2025 from 2018 is stunning to me. Because March 4, 2025 marked the publication date of this book, which the Lord asked us to write to convey the inauguration of a new era of history. *End Times in Real Time.*

Let me share one more portion of Chuck's Revolution word that you will find interesting:

God gave us this land, God will judge us according to stewardship of this land, He will judge us based upon righteous rule we bring into this land. He will judge us on how we multiply resources of this land.

God looks at that! When you look at judgment in the New Testament, judgment usually revolves around resistance to Holy Spirit, and when you've been given resources and don't multiply them.

The Lord says, we must see turnaround in multiplication of resources, find resources that have never been uncovered, and we must bring down the sound of Heaven to uncover the resources. And you're going to see a lot of new resources coming…

We are now battling confederations of demonic structures. We're not just dealing with a stronghold. And if you think you're just dealing with a stronghold, that was last season. This is a confederation where you see strongholds have aligned together forming a chord of resistance. It's just like a resistant strain that antibodies won't touch.

And you have to understand we must define our confederations from state to state. States in alignment, states not in alignment. What it take to bring states into alignment. Move of God in every state. Freedom outposts, glory gatherings, when this movement would hit freedom outposts, people will come in one way and come out seven times brighter!

And He showed me after Mr. Trump came into office, there was a determinedness by the Lord to RESET THE COURSE OF COVENANT WORLDWIDE—using this nation which has been the strongest covenant nation in the world. Whether you like it or don't like it, it has been. So it was amazing to see the realignment of Israel, Jerusalem from

America actually… Father we say Your goodness is about to rule across the land from this city. We say let realignment penetrate. Your mercy endures forever![7]

SEVEN PRIORITIES THIS SEASON

Given these prophetic words about glory meetings locally and nationally, and resetting the course of covenant worldwide, let me share some insider information. The following are a few key focuses for Lamplighters in 2025 and beyond.

1. Shining the Lamp from Washington, DC!

Beginning on inauguration day, expect both conflict and glory from our nation's capital as the future of our nation is framed. We continue serving as advisors, providing prophetic counsel, and prayer, etc. One overarching goal remains. Let this City on a Hill again become a Light to the Nations!

As part of these efforts, Jolene and I are bolstering our home fellowship and ministry headquarters—first to welcome God's governmental glory, second to better accommodate the demand for a safe place for leaders to connect and grow in Jesus. Our home also serves as an ambassadorial house, hosting high-level meetings as well as quarterly prophetic roundtables. But first and foremost, we want it to become a throne of glory!

Even given our best efforts locally, collaborating with you is what actually gets the job done! So we look forward to taking this journey together. Jolene and I will continue to provide resources for the body of Christ with key prophetic insights through broadcasts, postings, prayer calls, etc. Online teachings are also in production. Let's roll!

2. Burning Lamp Alliance

We have just launched a new collaborative partnership to empower you, featuring virtual prayer calls and more. Let's make covenant great again! We together are given a sacred task of rekindling this holy fire within the body of Christ during very challenging times. Our combined efforts will continue to impact the White House, Congress, our military and diplomatic communities, and our nation, first through watchman prayer.

And let's not forget Israel. Burning lamps for Zion's sake!

Resourcing is key and mandates a mutual investment. To meet the challenges, we have developed a vital new partnership program. You can find information on our website. Let's take this journey together!

3. Redeem America

Our broadcasts and prayer focus continue into 2026, partnering locally and nationally to see the covenant blessing and freedoms originally ordained for us secured once again. It's time to restore God's covenant covering in our nation. That's how we legitimately regain the title of One Nation under God.

4. Harvest Wars! Contending for Next-Gen Awakening

Yes there is a harvest war. Turning the hearts of the parents to their children and children to their parents is vital to redeem America from the X-out we have largely succumbed to. The good news is that Jesus is moving at a very high level to reveal Himself to your sons and daughters! Our prayer mobilization continues. Be sure to join us for Turnaround Tuesday broadcasts at 1 p.m. each Tuesday. And let's see God bring a turnaround!

5. Lampstand Summits

Jolene and I look forward to partnering with you, along with local churches across the nation, for weekend summits featuring End Times in Real Time, with an overarching focus on seeing God renew our burning lamps. It's time for God's mantle to be imparted. The Lord is raising up a new breed of spiritual revolutionaries who will keep their lamps lit and their vision set for Jesus as the end times progress.

6. Spirit of Elijah Tours—United States

Over the next two years at least, we will be hosting Spirit of Elijah convocations nationwide. Cindy Jacobs actually prophesied to us about a Spirit of Elijah tour in America that would usher in the next phase of God's revival, with miracles, signs, and wonders. She prophesied, it's time to ride. Beginning in 2025, it's time to get onboard!

Jolene and I will be joined by Chris Mitchell Jr., Ed "Wattage" Watts, Jamie Fitt, and others for these key regional gatherings. More information coming soon.

As part of these gatherings we will also be hosting regional prophetic roundtables. I feel it's important to model roundtables that genuinely engage Heaven and unlock real-time revelation critical to the areas we are visiting. Preparing people to prepare the way!

7. Redeem the Times! Major Announcement

I believe Chuck Pierce's word. God is determined to reset the course of covenant worldwide. Tick tock to the holy clock! And we've got some resetting to do.

May 2025 marks the 1700th anniversary of the Council of Nicaea, convened by the emperor Constantine. At Constantine's direction, the council decided to essentially divorce Christianity from our covenantal, Hebraic roots and plant the movement in the idolatry-laden soil of ancient Greece and Rome. So much syncretism has defiled our true faith as a result.

"It was declared to be particularly unworthy for, the holiest of all festivals (Passover), to follow the custom of the Jews, who had soiled their hands with the most fearful of crimes, and whose minds were blinded," declared Constantine to the Council of Nicaea. "We ought not, therefore, to have anything in common with the Jews, … [but] to separate ourselves from the detestable company of the Jews, for it is truly shameful for us to hear them boast that without their direction we could not keep this feast."

It is an understatement to say Constantine was antisemitic. Ironically, his assessment that Christians were unprepared to fully appreciate the Passover feast without a Jewish context proved fatally true. The Lamb of God was slain during Passover. He rose again during Passover. The holiday Easter, however, derives its name from the goddess Ishtar. The argument could be made that this syncretistic mix-up could have been entirely prevented had the Jewish context of the true Passover feast been embraced.

Remember, the antichrist spirit seeks to change times, seasons, and laws (Daniel 7:25). The forces behind Constantine accomplished a perfect trifecta in this regard. But the Lord is calling His people to come up higher! It's time to repent, reconcile, and reconnect with our covenant roots. Together we can see the Lord re-establish His cycles of biblical timing in the end times.

And it is now time for a collaborative strategy to restore the sacred covenantal roots that were severed by Constantine. Let's see the Lord rescue our lampstands and redeem the times! Please stay updated via our website for more information.

TURN THE STORM

It is amazing that Chuck Pierce referred to Daniel 7 in his prophecy and even invoked the Ancient of Days to be seated over Washington, DC. We are actively engaging with Him to confront the challenges ahead.

Daniel 7:21 reminds us that seasons may come where it appears dark forces are winning. Why? An antichrist spirit is waging war against the saints and prevailing until, as recorded in Daniel 7:22, judgment is rendered in their favor. This passage will find its ultimate fulfillment in the very last days. But the principle remains today. Heaven's Court remains open for business. Dare to approach the Bench and make a transaction. State your plea. Even in spaces where the forces of darkness seem to have prevailed, you and I can see turnaround.

Esther saw a turnaround. Just one generation after Daniel prophesied, judgment was rendered in her favor and the saints were literally released to possess the Kingdom. They were restored from exile back to their land. What Daniel saw for the very end of days gained initial fulfillment in Esther's day. It is still happening today. Because Hebraic time is cyclical. And His verdict becomes the final word through every generation.

What does this have to do with turning storms? Glad you asked.

In August 2022, Holy Spirit spoke to me a defining word for our time. *"Storms are coming that you cannot avert. But you CAN TURN THE STORM so the winds blow you, and the waves take you in the right direction."*

Here's a backstory that will inspire you. We immediately felt to mobilize an East Coast tour centered on this word. Within only weeks, the Turn the Storm Tour was launched. We felt led to retrace the paths of the 9-11-01 terrorists from Florida to Boston to New York City, asking God to turn both the storms of terrorism and storms in the natural.

On the final day of the tour, a hurricane formed in the Gulf of Mexico and began barreling toward Tampa. We prayed and decreed. At the last moment, the storm literally changed its trajectory! Much damage was still done. But a major population center was spared.

Storms are coming—both natural storms such as hurricanes, tornadoes, blizzards, and floods, and natural disasters such as earthquakes, pestilence, famine, etc. We are also facing human storms with the potential to be even more destructive. The weaponization of government for instance. Cyber wars, power grid failures, terrorism. Perhaps even the storm of a global war.

We saw firsthand how many storms can turn before impact and even be averted altogether. Sometimes it takes a storm to counter the perilous storm on the horizon. The good news is God's glory is a storm as well. Prayer generates this spiritual storm and empowers it to reach far beyond anything mankind can accomplish. Keep vigilant watch! And work to restore His glory to your land. Let's together generate an upper-atmospheric force that counters the storms ahead.

We have learned a vital lesson though. Just as the prophetic word conveyed, some storms cannot be averted. Many are actually going to make landfall before they can be turned or mitigated. Sometimes even in your own backyard.

As we've emphasized throughout the pages of this book, circumstances may not be easy. Birth pangs never are. But we are mandated to overcome, so never give up. Remember that the new birth of freedom, now at hand, will be worth it all. And in the midst of coming challenges you will discover that your word will have the prevailing influence over the enemy.

No excuses, friend. Just turn the storm.

REDEEM AMERICA

"That this nation, under God, shall have a new birth of freedom; and that government of the people, by the people, and for the people shall not perish from the earth." These words from the Gettysburg Address convey President Abraham Lincoln's solution to the dire storm of his day.

Engulfed by division and war, our very expression of freedom governance was on the verge of perishing. As noted in Chapter 1, Lincoln saw how the only thing that could save our Union was that America as a nation receive a "born-again experience" similar to an individual's redemptive transaction with God.

How should we pray? Following are seven essential decrees to help you intercede through the vulnerable season ahead. These thematic decrees will connect you with God's heart and secure Heaven's intervention on your behalf.

America needs these results. But as Lincoln observed, often the greatest need of our nation is mirrored by our own personal experiences. In other words, you need these results as well.

The book of Romans instructs us that God *"calls those things which do not exist as though they did"* (Romans 4:17 NKJV). This process is evident from the first pages of the Bible. As recorded in Genesis 1:3, the phrase *"Let there be light"* is literally a decree. The Hebrew translation *Hayah Or* addresses light and commands it to immediately exist. "Come forth, Light!" Another way of saying it is, "Light, exist!"

Of course when the decree was made by God, light shined and darkness had no choice but to yield. You will see similar results as you allow the Lord to make these decrees through you.

Remember to pray in the Spirit over each subject covered. Together we can set a new way forward for our nation—Jesus' way.

1. NO KING BUT JESUS!

Declare this in your prayer: *Our nation was founded by covenant with You, Lord. Therefore the thrones of this nation belong to You alone. Be the Throne behind the thrones of the White House, Capitol, Supreme Court, and the branches they direct. Uphold Your covenant through the new presidential administration. Deliver us by Your covenant!*

2. NO CROSS, NO CROWN!

Declare this in your prayer: *Lord, we declare the leaders of our land who have disqualified themselves like the biblical* *figure Shebna through compromise and corruption (Isaiah 22) must now be exposed and unseated. And we declare that You now endorse and promote leaders similar to Eliakim (Isaiah 22), who have gained Your heart to empower the constituents within their leadership for the betterment of our land. As portrayed in Isaiah 22, we say the Shebnas must now rescind the keys of leadership and restore them to Your Eliakims.*

3. CALL 911—RESTORE YOUR COVENANT COVERING!

Declare this in your prayer: *Lord, now sound Your alarm and awaken Your people to the reality now before us. Gather Your people in humility, repentance, and prayer, and set Your watch against our enemies in the spiritual and natural realms.*

We declare and invoke Your Psalm 91 protection over the United States, over each city and state. Including deliverance from the snare of all trappers and from deadly pestilence. We also claim Your protection over our president, our elected officials, our leaders and ambassadors, especially from assassination attempts. On a national level, restore Your covenant covering over our land!

4. LET MY PEOPLE GO!

Declare this in your prayer: *Lord, we forbid the spiritual manipulation of our nation's citizens through mass deception through occult manipulation tied to the political spirit. Break* *through and restrain every mesmerizing force, in Jesus' name. Reveal truth that sets America free, citizen by citizen, family by family, state by state.*

Lord Jesus, we reclaim our sons and daughters for You and for Your Kingdom, in Jesus' name. Reveal Yourself to them. Put Yourself across their path. Save them. "Even the captives…of a tyrant shall be rescued, for I will contend with the one who contends with you, and I will save your sons" (Isaiah 49:25 NASB). LET MY CHILDREN GO!

5. HEAVEN-RESCUED LAND!

Declare this in your prayer: *Lord, we declare our trust is in You. Now rescue us from the forces who would try to steal our freedom! Deliver us from unreasonable and wicked men who do not have faith! We forbid the sabotage of our election process by outside influences—such as cyber warfare from other nations, the release of viruses or other biological agents, by espionage and all terrorist cells. Let every attempt be exposed and brought to justice, in Jesus' name.*

You might be surprised to learn that the decree of a Heaven-Rescued Land is actually from our National Anthem. Though rarely cited, the final stanza of the Star Spangled Banner is perhaps the most powerful. As a "Heaven-rescued land," Francis Scott Key compels us to "praise the power that hath made us, and redeemed us a nation." May we again become a Heaven-Rescued Land in this perilous end-times hour. And may the new birth of freedom overtake our land.

6. TURN THE STORM

Declare this in your prayer: Lord Jesus, we have aligned ourselves covenantally with You. We now invoke Your covenant promise for our deliverance. According to 2 Kings 17:28-29, we remember and invoke the covenant You have made with us, not fearing but instead repudiating all other gods. We fear and reverence You, Lord Jesus Christ! Now deliver us from the hand of every adversary. Like a man on a chariot, take the reins of the storm we are facing. Disempower all evil sourcing the storm. Turn it for Your glory and for the protection of those You love. STORM BE TURNED IN JESUS' NAME.

7. NEW BIRTH OF FREEDOM

Declare this in your prayer: Lord, we realize that the challenges we now face defy solutions even the finest minds can devise. As in Abraham Lincoln's day, our nation must have a new birth of freedom so that we do not succumb to antichrist globalism but remain a nation under God. Remember Lincoln's prayers. Remember ours. LORD, REDEEM AMERICA! We decree that our "Hosea nation" now turns back to You. Our sons and daughters return to you. We plead the blood of Jesus over our land and decree that You bring to birth, protect, defend, and perpetuate the dream of Your heart for our land, even through the end of days. That this nation, under God, shall have a new birth of freedom—and that government of the people, by the people, and for the people shall not perish from the earth. IN JESUS' NAME, AMEN.

(TO BE CONTINUED)

NOTE

7. Chuck Pierce word from Revolution 2018. To read the full transcript see: https://jonandjolene.us/lampostings/border-wars-chuck-pierce-revolution -transcript/.

Jon & Jolene ministering

ABOUT JON AND JOLENE HAMILL

We hope you enjoyed our latest book, *End Times in Real Time.* We look forward to staying connected!

In 2007, Jon and Jolene Hamill launched Lamplighter Ministries to mentor and equip people to know Jesus better and in the process, become catalysts of His transformation in their world. They reside in metro Washington, DC, where they host a weekly home group and minister regularly to leaders.

In addition, Jon and Jolene have ministered extensively throughout the United States as well as in Israel, Italy, and the United Kingdom. They serve in many leadership capacities in prophetic communities and prayer networks.

Since 2022, Jon and Jolene have hosted the popular weekly broadcast *Turnaround Tuesday* which you can view on YouTube, Facebook, or on the homepage of their website. In 2024, they launched the new broadcast *Real Time DC.* They also write weekly updates featuring prophetic insights from Washington, DC as well as prayer points and ministry opportunities.

Most importantly, you are welcome to join Jon and Jolene live every Wednesday for their weekly prayer call covering the nation. No King but Jesus!

Jon and Jolene are the authors of five books: *End Times in Real Time*, published in March 2025 by Destiny Image; *Turnaround Decrees* published in summer 2022 by Destiny Image; *White House Watchmen*, published in 2020 by Destiny Image; and two self-published books *Midnight Cry* and *Crown & Throne*.

To stay connected with Jon and Jolene, please visit the Lamplighter website and sign up for their postings. Be sure to check out their partnership program. We look forward to staying in touch!

LAMPLIGHTER MINISTRIES WEBSITE:
https://lamplighterministries.net

JON & JOLENE'S YOUTUBE CHANNEL:
@jonjolenehamill8335

JON & JOLENE'S FACEBOOK PAGE:
https://www.facebook.com/jonathan.hamill1

JON & JOLENE ON TWITTER OR X:
@JonJoleneHamill

EMAIL CONTACT:
jon@lamplighterglobal.com

From
Jon & Jolene Hamill

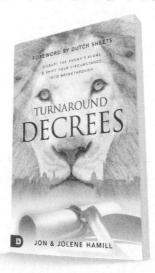

Interrupt the plans of darkness and shift circumstances to align with God's will!

In our culture, the powers of darkness have been working overtime to turn a generation away from God, discipling society in wickedness, destroying families, ravaging finances, afflicting bodies, and obstructing the advance of God's people.

The only solution is a supernatural turnaround. The good news is that you serve the God of the Turnaround!

In response to a radically unexpected prophetic word, Jon and Jolene Hamill have launched a turnaround movement to see supernatural breakthroughs take place. The results have been overwhelming. In this powerful new book they equip you with prayers, decrees, and activations that will render turnaround verdicts from Heaven on your behalf.

The destiny of generations are at stake... but you are the turnaround catalyst! Speak these powerful declarations over every impossibility, and watch as the God of the Turnaround brings supernatural breakthrough!

Purchase your copy wherever books are sold.

From
Jon & Jolene Hamill

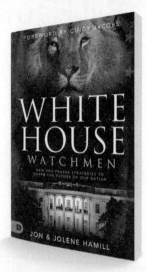

"This actually happened!" — Dutch Sheets

WITH LIBERTY AND JUSTICE FOR ALL.... Historic turnarounds are now in play. Yet at the same time, powerful forces seek to destroy the Judeo-Christian foundations which have secured America's greatness. *Awakening must prevail. Prayer must prevail. Life must prevail.*

The turnaround must be completed.

You are called to be a change-agent for this unprecedented prophetic moment. Your children and grandchildren are counting on it, your nation is waiting for it, the church is in desperate need of it. And this book will equip you for victory.

Long behind the scenes in Washington, DC, Jon and Jolene Hamill have come out of the shadows to expose the true battle and empower your success. In *White House Watchmen*, the Hamills share incredible untold stories, prophetic words, and revelatory encounters within the highest halls of government, where a genuine move of God is shaping the course of our nation.

Discover how to pray powerful, earth-shaking prayers for America that hit Heaven's target every time. It all starts with stepping into your assignment as a *White House Watchman*.

Purchase your copy wherever books are sold.

From
Dr. Bill Hamon

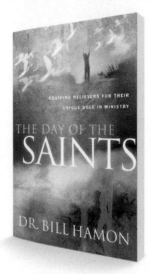

Many Christians are looking for "the Day of the Lord" but before that day comes the Lord is preparing His Bride for His Divine purposes in the earth. All creation longs for that day: *The Day of the Saints.* This day is on God's prophetic timetable and is the day when the Saints will fulfill all the Scriptures regarding Christ's glorious church.

The Day of the Saints is written with a sense of urgency and a surge of passion about God's great plans for His end-time people. With prophetic clarity, author Bill Hamon fits together the Biblical directives and the spiritual power that will prepare and propel the saints of God into the world. The saints of God are called to take the message of the Kingdom into the marketplaces of the world and Dr. Hamon shows how all of history has been moving towards this magnificent end.

Purchase your copy wherever books are sold.

From

Cindy Jacobs

This is your prophetic commissioning!

In these last days, the prophets foresee a great Holy Spirit out-pouring – a revival that will not be constrained by the four walls of an institution, but will shake the whole earth, shifting the very landscape of nations. This book is your prophetic commission-ing to take your place in God's imminent plan for mighty revival!

Cindy Jacobs is a renowned prophet to the nations with a heart that burns for revival and reformation. In this timely work, she steps into her office as a prophetic general, calling revived be-lievers to take their place as supernaturally-empowered agents for societal change.

In this freshly updated edition of her landmark book, *Reforma-tion Manifesto,* Cindy provides two new chapters that give pro-phetic insight on the present revival, coming awakening, and the great reformation that will see moves of God become societal transformation.

Rise up! It's time to take your place in Heaven's agenda for the world!

Purchase your copy wherever books are sold

From

Sid Roth

Your Prophetic Handbook to End-Times Events!

Sid Roth, host of *It's Supernatural!*, has gathered some of the leading experts and prophetic voices to take you on a powerful journey of upcoming events.

Each author shares a different part of the prophetic puzzle. By the time you finish reading this book, the pieces will come together and create a clear picture of God's unfolding agenda for the end-times.

Discover how this pivotal moment in history is your great opportunity to be on guard against the enemy's deception, experience God's power like never before, and participate in the greatest revival in history!

Purchase your copy wherever books are sold.

From

Larry Sparks

Do you pray prayers that, sometimes, feel like they hit the ceiling? Are you frustrated by religious praying that does not seem to produce results? Have you tried to start "decreeing and declaring" God's promises, only to feel like you are simply reciting spiritual formulas? It's time for you to unlock the force of Bible-based, prophetic decrees that release the breath, life and Spirit of Jesus!

Larry Sparks, publisher of Destiny Image, has personally assembled some of the top-teaching on speaking forth God's Word, coupled with topical decrees to help you release the power of these confessions.

Receive inspiration, revelatory teaching, and topical decrees from top leaders in the body of Christ who are practitioners at seeing the power of God manifest through their prayers and acts of faith.

Learn how to pray prayers that hit the mark and release the Spirit of Jesus. Your decrees will only carry anointing, presence, and power to the degree you say what God says about the situation. No more aimless prayers or formulaic declarations.

When you open up your mouth and boldly decree what God is saying, those words release the Spirit and life of Heaven!

Purchase your copy wherever books are sold

YOUR
Prophetic
COMMUNITY

Sign up for a **FREE** subscription to the Destiny Image digital magazine and get awesome content delivered directly to your inbox!

destinyimage.com/signup

Sign up for Cutting-Edge Messages that Supernaturally Empower You

- Gain valuable insights and guidance based on biblical principles
- Deepen your faith and understanding of God's plan for your life
- Receive regular updates and prophetic messages
- Connect with a community of believers who share your values and beliefs

Experience Fresh Video Content that Reveals Your Prophetic Inheritance

- Receive prophetic messages and insights
- Connect with a powerful tool for spiritual growth and development
- Stay connected and inspired on your faith journey

Listen to Powerful Podcasts that Propel You into God's Presence Every Day

- Deepen your understanding of God's prophetic assignment
- Experience God's revival power throughout your day
- Learn how to grow spiritually in your walk with God

In the Right Hands, This Book Will Change Lives!

Most of the people who need this message will not be looking for this book. To change their lives, you need to **put a copy of this book in their hands.**

Our ministry is constantly seeking methods to find the people who need this anointed message to change their lives. **Will you help us reach these people?**

Extend this ministry by sowing three, five, ten, or *even more* books today and change people's lives for the better! Your generosity will be part of catalyzing the Great Awakening that many have been prophesying and praying for.